Occult Hunting and Supernatural Play in Japan

Occult Hunting and Supernatural Play in Japan

LAURA MILLER

University of Hawai'i Press
HONOLULU

Printed in the United States of America

First printed, 2024

Library of Congress Cataloging-in-Publication Data

Names: Miller, Laura, author.
Title: Occult hunting and supernatural play in Japan / Laura Miller.
Description: Honolulu : University of Hawaiʻi Press, [2024] | Includes bibliographical references and index.
Identifiers: LCCN 2023053667 | ISBN 9780824896164 (hardback) | ISBN 9780824898410 (trade paperback) | ISBN 9780824898328 (epub) | ISBN 9780824898335 (kindle edition) | ISBN 9780824898311 (pdf)
Subjects: LCSH: Occultism—Japan. | Women occultists—Japan. | Japan—Religious life and customs.
Classification: LCC BF1434.J3 M55 2024 | DDC 130.952—dc23/eng/20240308
LC record available at https://lccn.loc.gov/2023053667

Cover art: Collection of *magatama* beads, Taoist paper talismans, and Japan-made tarot cards. Photograph by the author.

University of Hawaiʻi Press books are printed on acid-free paper and meet the guidelines for permanence and durability of the Council on Library Resources.

Contents

Acknowledgments

I owe gratitude to many people who assisted me while I was working on this project. I will always be grateful to the friends and strangers in Japan who patiently endured my questions for more than a decade. My research was primarily made possible because of the Ei'ichi Shibusawa-Seigo Arai Endowed Professorship at the University of Missouri-Saint Louis (UMSL) that I accepted in 2010. The staff at UMSL Global, especially Liane Constantine and Bob Ell, were always supportive and amazing. Abby Naumann gave me valuable help as my research assistant in spring 2022.

I am grateful to Hideko Abe, Linda Chance, Kathryn Goldfarb, Sonia Ryang, Tobias Zürn, and others for the opportunities to present aspects of this book on their campuses. For chapter 1 thanks go to Scott Youngstedt for comments. Parts of chapter 1 and chapter 2 were presented at the annual meetings of the American Anthropological Association in 2008 and 2023. I thank all the panel members and the discussants for feedback. I would like to thank Abby Naumann for feedback on chapter 2 as well as Satsuki Kawano, Susan Long, and Glenda Roberts for comments on some material from an earlier iteration of it. Debra Occhi gifted me several cool divination books that were very useful. I greatly appreciate the useful feedback on early drafts of chapter 3 that I received from Masafumi Monden and Carolyn Stevens. Many thanks to Kaoru Rudlin for going with me to Tarot Bar Rosy. I appreciate the feedback or help with chapter 4 from Marc Moskowitz and Kathryn Ugoretz. For helpful comments on chapter 5, I thank Joseph Elacqua, Paul Manning, Anne Meneley, Abby Naumann, Noriko Sugimori, and Tobias Zürn. Members of the Midwest Japan Seminar also provided valuable feedback when I presented an early version of this chapter in 2019. I am grateful to Middlebury College for the invitation to present at its conference in 2017. I received excellent feedback from Tamar Mayer, Marybeth Nevins, Stephen Snyder, Linda White, and other participants. I received helpful comments on early drafts of chapter 6 from Teri Silvio and participants in a history faculty symposium at UMSL. I wish to thank Masafumi Monden and Cindi SturtzSreetharan for helping me track down the start of the huge *ema* trend. Thanks are due to many people for suggestions on chapter 7: Jan Bardsley, Brian Bergstrom, Deborah Cohen, Gergana Ivanova, Edward Kamens, Paul Manning, Deborah Occhi, and Teri Silvio. Colleagues in the history department at my university were also generous in giving useful comments at a faculty colloquium. I also benefited greatly from conversations and assistance from people in Tamatsukuri Onsen, including Murata-san at Izumo Magatama no Sato Denshōkan and Endō-Gūji at Tamasukuriyu Jinja. In Osaka I am grateful to Suzuki-Gūji at Tamatsukuri Inari Jinja. I will never forget the generosity of the two Shinto priests in allowing me to enter their *magatama* museums and take photographs. For chapter 8 thanks are due to Abby Naumann and Genevieve Sawicz for their comments. Old friends helped me get to a few of the locations: Justin Ho drove me to Murōji in Nara Prefecture and to the Hoshida Myōken-Gū in Osaka. Kay Ikeda has accompanied me to several sites over the years and drove me to Kurumazaki Jinja and Kanga-An in Kyoto.

Chapter 1 further develops arguments from Miller (2014b), and chapter 3 is a significantly revised version of ideas published in Miller (2017b) and Miller (2011b). Photos and images without a source listed are by the author or from scanned images of objects owned by the author. Sources for all others are given. I am grateful for the permission to use figure 20 from Yuanyuan Zheng and East Press Co. in Tokyo. I appreciate the effort made by Tomoki Hayashi at PHP Institute Inc. for making an effort to find the artist who drew a comic they published twenty years ago.

Most of all I am grateful to my friend Rebecca Copeland for all her years of support and enthusiasm for this project. I may have given up long ago without our writing retreats and hours of conversation over Silk Road cocktails and bowls of green pozole. She read every chapter and provided detailed feedback on each with both wit and precision. Rebecca was my traveling companion on trips to both Tamatsukuri Onsen and Izumo Taisha, surely one of the highlights of my work on this book.

Occult Hunting and Supernatural Play in Japan

Introduction

I had been invited to meet with three visiting business school professors from a university in Tokyo. Out of politeness one of the men asked about my research, and when I mentioned the divination industry, they all laughed out loud! Why on earth would someone waste time on such a frivolous subject? One aim of *Occult Hunting and Supernatural Play in Japan* is to assert that divination and other related activities are not a trivial part of Japanese culture. Rather, they provide insights into realms of pleasure, creative exploration, and spiritual development, in addition to being extraordinarily lucrative. Occult hunters seek out locations imbued with charged energy. They desire magical goods and engage in activities such as reading tarot cards, collecting religious charms, and visiting locations thought to have spiritual energy.

A second goal of *Occult Hunting* is to argue that because women and girls are the primary drivers of transformed enchantment, they have inspired shrines, temples, and the media industries to accommodate their interests and tastes. Many religious objects and activities have become *feminized,* even if men and boys also participate. Female seekers have thus had a major impact on how religious sites, texts, and objects are fashioned and marketed. As my meeting with the business school professors made clear, although this domain is a huge part of the Japanese economy, it is often stigmatized as unworthy of study. There may be different reasons for this. I suspect that one reason it is an underanalyzed sphere of economic activity is because women are the primary providers and seekers of such services, goods, and experiences. Similarly, in another study I found that the profits and energy devoted to the beauty industry (aesthetic salons, cosmetics, weight loss products, etc.) far exceeded those of the wedding industry, the funeral industry, the car repair industry, and all software-related businesses (L. Miller 2006). Yet scholarly and business reporting focused intensely on these other less profitable domains, and the beauty industry remained virtually invisible aside from occasional articles mocking cosmetic trends. In regard to divination and related occult pursuits there might also be some embarrassment that so many people in purportedly hypermodern Japan continue to pursue nonscientific pastimes, especially those believed to be entangled with "ancient traditions."

Feminist scholarship asks us to treat the lives, employment, preoccupations, and consumption patterns of women and girls as worthy of investigation. Female investment in occult interests takes us beyond some assumptions about religious and spiritual pursuits. It is a domain that can be about sociality, creativity, rebellion, and relaxation and a space for decisions about self-exploration and life trajectory. Within the study of gender in folk religion, scholars have primarily focused on the role of female shamans in Okinawa (Blacker 1975; Hori 1968). Kawahashi (2000) offers a succinct reexamination of this existing literature, in which she reflects on the problems with both terminology and the treatment of gender. Ambros (2015) provides a needed corrective to the predominantly androcentric scholarship on religion in Japan. Silvio's (2019) study of religion, puppetry, toys, and cosplay in Taiwan is close to the intent of *Occult Hunting*. It takes female interest and fan efforts seriously and treats the material and visual aspects of religion as worthy of analysis.

Some scholars like to ascribe the predominance of women as occult hunters to ongoing gender inequality. According to much contemporary scholarship, Japanese women experience lives of exploited instability and anxiety (Allison 2013). While there is no denying that the changed labor market and the trauma of the triple disasters in 2011 (earthquake, tsunami, nuclear accident) had a negative impact on most people both economically and psychologically, it is not the case that tales of misery dominate social and cultural life. *Occult Hunting* seeks to capture another aspect of everyday life—the optimistic, positive, and pleasurable dimensions of spiritual endeavors. Occult hunters are able to experience agency and energy and to pursue the self-development and spiritual exploration that might be missing in jobs or family life. This arena of pleasure also surfaces in a variety of popular culture media and activities. The quest for spiritual meaning and enjoyment is important to acknowledge because other research has focused on women tasked with caring for aging parents, continuously struggling to resist constricting social roles, and experiencing great economic marginality (Alexy and Cook 2019; Long 2005; Rosenberger 2013). Women and girls from all economic classes and age cohorts occasionally participate in some form of occult activity, such as obtaining a fortune slip at a shrine. Because occult hunting is not at all new, ascribing the entire phenomena to a functionalist argument about topical anxiety is not useful. Astrological and other schema that are popular today were also enjoyed in the 1990s (L. Miller 1997a). Linking occult hunting to precarity or the COVID-19 pandemic will not get us very far in understanding its various attractions. In separate chapters I share polls, expert commentary, and individual justifications for the developments described. For example, some people admit that visiting places of spiritual energy legitimizes free time away from duties, and some religious artifacts are collected because they constitute beautiful and inexpensive art.

A third goal of *Occult Hunting* is to include popular culture, particularly material and visual artifacts, in the analysis. I continue to hear scholars complain that looking at popular culture detracts from "serious" research. Once I shared an image of a *tenugui* towel fashioned with charming cats representing graphs of the *Heart Sutra,* and a scholar of religion insisted that it did not further our understanding of Buddhism. My attitude is that popular culture and religion are deeply intertwined and embedded in the everyday world and should not be ignored. Reframing a sutra as a cute artifact marks it as something any young woman would like. A writer known for her books on pilgrim stamps discusses the monumental statue of the historic Buddha at Asukadera in Nara (Nishimura Yumiko 2016). She refers to it as an *ikemen* buddha. *Ikemen* means "good-looking guy" or sometimes "hot dude." Numerous tweets and blogs provide rankings for the top *ikemen* Buddha statues. Naming like this relocates an ancient bronze Buddha from centuries ago to the realm of contemporary culture, combining the religious and the popular. Thomas (2013) provided solid evidence that we should make a connection between religion and popular culture, but unlike his work, which hunts for traces of religion in manga and anime, *Occult Hunting* does not take popular culture as the starting point for analysis. Rather, I begin with religious and occult sites, imagery, and artifacts first and then note where popular culture might have influenced their form or production. The manner in which Thomas acknowledged the key aspect of play in religious representation was a critical innovation in the scholarship that will also be a core theme in *Occult Hunting.*

Occult Hunting is written from an interdisciplinary cultural studies perspective derived from history, art history, literature, media studies, and anthropology. My PhD training in linguistic anthropology is especially useful for discussing written artifacts. Melded with ethnographic fieldwork in Japan are my own outsider/etic analyses. I will occasionally adopt the perspective of art historians, who assess visual and material culture without including a native person's direct commentary on those materials. I will treat some artifacts from a semiotic perspective, as objects that embody sign systems and cultural meanings that can be traced through historical knowledge and cultural context. While some chapters incorporate findings from ethnographic research, this is not "an ethnography" (one is a method and the other is a specific type of product). I, too, am a hunter who went looking for the spaces, objects, and behaviors related to the topics covered in this book. Beginning in 2007, annual visits to Tokyo allowed me to explore broad aspects of divination and to visit sites thought to have special spiritual energy. In 2015 I shifted focus to the Kansai region during annual visits and in 2019 did fieldwork in Ise, Izumo, Tamatsukuri Onsen, Osaka, and Nara.

When I teach an undergraduate course on the visual and material culture of Japan, I often compare similar images that have different meanings depending on the cultural context. One example is the Japanese five-pointed symbol borrowed from the mainland at the start of the sixth century to represent the five elements or phases (*gogyō*), a balance of wood, fire, earth, metal, and water.[1] It has no historic relationship to the pentagram in Christian contexts, with its connotations of witchcraft and Satanism. One student vehemently insisted that the symbol is always a form of superstition. Encountering students who label anything outside their own religion "superstition" is more common than not. My underlying stance is that none of the things that people in any society do are forms of superstition (or we would need to categorize all religion as superstition). Within some quarters of anthropological thinking, all ideas, efforts, and activities related to the supernatural world are forms of religious behavior. When people use the semantic category "superstition," it is generally reserved for nonmainstream religious behavior or the religious activities of people other than their own. Since ancient times there has been bickering about the very concept of "religion" and whether "belief" is a required component. Although debates continue about the usefulness of universal definitions in the study of religion, the starting point for a definition of religion presented here is one found in many anthropology texts: "An organized system of shared supernatural beliefs and ritualized behaviors." But now I encounter another controversy!

Although the terms and concepts related to the hidden world and the supernatural have shifted throughout history, among the possible terms in Japanese is *chōshizen-teki* (supernatural). Terms for the supernatural were coined in the nineteenth century, and they continue to be used widely in scholarly writing and popular media to mean the mystical, mysterious, or otherworldly. I use "supernatural" as it is understood in this sense. Thus, I am not using the term to denote the primitive, strange, or irrational. In contemporary anthropological writing, many scholars use "supernatural" in definitions of religion, intended to encompass all beliefs related to those beyond or outside the natural world. However, debate exists about this term, and some academics insist that the distinction is not universal among all human groups (Dein 2016). For this study it is important to note that the adoption of an originally Western framing device into Japanese thinking occurred more than 130 years ago and has now been fully domesticated. Although supernatural beings, energies, and objects are thought to be imbricated within the world of humans, they are separate from humans as a category, even if the boundaries between these levels of existence are not fixed. Drawing from classic Durkheimian theory, Hultkranz (1983, 231) insists that we acknowledge a fundamental dichotomy between two levels of existence, the ordinary and the extraordinary, or supernatural. Although the Japanese terms and concepts related to the hidden world and the supernatural have shifted throughout history, I use "supernatural" to encompass a range of transcendental phenomenon and to mean mystical, mysterious, or otherworldly.

Occult Hunting builds on the landmark book *Practically Religious: Worldly Beliefs and the Common Religion of Japan* by Reader and Tanabe (1998, 7). It moved the discussion of religion away from formal texts and doctrine to the everyday practices and rituals that are familiar to most people, emphasizing that "indeed, Japanese religion is less a matter of belief than it is of activity, ritual and custom." Their book continues to have a strong influence on our understanding of religion in Japan. Reader and Tanabe were also pioneers because they analyzed material aspects of religious behavior. Attention to "material religion" was later taken up by scholars in the humanities (anthropologists have always looked at material forms of religion), such as Morgan (2021). In 2005 Morgan cofounded the journal *Material Religion,* establishing it as a legitimate field of inquiry. I also aim to look beyond the usual assumptions that religion is about "belief" or participation in official forms of worship. Rather, the diverse arenas for occult hunting encompass both official modes of ritual behavior as well as marginal avenues for spiritual exploration. Asking if people believe something would have deformed my perspective. Unlike Reader and Tanabe, however, this book highlights the gendered nature of many recent developments in religious behaviors and consumption.[2]

In the chapters that follow I view whatever people practice as forms of religion even when they are not linked to organized religious institutions and are in opposition to established doctrine. Religion in Japan is characterized by an acceptance of a variety of supernatural beings and essences, its accessibility to everyone without the need to profess belief or demonstrate affiliation, and its availability to anyone who seeks the aid of any supernatural being at any shrine or temple at nearly any time. Although what I am describing fits my case for "religion," I often use the term "occult" in its place in a deliberately expansive manner. If I began with or solely relied on well-established scholarly categories such as "religion," my analysis would already be limited to the existing borders of those categories and definitions and would carry culturally loaded baggage. For example, in other contexts people have expressed difficulty understanding or accepting that religion or spiritualism can exist without faith or belief. Following advice from Becker (1998, 123), I am allowing the case to define the category. Here the case is interest in the supernatural in Japan. My case includes a wide-ranging spectrum of religious activities, including divination, tarot cards, and fascination with a reified bead called *magatama*. Many academics and critics, like the Japanese business professors mentioned above, normally consider these to be outside the domain of religion (not to mention outside proper academic inquiry). Beginning with religion as the category would exclude many activities and interests that are central to female-oriented cultural domains. For instance, tarot cards or *magatama* beads might be considered extraneous to the category "religion." I made the error of trying to "make the case fit the category" when I first began writing about amulets. I saw a continuum of objects from sacred *omamori* to *omamori*-like secular objects and imagery that all shared some symbolic meanings. At first, I labeled these "real *omamori*" and "fake *omamori*." Smart friends asked me what purpose it served to make category distinctions if my argument was that all *omamori*-styled objects and imagery participated in shared meanings. Although *omamori*, either obtained from shrines or made at home by fans, are carried by many people, they are not ordinary in the same way as pens or lunch boxes. It made sense to treat them as comembers of a category. Kendall (2021) encountered a similar problem in her study of material objects and images in Vietnam, Myanmar, Bali, and South Korea through an investigation of how these things might be viewed differently. Depending on the context and the person, the same items could be treated as fabricated commodities, museum artifacts, or venerated objects.

The English word "occult" is a long-established loanword in Japanese that denotes the esoteric, mysterious, or supernatural. Introduced in the nineteenth century, *okaruto* originally meant unconventional religious beliefs, folk religions, and theosophy.[3] In recent years it is used for the broader, general meanings of uncommon knowledge or esoterica (linguists call this sematic broadening). It is this expanded and nebulous meaning that I intend in this study. Hundreds of recent books and articles use the loanword in their titles, and one may even consult the *Dictionary of Occult Mysteries* (Terai 2021). A series of "occult booms" (*okaruto būmu*) began in the 1970s, which Ryūhe Hirota (2021) believes evolved from the explosion of imps and goblins called *yōkai* in popular culture. People also became fascinated by astrology, mediums, theories about Atlantis, and divination such as tarot cards. One consequence today is that previously devalued or avoided folk religion and nonmainstream religious beliefs are no longer quite as stigmatized. This shift is illustrated in a study of the shamans of northern Japan, who became a positive instance of the unique "mysterious knowledge" of Japan rather than representing backwoods irrationality (Ōmichi 2016).

The wide-ranging domain I label "occult" contains objects such as *magatama* beads and pilgrim stamps, which might not fit well in traditional categories such as "religious objects" or "calligraphy art." Occult implies the extraordinary, the not ordinary. An *omamori*-like object used on stationery is not a religious object, yet it belongs in a discussion of *omamori* because it shares imagery and meanings. A *magatama* bead may be a sacred symbol for some people or a touristic key chain bauble for others, yet all *magatama* share historical and other associations. I am interested in all aspects of selected objects or activities and think that using "occult" allows me to explore them fully, including humorous, ironic, or irreverent uses. I also include instances in which the intended meaning is deliberately crass. The same object or behavior, be it collecting pilgrim stamps or writing a votive plaque, might address multiple needs and interests concurrently for the same person.

Readers will notice that many of the Japanese terms encountered in this book are loanwords from English. Foreign word borrowing has a long history in Japan, and English loanwords in particular have been adopted extensively in all realms of life. Once added to the lexicon, they normally undergo a change in meaning or other alterations. A few loanwords in the occult domain were first popularized in the 1990s as part of the "healing boom" (*iyashi būmu*), which focused on psychological and physical soothing through the consumption of a variety of services, products, and media. Beginning with the adoption of the New Age movement's practices and beliefs in healing crystals, yoga, and aromatherapy, the domain escalated to include powerstones, cat cafés, and the visitation to sites of spiritual energy. We know one thing from research on loanwords in Japanese: there are countless reasons for adopting foreign terms, including aesthetic value, humor, taboo avoidance, wordplay, specificity, ambiguity, and prestige (L. Miller 1997b). For loanwords related to the occult, many of these motivations are in play, some of them simultaneously. The desire to use the borrowed terminology may also be evidence of an insider language used to signal knowledge of esoteric culture. A concept that surfaces in many chapters is the idea that impersonal supernatural power may attach to or reside in some living beings, inanimate objects, or special places.[4] In general, most occult hunters use the loanwords *pawā* (power) and *enerugii* (energy) for this supernatural power. In some cases, these terms are combined with the loanword for "spiritual." They are preferred over technical terms from religious texts or doctrine to refer to life-force energy, sacred power, or mysterious power. In some specific contexts, however, more specialized terminology might be used as well.

Many people in Japan visit both Buddhist temples and Shinto shrines yet do not regard themselves as "members" of a particular religion. Although very different, Buddhism and Shinto have been coexisting in Japan since the sixth century, when Buddhism was adopted from the Korean Peninsula. Shinto is the name now attached to the preexisting religious landscape prevalent before the arrival of Buddhism. The majority of Japanese are familiar with a number of different supernatural beings, such as Shinto kami, various buddhas and bodhisattvas, and other supernatural entities. Many locations are dedicated to more than one supernatural being. The largest category is the kami of deified entities and spirits, once living humans, objects, and natural phenomena. The difference between these traditions and their doctrines or cosmologies does not mean much to the majority of occult hunters. They indiscriminately visit Buddhist, Shinto, and other locations and collect pilgrim stamps and amulets from any religious site.

Specialists have documented the ways that Shinto, in both its institutional forms and its folk religious forms, has been molded and manipulated by different groups of people throughout history. Scholars of religion have taken various perspectives when it comes to the nature and history of Shinto, debates that are beyond the intent of this study.[5] The view presented here is that Shinto exists as a religious tradition that has links to historical precedents. Similar to other anthropologists who have studied everyday behaviors related to notions of purity and pollution, I see traces of Shinto in the many occult domains described in this book that render them nonequivalent to the religious situation in China or Korea. Japan differs because the focus is not necessarily centered on named deities or supernatural beings but rather on *pawā* (power) and *energii* (energy) that derive from Shinto ideas about kami and supernatural power. It is important to keep in mind that kami are not necessarily "beings" and that the kami spirit may inhabit various natural phenomena, such as large trees, storms, and other aspects of the natural world (Kasulis 2004). Nonspecific supernatural power is often claimed to reside in objects such as *reifu* paper charms, *magatama* beads, or other objects examined in this book. This is somewhat different from Silvio's (2019) case in Taiwan. One class of objects she focused on are anthropomorphic figurines called *ang-a,* which are animated and given agency. Even so, her discussion of the cuteness and commercialization of religious deities, and the dominance of woman and girls in some fandoms, is reminiscent of what I found in Japan. However, it is necessary to note that Japan is often different from Korea, Taiwan, and China in some aspects of its religious landscape despite centuries of contact and borrowing.

As a model of how to approach and describe the religious or spiritual life of others, I kept in mind a study of the Rastafarians by Lewis (1993). Trained as an anthropologist, he described Rasta lives and ideas based on fieldwork in Jamaica, where he participated in numerous "reasoning sessions," smoking ganja and engaging in the interpretation of scripture with many people. Although he himself was a Franciscan brother and a Catholic priest, he never presented Rasta views through a Christian interpretive framework. Other than visits to shrines and temples in Japan, I do not participate in any organized religion. I have attempted to avoid using models from Christian-dominant Euro-American cultures as a yardstick for my interpretations. Kasulis (2004, 31) pointed out that some questions about Japanese religious practices tell us more about Euro-America or Christian expectations than about religion in Japan. I first visited Japan in 1972, the same year I began the formal study of Japanese language, history, and culture. Thereafter I spent many years working, doing research, and teaching in Japan. Over five decades I frequently visited religious sites and participated in rituals and other activities.

Some chapters in *Occult Hunting* are primarily organized around activities such as having one's fortune told (see chapter 2 and chapter 3), visiting locations thought to hold exceptional spiritual energy (chapter 9), or playing with tarot cards (chapter 4). Other chapters focus on material and visual artifacts, including good luck amulets and votive plaques (chapter 7) and curved beads (chapter 8). Two chapters consider specific types of written artifacts: Taoist paper charms (chapter 6) and pilgrim stamps (chapter 5). Both are entangled with symbolic meanings and developments in calligraphic styling and script innovation. The themes and trends found in all the chapters are not suggesting a simple narrative about loss and recovery of religion.

According to early social theory, modernization and its rationalistic mode resulted in a high regard for scientific understanding and a devaluation of religion. This "disenchantment" is a sociological formulation that Max Weber proposes about the modern condition after the departure of magic and myth (the "enchantment") from everyday life for the modern, urban person in industrialized societies: "The fate of our times is characterized by rationalization and intellectualization and, above all, by the 'disenchantment of the world'" (Weber 1946, 155).[6] In this model, "wonders and marvels have been demystified by science, spirituality has been supplanted by secularism, spontaneity has been replaced by bureaucratization, and the imagination has been subordinated to instrumental reason" (Saler 2006, 692). Even a highly modernized, bureaucratic, and technologically sophisticated society such as Japan, however, never adequately fit this Weberian "disenchantment of the world" model, which was firmly grounded in EuroAmerican thinking and culture. Instead, *Occult Hunting* describes a refurbishing of long-standing religious tropes and a renewed respect for enchantment. In addition, many innovative forms of enchantment have become commodified and monetized by individuals, religious institutions, and media industries. Pursuit of the occult, however, does occur within a context of cultural tension. There is a contrast between spiritual and mystical preoccupations, which are openly endorsed in female culture, and mainstream productivity-oriented, androcentric society. Participation and interest in supernatural play and occult consumption shift orientation away from the habitual routines of orderly and bureaucratized school and work environments. Ironically, the occult hunter's search has generated enormous profit for capitalist industries that offer hundreds of novel travel experiences, products, media, and divination services. Although a contingent of scholars continue to deliver pronouncements on religion in Japan, women are busy playing with and modifying the textual, philosophical, visual, and material basis of their knowledge.

CHAPTER 1

Divination

A friend in Japan complained about his daughter's interest in divination. He said something like "I know ancient people did *bokkotsu* [divination with animal bones and tortoise shells], but now we live in modern times with science, so it's a waste of time." Of course, he was correct in thinking that scientific understanding of how the universe operates has replaced former attempts to comprehend it through magic, divination, and mythology (although he misses the point of why people continue to do divination, in Japan and everywhere else in the world). When I gave a lecture on contemporary divination years ago, I jokingly said that while many archaic forms of divination are still performed, people were not doing divination with tortoise shells as they did in ancient history. It turns out that I was wrong. I was unaware then, as perhaps was my friend (or maybe he was too embarrassed to admit it?) that a type of *bokkotsu* was performed in Japan's Imperial Palace in 1990 and again in 2019. Because it only occurs when a new emperor is enthroned, it is easy to overlook this type of imperial ritual. In any case, there is also the probability that my friend had more than once selected a paper lottery slip called *omikuji* on visits to a shrine, which is a form of divination. What invites the disapproval he and others express is most likely that popular divination, unlike the imperial *bokkotsu* ritual and the *omikuji,* is normally untethered to state or religious institutions. In addition, it is primarily pursued by women. In other words, what seems to be irritating is not the act of divination itself but rather the types of divination and the people who are doing it.

In this chapter I am interested in divination not only because it is an enormous part of the economy; it is also underanalyzed in many studies of Japan. We should pay attention to it not simply because of its incredible profits but because it is a highly female-oriented market and therefore provides recognition of their interests and activities. Divination may have real-life consequences in how people navigate jobs, marriage selection, births, and other decisions. For example, the birth rate declined dramatically in 1966 because it was the Year of the Fire Horse, according to the Chinese zodiac. Women born in that year are considered difficult marriage partners, and births plummeted as a result. Finally, female investment in divination often counters mainstream ideals about proper economic behavior and use of time. A close look at the integral role of divination in mythology and ancient history will also provide a comparative context.

I use the concept of divination to mean practices that intend to predict future events or discover hidden knowledge that will inform decision-making. Contemporary divination products, media, and services are usually categorized under the term *uranai* (divination). I begin with ancient *bokkotsu* divination, followed by discussion of the paper lottery slip, the *omikuji* mentioned above. Then I turn to other contemporary forms of divination. A noticeable escalation of interest in divination and other occult pursuits became evident during the 1980s, when critics began talking about an *uranai būmu* (divination boom). Many scholars, including Suzuki (1995), Kawano (1995), and L. Miller (1997a), noticed the preponderance of women as consumers of divination schemas and services. Taneda (2000) also described the divination industry as being under the control of women as both producers and consumers of services. Time-consuming and occasionally expensive divination activities have, therefore, been dominated by girls and women for many years. My aim is not to discover the degree to which people believe in the efficacy of such practices. Rather, I want to explore the ways in which the divination industry has accommodated feminized aesthetics and female-oriented social and entertainment interests.

The feminization of divination results in a preponderance of female aesthetics and tastes being channeled into a diverse range of new or refurbished businesses.[1] While older women continue to be interested in old-fashioned types such as palmistry, face reading, and Chinese-style astrology, younger women create and consume multiple genres of creolized and sometimes humorous divination. The occult hunter's search for divination entertainment has generated enormous profit for businesses that offer novel and amusing products, media, and services.

Women may buy books on feng shui for their cars or access automated forecasts in booths at entertainment parks. Women resurrect some archaic forms of divination yet concurrently create and consume thoroughly modern innovations. Even so, they have not yet shown much interest in *bokkotsu,* which I turn to in the next section.

Ancient Divination

The famous Shinto scholar Ban Nobutomo (1773–1846) published widely on religious and esoteric topics, including his compilation on tortoise shell divination (*kiboku*). He detailed the tools used for preparation, explained how the turtles were obtained, and demonstrated how the plastron should be cut into the shape of a pentagon. In one illustration (figure 1), he shows the possible crack patterns that might appear after the application of heat with a piece of wood. In general, if the cracks spread straight upward or to the right, they were considered positive answers, while cracks going downward or to the left were interpreted as negative omens. In media surrounding the 2019 Daijōsai enthronement ritual were many images of the cut and polished turtle shells used in the divination, and they were exactly this shape.

Unlike forms of ancient divination such as those used by Heian-era (794–1185) court wizards, divination with animal bones and tortoise shells has not made a noticeable appearance in popular manga and anime. One intriguing exception is a drawing of the third-century female ruler Himiko

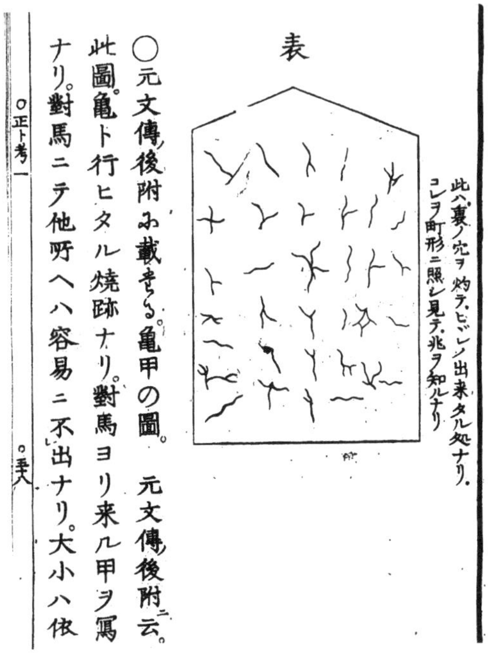

Figure 1. Possible crack patterns in tortoise shell divination (Ban 1903, 59)

(ca. 170–248 CE) that apparently shows her engaged in a plastromancy ritual (divination with tortoise shells). It is found in an unlikely context, a manga by Kobayashi (2010). Kobayashi is a nationalist who advocates for the remasculinization of men along the lines of the prewar militarists. In a manga on "new emperorism," he deviates from his usual misogyny and supports the idea of allowing the granddaughter of Emperor Emeritus Akihito to be part of the succession (Kobayashi 2010). His manga justifies female emperorship by highlighting female rulers from Japanese history. Although Himiko is not considered one of the female emperors by Kobayashi, he highlights her as an ancient shaman-ruler who was close to the deities despite the "primitive" nature of her power. Kobayashi's image is possibly flawed in at least one respect: most likely Himiko did not use tortoise shells for divination but rather the shoulder bone of a deer or a wild boar. We know this from many archaeological excavations but particularly one discovery from the proposed site of her palace. Archaeologists discovered a boar bone that had been used for scapulimancy at the Makimuku ruins, considered to have been the location of Himiko's palace in Nara Prefecture (Hayashi 2015). The terminology for these ancient forms of divination is a little confusing. The general category *bokkotsu* is a cover term for two different types of divination from the ancient period that utilize the same method of analyzing cracks in either animal bones or tortoise shells. The main distinction is between the use of animal bones and tortoise shells. The confusion also rests on multiple terms for these different types of divination. A few of them are listed in table 1.[2]

There is archaeological evidence of animal bone pyro-scapulimancy from the Yayoi era (ca. 300 BCE–250 CE). The bones were cut and polished, then subjected to a hot ember inserted into grooves until it cracked. The pattern of fissures was interpreted for the prognosis or answer. This type of divination was called *futomani* in ancient texts and *katayaki* in the poetry anthology named *Man'yōshū* (ca. AD 759).[3] *Futomani* were mainly

Table 1. Types of ancient divination using animal bones or turtle shells

bokkotsu	Divination using either animal bones or turtle shells
futomani	Deer scapula or boar scapula divination
rokuboku	Deer scapula divination
katayaki	Deer scapula divination term used in the *Man'yōshū*
kiboku	Tortoise shell divination

deer shoulder bones but also wild boar and occasionally porpoise bones. Early mentions of this type of divination in Japan are found in the Chinese historical accounts. One description is in a section of the *Wei zhi* (297 CE) titled "Account of the Eastern Barbarians" and compiled by Chen Shou (233–297; *Gishi wajinden* in Japanese). The history describes the ethnology of the people of Wa (Japan) and mentions tattooing, weaving, drinking, and divination: "It is the custom on the occasion of an event or trip, whatever they do, to divine by baking bones so as to determine future good or bad fortune. The words are the same as those for tortoise shell divination. The fire cracks are examined for signs" (Kidder 2007, 15).

The Chinese ethnohistorians refer to "words" for spoken forms of language, as there was no writing system in Japan during that time. The early mythological histories *Kojiki* (Records of Ancient Matters, 711–712) and the *Nihon shoki* (The Chronicles of Japan, 720 CE) contain several mentions of *futomani* divination. One story is about the anxiety felt by the deities Izanami and Izanagi, who asked the other celestial beings to help them determine why they had produced an abnormal baby. Another refers to the time when Amaterasu, the sun deity, hid in the heavenly stone chamber, and a deity named Ame no Koyane used the shoulder bone of a deer in his divination efforts to lure her out: "The heavenly deities led by Ame no koyane no Mikoto (ancestral deity of the Nakatomi clan, later called Fujiwara) took counsel about how to restore Amaterasu. They caused birds to cry. They brought iron to a smith and had him make a mirror. They had *magatama* beads made. They performed a divination with the shoulder bones of a deer" (Hardacre 2016, 53–54). By the Heian era (794–1185) *kiboku,* tortoise shell divination had completely replaced the older forms of animal bone divination. Kory (2015) investigated this shift and relates the change to political strivings on the part of the powerful clan-based divination guilds and perhaps also to the prestige value of knowing about Chinese models. Chinese plastromancy (tortoise shell divination) dates to at least the Shang era (1200–1050 BCE), but unlike the Japanese versions, they have the earliest Chinese script inscribed on them, while the Japanese ones never had writing on them at all.

The most recent *kiboku* divination using tortoise shells took place as part of imperial succession rituals for Emperor Naruhito. In order to determine the location for growing rice for the Great Thanksgiving Ceremony (Daijōsai), the ritual called Saiden Tentei no Gi (Imperial Tortoise Shell Ritual) was held May 13, 2019. It took place in a curtained-off area in front of an imperial sanctuary at the Imperial Palace, conducted by priests without the emperor present. In the ceremony, all forty-seven prefectures were grouped into either eastern or western locations, and two were chosen as the sites for growing the rice for the ritual: Kyoto as the western site (Yuki) and Tochigi as the eastern site (Suki). Nearly a year prior to the ritual, a morning news program aired a detailed story about the event, showing images of the green sea turtles that would be taken from a rookery in the Ogasawara Islands (Nippon Hōsō Kyōkai 2018). The priests required a total of eight pieces from three plastrons for the ritual, but they had to find someone to prepare them. They recruited a sixty-eight-year-old shell craftsman named Morita Takao, who told interviewers that "I had to learn through trial and error as it was my first time (making them)" (*Kyodo News* 2019b).[4]

Historical manga and ancient mythology manga occasionally depict representations of *bokkotsu* bone divination. An unusual manga version of the *Kojiki* equates it with an aspect of contemporary funeral rites known as *kotsuage,* although this seems highly unlikely. Most families have deceased members cremated, and the remaining pieces of bone are gathered by family members and placed in an urn. They use long, often unmatched chopsticks in tandem, such that two people lift up the bone at the same time. Outside the context of the crematorium, this behavior is highly taboo. In *Tales of the Deities: Kojiki Dramatic Comic* (Tobe and Takamuro 2006, 34–35, 124), two instances of *futomani* are shown as identical to *kotsuage.* Izanagi and Izanami together lift the scorched deer shoulder bone with long chopsticks, while for the ritual outside Amaterasu's hiding place a cracked deer bone is held aloft by two pairs of chopsticks. This is interesting fantasy because chopsticks were not introduced to Japan from the mainland until around the third century. I have not come across many references to *bokkotsu* divination in manga but expect this may change in the coming years. Now that some of the details of the imperial ritual have been broadcast in the press and on TV, it is inevitable that plastromantic omens will eventually surface more frequently.

Historians and ethnologists have documented other types of antique Japanese divination as well. Taken out of context, mentioning them looks like "weird Japan" discourse. Yet many of these forms of divination are found worldwide. An example is bird divination, called *toriura.* It is the interpretation of bird chirps, bird directional movements, and the branches they land on. It is common enough that there is a technical term in English—"ornithomancy," for the reading of calls or actions of birds to gain information about the future. It was especially customary among the ancient Mesopotamians, Hittites, Greeks, Romans, and Egyptians. Bird divination was introduced to Japan by immigrants, perhaps in the early Yayoi era (ca. 300 BCE–250 CE). It continues to be popular in Taiwan and China, and there is at least one bird divination specialist in Japan. At a divination shop in Nagoya named Iyashi no Uranai Kan Mire Fortune, the woman who runs the place will do bird divination using Java sparrows (*bunchō uranai*). Other types of divination in the past included bridge divination, crossroads divination, foot divination, stone divination, and various kinds of archery divination, which are still conducted at shrines as part of ritual events (Yagi and Masaoka 2004). The form of divination with paper lottery slips, *omikuji,* does not have ancient roots, but it is something nearly every Japanese person, including my skeptical friend, has done at least once.

Omikuji

I watched a group of young women standing next to the shrine kiosk at Tokyo Daijingū trying to figure out what to do with the paper lottery fortune. I heard them debating whether a good fortune or a bad fortune meant they were supposed to tie the slips of paper to a wooden stand in the shrine precincts. They giggled and appeared to be greatly enjoying themselves, not alone in their relish of one of the most popular forms of divination today. Named *omikuji,* these lottery slips are accessible at most Shinto shrines and many Buddhist temples. Of course, the fact that they are an easy source of revenue for both shrines and temples is an additional boost. The ambiguity of the prognoses means that anyone can read their own situation into the prophesy. In this section I will begin with a brief history of *omikuji,* followed by discussion of the variations in their formats that, I believe, have mainly been shaped by the aesthetics and desires of women and girls.

Omikuji are categorized as a type of cleromancy, the practice of foretelling from a card or other item drawn at random from a collection. Kaburagi (2017, 13) states that they were originally interpretations of the "voice of the *kami* [deities]" through the intermediary of a shaman. Tracing the provenance of *omikuji* through this concept is not possible, and written sources provide a somewhat different story. The original models for Japanese ones are unquestionably from China (Nakamura 1999). Chinese versions of the same method are still prevalent in Hong Kong, where they are called Kao Chim in Cantonese.[5] The majority of origin stories about *omikuji,* some of them quite convoluted, generally ignore their Chinese origins. For example, one theory is that they derive from Japanese officials drawing lots when facing important decisions such as succession. Ganzan Daishi (912–985), abbot of the Buddhist temple Enryakuji, is credited with the first compilation of *omikuji,* a collection of models now named Ganzan Daishi's *One Hundred Lots* (*Ganzan daishi hyakusen*).[6] The book was reprinted and used as a resource for centuries. At the temple is a monument declaring "The birthplace of *omikuji*" in front of the hall in his honor, the Ganzan Daishi-do (Nakamura 1999).

Table 2. Available *omikuji* at Kanda Myōjin

大吉	*daikichi*	great good fortune
中吉	*chūkichi*	middle good fortune
吉	*kichi*	good fortune
小吉	*shōkichi*	small good fortune
末吉	*suekichi*	uncertain
半凶	*han-kyō*	half misfortune
凶	*kyō*	misfortune

Source: Kanda Myōjin Kanshō 2008, 71.

A Buddhist temple in Takatsuki, Osaka, named Kabusanji takes the history of *omikuji* linked to Ganzan seriously by providing some that have not changed in centuries. They offer thirty-two fortunes printed from woodblocks dating to the Edo period. Because they are incomprehensible to most people today and allude to obscure meanings, each person may receive a private session with a resident monk who will read aloud and explain the *omikuji.* They will talk about the cryptic meanings and also tender advice for the future. The temple is aware that the majority of its *omikuji* are negative and asserts that they are meant to bring awareness of things one might be unconscious of or might be unreasonable about in daily life.

What forms do *omikuji* take? Most of the oracles are small slips of paper drawn at random, each with one or more Chinese characters denoting different levels of luck. The scale may span as many as twelve possibilities, from great good fortune to great misfortune. At Kanda Myōjin in Tokyo, there are seven possible categories (table 2).

It is notable that there are no *daikyō* (great misfortune) slips at this shrine. Most Shinto shrines do not have any *omikuji* with great misfortune written on them. On the other hand, most Buddhist temples, such as Sensōji in Asakusa, have a reputation for having a high percentage of *omikuji* on the less lucky scale. Kaburagi (2017, 223) suggests that this is because they are modeled on the text by the Buddhist abbot mentioned above, the *Gansan Daishi's One Hundred Lots* (19). She provides the estimates for *omikuji* fortunes at Buddhist temples (table 3).

Compared to Shinto shrines that do not offer great misfortune (*daikyō*) *omikuji,* the 30 percent rate for Buddhist temples is comparatively high. The Buddhists want the *omikuji* to serve as a teaching device, while priests at Shinto shrines are less interested in preaching lessons. In the past these fortune slips

Table 3. Percentages of *omikuji* fortunes at Buddhist temples

35% 吉	*kichi*	good fortune
17% 大吉	*daikichi*	great good fortune
30 % 大凶	*daikyō*	great misfortune
18%		other

Source: Kaburagi 2017, 223.

most often carried a poem together with the forecasts written on them. There would be four or five "commentaries," or subsections, related to different areas of life, such as health, wealth, family, and marriage. One or more divination schemes might also be listed, such as the Chinese zodiac or the ancient directional divination system called *katatagae.* The poems on *omikuji* are written in either *kanshi* (poetry written in Chinese) or Japanese *waka* poems.[7] Generally, Buddhist temples use *kanshi* poems, while Shinto shrines use *waka.*

Shrine functionaries at Kanda Myōjin instruct aspiring shrine attendants to keep in mind that *omikuji* contain advice from the deities and are not predictions. The *waka* poems are not intended to provide black or white or yes or no answers but are for petitioners to study possible meanings (Kanda Myōjin Kanshō 2008, 70–71). In essence, no *omikuji* are truly bad; they are intended to provide guidance for decision-making. Advice given to new shrine attendants cautions that if a "bad" luck slip is drawn, it is not entirely bad but simply means to pay attention to things. There are two main methods for receiving *omikuji.* A hexagonal oblong container with numbered sticks inside, closed except for a small hole, is shaken until one stick emerges. The number on the stick is used to obtain the paper *omikuji* with the corresponding number from the shrine attendant. Many places, however, simply leave a pile of rolled slips in a box or basket, and the petitioner selects one and then offers a remittance.[8] *Omikuji* may differ linguistically. There are special ones for children, with simplified language. Because *omikuji* are popular with foreign tourists, some shrines and temples offer bilingual versions or language-specific versions. At Kifune Jinja in Kyoto, they add a QR code to the *omikuji,* which allows foreign visitors to scan them to find online translations in Korean, Mandarin, and English.[9]

Similar to the women I observed at Tokyo Daijingū, many people are not certain what to do with the *omikuji* after it has been read. Does one take it home or leave it at the shrine or temple? There is conflicting advice about this depending on the source. At some shrines the attendants suggest that the visitors leave them, while others say it is up to the individual. One writer offers this advice: "What to do with an *omikuji?* Do I have to tie it there? If it's a good one, it's okay to take it home" (Kurabayashi 2010, 73). But some experts say, "Good or bad, take it or leave it, do as you like" (Kaburagi 2017, 28). If one decides to carry it home, it is permissible to place it somewhere as a reminder of the visit, such as on a desk, in a wallet, or in a scrapbook album. Some occult hunters save them in small cloth-covered books. They are called *omikuji-chō* and use a system of slots to keep the papers folded without fraying or becoming damaged with glue or tape. There has been a change in thinking about the old method of tying the *omikuji* to a tree. These days many are finding it unacceptable, as it damages the tree. Instead, people are asked to tie the *omikuji* to a stand that is usually provided. At Seimei Jinja in Kyoto, they have a box for depositing negative fortunes. Concern for recycling is also seen in a collaboration between the Asakusa Jinja and a local artisan who makes paper and papercraft art using the *omikuji* visitors have left that have been ritually purified.

A common question is whether it is acceptable to draw more than one *omikuji* during a single visit to a shrine or temple. Most etiquette literature and shrine guides advise against it. A writer named Ōtawa (2006) collected advice for badly behaving women titled *Medicine for the Super Hideous Woman.* Chapters profile deviant or repulsive behaviors, followed by the prescriptions for fixing them. One of the horrible types is the Divination Maniac, which includes women who visit shrines and take one *omikuji* after another until they select a good one. The woman in the accompanying drawing is reaching into the *omikuji* box while saying "A *daikichi* [great good fortune] will definitely come out" while a shrine attendant nearby protests the action (see figure 2; Ōtawa 2006, 151). However, going to different shrines in one day and receiving *omikuji* from each site is not taboo. The logic of this, according to Kaburagi (2017, 26), is that each shrine has its own resident deities, and therefore the oracles are generated from different sources.

Shrines and temples once printed their own *omikuji,* but eventually specialized companies began to mass produce them. Joshidō-sha (Women's Road Company) at one time accounted for almost 70 percent of the mass-printed *omikuji* used all over Japan (Joshidō-sha, n.d.). It has an interesting history linked to early women's rights efforts. A man named Miyamoto Shigetane (1881–1959) started a magazine in 1906 titled *Joshidō* (Women's Road) in order to support the organization he founded to promote female education and independence (Odaira 2015). His efforts failed and he went on to became a Shinto priest. He decided to use the printing technology from the defunct magazine to manufacture *omikuji* to fund his women's association. He also advocated for allowing women to become part of the Shinto priesthood, but as Ambros (2015, 126) points out, that effort was not successful.

Figure 2. The Divination Maniac (Ōtawa 2006, 151; drawing by Saitō Yoshiko)

Today Joshidō-sha continues to produce *omikuji* for wide distribution, but many shrines and temples are opting to have specialized ones made instead.

Thousands of unusual, cute, or pretty *omikuji* are available today. One of the most comprehensive and beautifully illustrated guides to their diversity is Kaburagi's (2017) *Japanese Omikuji: Take One of the Two-Hundred and Thirty-Two Omikuji from All Over Japan.*[10] Kaburagi describes individual *omikuji* as romantic, historical, spiritual, manga-illustrated, or retro style. It is clear from looking at page after page of the more than two hundred *omikuji* that the majority of them have adopted the kawaii (cute) aesthetic that characterizes mass culture and media.

One day in the early 2000s, I saw three schoolgirls buying *omikuji* at Kameido Tenmangū, a Shinto shrine dedicated to Tenjin, the deity of scholarship. At this shrine are two options for *omikuji:* a typical one for ¥300 and a more elaborate one for ¥500. The expensive alternative comes tied together with a small origami girl in a kimono. I wondered if perhaps a female shrine attendant (*miko*) had come up with the idea of using the cute wrapping in order to appeal to female visitors. When I asked, however, no one in the amulet office (*juyosho*) knew when this new style got started. But they did say that these origami-style oracles were proving to be extremely popular, especially with women and schoolgirls. The oracle itself, however, is of interest because it lists different types of divination forecasts, including Chinese astrology, Western astrology, and blood typology.

Cute and unusual *omikuji* have greatly proliferated. A few shrines offer a type of divination called *mizuura* (water divination).[11] The *omikuji* paper appears to be blank, but once it is placed in a fountain or water basin, the written forecast appears. An example is the *omikuji* from Meoto Daikokusha, a subshrine at the Kasuga Taisha in Nara. Set among a forest of cedars, pine, and maples, its *omikuji* is decorated with pink hearts and deer (figure 3). Once I joined a few other women at the fountain, where we submerged our *omikuji* in the water until the characters were visible. One of them exclaimed, "Wow, how cool!" A unique variation is found at Ako Oishi Jinja in Hyōgo Prefecture. The visitor writes a character on a slip of water-soluble paper and places it in a stone water basin to dissolve, taking the bad luck and negative energy with it. Women have written things such as ache (*tsu*), disease (*yami*), and man (*otoko*). According to *Yomiuri shinbun* (2009), "As this mind-refreshing practice is easier than a purification ceremony, it is popular among female university students and office workers as well as housewives."

A beautiful *omikuji* is available at Imamiya Jinja in Kyoto. It is called *waka-hime mikuji* (poem-princess paper lottery fortune) elsewhere and is

Figure 3. Water lottery fortune, Meoto Daikokusha

made of scented paper artfully folded in thirds. Inside is a *waka* and an illustration of a woman wearing the twelve-layer robes (*jūnihitoe*) of a high-ranking court lady. It is intended for visitors to take home, perhaps to use as a bookmark. Blogs are crammed with women talking about how much they love this poem-princess *omikuji*. An example is a blogger who wrote: "Now I'm going to introduce the history and things like the cute *omamori* at Imamiya Jinja that will fulfill the wishes of self-indulgent girls. Also information, so please check it out. . . . At Imamiya Jinja, there is the *waka-hime omikuji* in addition to the usual *omikuji*. Because they are cute, definitely try taking one. It has a shape like a bookmark, and inside is written a *waka* and the fortune. It is a pale, pastel shade with a cuteness that you will want to carry in your wallet or purse" (Yamada 2016).[12]

The aesthetic of cute is evident in the number of shrines and temples that now include adorable, tiny figurines with their *omikuji*. The slip of paper is placed into an envelope or plastic wrapper together with the tiny figures. At times it may be rolled up and placed in the mouth of an animal figurine. They may be animals of the Chinese zodiac or others such as a cat, bear, fish, bird, fox, or beckoning cat (*maneki neko*). Kasuga Taisha has one with a deer holding the *omikuji* in its mouth. At Tokyo Daijungū one may obtain a dainty washi paper packet that has three different pieces inside: a yellow paper with blood typology divination, a regular *omikuji* printed on elegant washi paper, and a small golden charm.[13]

City halls, stores, and many other nonreligious sites make their own secular *omikuji*. They are easily adopted for advertising and gimmicks outside the domain of shrines and temples. They are inexpensive to produce, with ample room for tweaking the form and for printing interesting text and images.[14] For example, *omikuji* are printed on bulk chopsticks for handing out at parties, and candy companies add *omikuji* to their individual packages of sweets. The Kobe Animal Kingdom created an unusual event that featured a resident parrot retrieving *omikuji*. The bird, named Harumi, accepted a ¥100 coin from visitors, walked to an offering box through a miniature Shinto gate, deposited the coin, selected an *omikuji* from a box, and returned to present it to the guest. Another memorable occurrence was the installation of an *omikuji* robot at JR Kurosaki station in Fukuoka. The "only fortune robot in the world" was unveiled in 2015 (*Afro Fukuoka* 2016). It has proven to be popular if judged by the number of Instagram photos, tweets, and other social media posts about it. It is free for passengers who have their train tickets in hand and have passed through the gate. Those who want to access the robot without traveling may get a ¥160 admission ticket. The robot performs a series of amusing actions involving a red ball that tells it which of three fortunes to select.

Only three fortunes are available: great good fortune (*daikichi*), middle good fortune (*chūkichi*), and good fortune (*kichi*), which are printed on slips of paper to resemble a train ticket.[15]

While the *omikuji* innovations and appropriations might be amusing, they are not nearly as extensive or hybrid as other types of divination not restricted to a known format. The next section will look at some of the types of divination that are popular.

Exploring Divination Texts and Spaces

For decades there has been an expansion of divination themes and images in all forms of popular culture, especially in ways intended to appeal to a female consumer. This shift is partly because the majority of divination production is now in the hands of women. Many of the trendy divination salons are owned and run by women, and the divination booths in malls are mainly staffed by women. Women are the primary artists, creators, and producers behind the recent flood of new tarot card design, occult goods, websites, and divination magazines and books. The Ministry of Economy, Trade and Industry does not provide statistical information about the divination industry, but according to one estimate a few decades ago, it generated the equivalent of more than $8 billion US dollars a year (Brasor 2006). Japanese critics are generally contemptuous of anything related to divination, dismissing it as nothing more than silly "superstition." For example, in an article in the *Asahi shinbun* (Matsukawa and Ogawa 2011), the writers warn about the dangers of divination and the occult, suggesting that dabbling in them leads to religious cult entrapment.

When we approach the subject from a scholarly perspective, however, we try to understand it on its own terms and from the insider's stance rather than from the perspective of an outsider's norms and ideas. In this case, older men who are not active participants often project their own ideas and attitudes onto their descriptions of female cultural activities. Unfortunately, most news reporting on the popularity of divination narrowly focuses on street fortune tellers and their potential exploitation of clients. Murata (2012) only interviewed female divination enthusiasts who are characterized as "addicted" to the services provided by street fortune tellers, noting the escalation in complaints submitted to the National Consumer Affairs Center of Japan. A common stereotype about divination, which journalists such as Murata perpetuate, continues to be that it is a sketchy business provided by stigmatized social groups who set up temporary tables near high-traffic train stations. Contrary to this portrait, my research reveals a much broader range of services, from upscale and trendy divination salons to corporation-owned stalls in elegant shopping malls where women enjoy divination not as a type of addiction or irrational belief but as an enjoyable social activity with entertainment value.

Divination is a social practice found among many women who enjoy exploring a multitude of augury styles and types. As one twenty-two-year-old woman told me, "I like tarot cards, *I Ching* [Book of Changes], and runes, because they are ancient types of divination and are also fun to do with my friends." My understanding of divination is based on multi-site fieldwork at bookstores, shops, bars, game centers, and schools and analysis of texts conducted sporadically since 2000. Rather than concern with individual beliefs about the efficacy of divination, I view it as a meaningful social practice that we can learn about through a variety of media and observations.

During a fieldwork visit in 2008, I spoke to or interviewed ten young women and girls between the ages of fifteen and twenty-two. My encounter with divination is also based on the observation of behavior in explicitly marked divination booths and shops and derives from participant observation in other venues as well, including shrines, bead shops, bookstores, and game arcades. I discovered divination subjects and imagery whenever I entered female-oriented consumption spaces. For example, Neko no Mise, a Tokyo café featuring resident cats that customers can play with while sipping a cup of coffee, once offered tarot card readings a few times a month by a fortune teller named Ririco. Two women I encountered in the café had originally gone there simply to visit with the cats and catch up with each other's news, but on learning that someone on the premises was giving tarot readings, they thought that would be fascinating to try. After the reading they spent more than thirty minutes talking to each other about what the tarot reader had said, trying to tie her words to specific events in their lives. Similarly, while doing research on annotated self-photography, I often saw photos on which women had written their divination blood type (*ketsueki-gata*) or a Chinese or Western zodiac sign (L. Miller 2005). For example, four young women getting their photo stickers made in an arcade each added the image of their Chinese zodiac animal above their heads. Since there is not much time allowed to add graphics and text to the photos before they are printed, the foursome had decided to add the zodiac animals before they even entered the booth.

Several long-standing and popular divination types are astrology, feng shui, tarot cards, *I Ching*, and physiognomy (reading the traits of the face and body). Western-style astrology has been fully assimilated in

Japan and is included in most monthly women's magazines and broadcast on TV. Chinese feng shui, introduced to Japan many centuries ago, is now popular among women seeking advice on how best to use specific spaces, such as Itō Yumi's (2007) guide to "car feng shui" for female car owners. Itō provides tips for a car's interior design and furnishings that will improve one's future prospects and financial outlook. Specialized feng shui such as Itō's are well represented among the thousands of books in this genre. There are, for example, books and courses on workplace feng shui, makeup feng shui, and toilet feng shui. Some of the women I spoke to understood feng shui to include the use of colors to aid in success. One duo I met always carried yellow charms on shopping days because they read in a shared book that the color yellow attracts wealth. A woman in her twenties named Aya told me about a book she shared with her friend Reiko titled *Girly Feng Shui Magic Make-up* (Takako and Mirey 2008). They experimented with some of the book's suggestions, such as hairstyles and nail polish colors that would enhance their careers or relationships. They did not view the book as something that should be taken seriously but simply thought it might be fun to play around with its ideas.

What is it about divination that women find so attractive? Scholars of religion and ritual have probed the diverse functions of divination from a variety of perspectives. For example, Kawano (1995) investigated the relationship between single women and their interest in divination during a liminal period in the years after graduation and before marriage. She also noted that divination was a social endeavor for women during gatherings at holidays, a continuing aspect of its appeal. For young women, divination is available as an imaginative activity that readily caters to their tastes and aesthetics. Divination is popular because it is something women can do with others, facilitating sharing and bonding.

Playing with Divinatory Genres

A schoolgirl named Naoko told me about the sheet of stickers with tiny photos on it that she and her friend Tomoko had just printed from a self-photography booth.[16] We were in a Harajuku arcade in the popular shopping and entertainment area. It was crammed with photo sticker machines called print club (*purikura*). Suddenly, Tomoko began laughing at something on her cell phone. Tomoko revealed that it was an online divination site that provides a forecast based on a person's "cake" personality. Looking into it, I found that the system works in this way: You go to the cake divination website and enter your name

Table 4. "Most want to do" internet divination types

1.	Wizard (*onmyōji*) divination
2.	Cake divination
3.	Conveyor belt sushi divination
4.	Movie divination
5.	Disney movie divination
6.	Rāmen divination

Source: Goo Research 2011.

and date of birth, and you are assigned a cake type (such as chocolate cake, chiffon cake, baked cheesecake, fruit tart, and others) that best captures your personality type. For example, someone who is the shortcake is said to have the qualities of a fashion leader. Although shortcake folks have a policy of being fashionable, they are not gaudy or ostentatious—they are good at casually combining accessories and dressing according to the time, place, and occasion. Cake divination can easily be accessed via a cell phone and was one of many popular internet divination types linked to female cell phone and internet culture. Indeed, according to Goo Research (2011), an internet marketing research firm, cake divination was number two on a list of the ten "most want to do" internet divination types based on a poll of 1,663 people (56 percent female) in 2005 (table 4).

The examples of cake divination, conveyor belt sushi divination, and some of the other intentionally amusing types lead me to wonder about methods for organizing or classifying the many forms of divination available. How should I group them? Although some occult hunters make a distinction between "fun" types such as cake divination and older forms such as astrology or blood typology, this manner of classification is problematic because it depends on the classifier's attitudes or belief system. Suzuki (1995) used the distinction of face-to-face or non–face-to-face channels to organize his discussion. Face-to-face channels include home fortune tellers, street fortune tellers, touring fortune tellers, and telephone fortune tellers. Non-face-to-face divination forms are accessed through media: magazines, books, TV, radio, the internet, and monthly journals. Although nicely human-centered, this system shifts away from the actual form of divination to the manner in which it is consumed. In looking at how divination is understood in female-oriented settings, I often found that these categories are interwoven in how people think about and use them.

A common scheme for classifying the divination arts is to rely on how the divination method operates as the main criteria. This is the way many popular divination manuals and divination schools arrange their descriptions and offerings. For example, a vocational school in Ebisu named Akademeia College trains students to be professionals in the divination industry. Their curriculum divides the "divination arts" into categories depending on whether the person's birth date, the person's physical traits, or the manipulation of objects is used. Divination that begins with the seeker's birth date is found in many older forms as well as newer types. Conservative author and TV personality Hosoki Kazuko (1938–2021) was one of the most well known, and perhaps most vilified, of the divination experts to often appear on TV in the 2000s. She authored more than one hundred books that use birth date as the basis for a modified Chinese-style astrological system called six-star astrology (*rokusei senjutsu*). Dorman (2007) tracked the ways in which Hosoki manipulated her system in order to make it more appealing to conservatives and those concerned about the loss of "Japaneseness." Although she was grouped with other "charisma fortune tellers," most young women told me they thought she was creepy or old-fashioned. Whenever I browsed through the divination sections of bookstores, I rarely saw women under twenty reaching for any of her books. Instead, they thumbed through cute editions describing newly invented divination types such as penguin divination (T. Ono 2007), panda divination (Midori 2007), and Yamanote Train Line divination (Isshūkan Henshūbuhen 2007).

One Japan-made birth and date divination craze popular among women is animal divination (*dōbutsu uranai*), a new zoomancy that is quite different from the borrowed Chinese zodiac, which also aligns animals with birth years. In this new system, the twelve animals are Pegasus, elephant, lion, cheetah, tiger, wolf, monkey, koala, black panther, sheep, racoon dog, and fawn, and each is associated with one of four elements (earth, sun, full moon, and new moon). The comic artist Kubo Kiriko (1999 and several subsequent years) created loveable illustrations for a series of *dōbutsu uranai* books that sold millions of copies. Animal divination systems are so popular that new ones are always being created.[17]

A second classification for divination uses traits from the seeker's body or physical components. The common indigenous typological system called *ketsueki-gata* is based on personality characterization according to blood types A, B, AB, and O. This type of classification is thought to have originated during the Taishō era (1879–1926) and became popular in later decades when it was proposed as a reliable method for understanding personality types. It has had immense cultural impact: numerous schools, corporations, and other institutions once used the system to organize work or study groups, and some ask for the applicant's blood type on job applications.[18] Every person I have ever met in Japan knows their own blood type. One may buy condoms, Hello Kitty good luck charms, and diet pills geared to each of the four blood types. In many of the female-oriented spaces, blood typology often emerges as a motif or gimmick. One divination fad that several women mentioned to me as a droll, nonserious sort they enjoyed with their friends is Gundam (Gandamu) fortune telling, in which characters from the famous animation series are paired with blood types A, B, AB, and O to yield forty-eight personality types (Gandamu Uranai Chō Seisaku Iinkai 2001).

A third method for organizing divination uses cards, stones, or other objects that are manipulated or selected at random and are thought to be material manifestations of prophecy. Older and imported divination forms such as *I Ching,* tarot cards, and crystals are examples of this object-based category. While I was hanging around a divination shop named Wiz Note, I saw two schoolgirls spend almost thirty minutes debating whether or not one of them should buy a deck of "rune" oracle cards, a good example of this category. They left the shop but returned a few minutes later to buy them. The alphabetic runes have long been associated with divination in Europe, and this deck, created by charisma fortune teller Kagami (2000), was antique looking with Renaissance-style art together with the Nordic runes.

Magazine companies, government agencies, university researchers, and marketing firms all routinely conduct surveys to determine people's beliefs about the efficacy of divination. A poll conducted by Goo Research (2010) shows that divination methods from each of the three categories are considered reliable (table 5). People who participated in the survey asking which divination system they think has the greatest chance of predicting the future ranked palmistry as the most reliable. The female respondents accounted for a little more than half those polled, nearly half of them under thirty. Two types, four pillars divination and name divination, tied for the number two spot. Four pillars divination (*shichū suimei*) was originally from China and uses the seeker's year, month, day, and hour of birth to predict the future. Name divination (*seimei handan*) can take different forms but most often is a type of numerology derived from the character strokes found in the person's written name.

Table 5. Which divination type do you think has the highest predictive value?

1.	Palmistry
2.	Four Pillars divination (tied)
3.	Name divination (tied)
4.	Six Star astrology
5.	Tarot cards
6.	Blood typology
7.	Geomancy (feng shui)
8.	Physiognomy
9.	Dream interpretation
10.	Western zodiac

Source: Goo Research 2010.

In addition to the three categories of divination discussed above (birth date, physical traits, or manipulation of objects), the poll also includes novel types that originated in Japan. Such an eclectic mix illustrates another problem in the classification of divination: many of the types that are most popular among women are hybrid forms that exploit multiple strategies and current interests. Consider cat characters divination (Tomono 2007). The seeker starts with their Western zodiac sign and cross-checks it against his or her blood type, which yields one of twelve alphabet letters. Depending on one's sex, one looks up one's type under the assigned letter to determine which of twelve possible cat characters represent one's forecast. The cats are manga characters such as Yume, Michael, Yukipon, Kuro, and Fukukuku. Manga drawings for each character are found throughout the book, and the presentation suggests that young women are the primary target audience. These types of ultracute divination schemas are plentiful.[19]

Divination products and services are often linked to cultural trends and combine imagery and meanings from different realms. An example is the combination of systems used to create Korean Wave face divination (Yanagi 2005). This system introduced Korean-style face reading with famous Korean pop stars as examples of particular facial types. The term "Korean Wave" was coined to describe the influx of Korean popular culture into Japan, especially hit TV dramas, and the increase in fans of Korean cultural products from 2003 (L. Miller 2008b). There are associated fortunes based on variation in eyebrow shape, nose type, ear type, mouth shape, eye shape, facial structure, and hairline pattern. One schoolgirl named Masako told me she liked this divination book because the illustrations reminded her of the main character in the TV drama *Dae jang geum* (Jewel in the Palace), a historical series that follows the life of the first female imperial physician in Korean history (Lee Byung-Hoon 2003). The book also includes information and maps for visiting divination cafés in Seoul, with directions and explanations of the types of divination services found in various specialized coffee shops. This aspect of the divination industry—combining other amusements with fortune-telling—characterizes how divination is frequently consumed in tandem with other leisure pursuits.

The spectrum of divination-driven activities or divination-oriented goods and entertainment has generated enormous profit, yet it remains an industry that receives little attention in mainstream business reporting. In addition, the divination industry is almost always the focus of negative reporting in media, where it is trivialized or demonized.

The role of print media, especially magazines and manga, is critical to understanding the escalation of interest in divination. Monthly magazines often include free specially inserted giveaways called *furoku*. In the divination magazines *Kaiunchō* and *Koiunreiki*, the inserts take the form of punch-out divination goods, oracle cards, or tarot cards. Many avid women connoisseurs of beautiful tarot card decks said they became interested in studying this art because their girlhood magazines often carried tear-out *furoku* sheets of colorful and unusual cards that fascinated them. They recalled that the free cards were something they and their friends talked about and shared.

By looking at some of the newer forms of divination, particularly the varieties of borrowed, hybrid, and reinvented occult practices that have emerged in recent years, we attend to an underanalyzed industry. I hope we might understand the function of divination as a form of entertainment or social play. Tanabe (2007) mentioned the manner in which religion and entertainment are locked in an interactive relationship, and Thomas (2007) wrote about Miyazaki anime films as a conflation of religion and entertainment. I, too, see occult play and the revitalized divination industry as aspects of the religious landscape.

Similar to divination systems everywhere in the world, those consumed by women in Japan are presented in such a way that the prognoses might suit almost anyone. Rather than advocating the efficacy of their forecasting results, most people say that whether or not divination is true or accurate, they are able to gain some useful insight into a personal situation just by virtue of thinking about it in a focused manner. When they talk about their worries and concerns with someone, such as a divination provider or friends who participate in a divination activity with them, they feel they have taken a step toward understanding the issue from a more dispassionate stance, which in turn aids them in decision-making. Thus, talking about their worries within the framework of the divination activity is seen as a legitimate move rather than as self-centered monopolization of a conversation. When the divination activity is framed as a fun, entertaining friendship activity, it also shifts the orientation away from behavior that might otherwise be seen as egotistical self-involvement.

Participating in the divination business, as a provider or a consumer, replaces the orderly domains of school and work with a new universe of magical possibility and action. I believe that creativity in the *uranai* industry also offers a counterargument to the better-known and officially promoted idea that androcentric otaku (nerd) culture is at the core of Japanese cultural innovation. While Asami (2007) and others investigate possible reasons for the divination boom, they rarely discuss the major shift in the concerns seen in occult consumption. In the past the focus of divination was on the family or nation, but these days it is firmly located on the individual and their own life trajectories, love interests, and self-development. In Figal's (1999, 7) study of the supernatural and the occult during the Meiji period, he argues that "a discourse on the supernatural, the mysterious, and the fantastic—what I refer to as *fushigi*—was constitutive of Japan's modern transformation." He tracked how worries about monsters and demons co-occur with periods of social transition and how Meiji-era "monsterology" was essential to the creation of modernity. While his work was certainly a major contribution to the scholarship, I wondered about the role of gender in this fascinating history. Gender is hard to ignore in the contemporary turn to the occult. The unstable nature of the concept of *uranai*/divination, which may encompass occult play to serious advice seeking, offers models and identities that run counter to mainstream versions of proper female roles, effort, and behavior. The subversions of this domain are also found in its opposition to an epistemology of scientific reasoning.

CHAPTER 2

Occult Business

The types of divination consumed in Japan are diverse and plentiful. Some forms are ancient, while others are a creolized melding from different cultures or traditions. In addition, there are entertaining divination pastimes meant to be humorous. In this chapter I discuss a few of the places on the ground where this spectrum of services is delivered to paying clients and readers. These brick-and-mortar divination shops and booths differ from the older model of how one goes about getting one's fortune told. Unlike the freelance, individual fortune tellers who would set up impromptu tables near train stations and charge variable fees, the majority of divination providers today are part of an established group or shop and have had some type of professional training and screening. Additionally, new spaces where occult hunters pay for divination, such as game centers and while traveling to other countries, have arisen. Divination services are also offered online and by telephone. Finally, I introduce some occult entrepreneurs who use figures from ancient history to legitimize or exoticize their divination services or publications.

Anywhere in Tokyo it is easy to find divination boutiques and shops where occult hunters purchase tarot cards, crystals, divination compasses, amulets, and other goods. Since 2008 I have visited many of these sites to receive a divination service or simply observe the type of services being offered and the interactions between providers and clients. I also stumbled on divination booths in shopping malls, which are usually called "divination corners." Most of the booths are operated by corporations that have a stable menu of divination experts who rotate between booths at different malls on different days of the week. One of the better-known companies is Mari Fortune. The schedules are easily accessed online and list multiple types of divination, from the old-fashioned to newer hybrid types. Each booth seats one to three diviners, and there is a standardized price structure based on time. The standardized prices are posted and are the same at all locations. Having uniform posted fees has made these businesses quite successful. They are especially attractive to women who do not want to worry about being bamboozled. Unlike the street soothsayers maligned by Murata (2012), these clean and bright divination booths never generate complaints about fees or services. I received tarot readings (Western Tarot and *I Ching* Tarot) from Mari Fortune booths at the Central Plaza in Iidabashi, at Mylord at Shinjuku Station, and at Metropolitan Plaza in Ikebukuro. The booths were set up in open areas of the shopping malls against a building wall, with curtains or screens blocking two sides. The readings were more or less public. The divination providers for my readings were all women who were cheerful, talkative, and warm. I did not see any waiting clients who appeared to be distressed. Everyone I saw was smiling and often laughing with the divination provider, seemingly enjoying this type of counseling session. Perhaps the luxury of talking about themselves and their own dreams was worth the low fee? A woman I spoke to said she always went to a nearby Mari Fortune location whenever her favorite divination specialist was doing a rotation there. She told me that Mitsuhana-sensei provides a type of tarot card reading using Inspiration Tarot, which she found especially attractive and meaningful. This variety of tarot incorporates the person's affect together with the reader's interpretations to predict the short-term future. Mitsuhana offers other divination services, including Chinese nine-star astrology, palm reading, directional divination, and *I Ching* Tarot readings. Many divination providers like Mitsuhana have a solid reputation and a loyal fan following. Their followers always address or refer to these divination specialists with the title *sensei* (teacher). What I saw in many divination service spaces was unlike the media portrayal of this business, which is usually depicted as run by sketchy scam artists who individually set up tables on the street.

In addition to the booths found in malls are small divination shops located in office buildings and along busy streets. They sell goods and provide readings and other services. One place that particularly appealed to schoolgirls and young women was a trendy shop named Wiz Note. It was later relocated to an office building, but in 2008 it was still crammed in among other businesses found on the main pedestrian-only shopping street in the section of Tokyo called Ikebukuro. The shop was always crowded with foot traffic because of its location near a popular store and shopping center. I entered the shop more than ten times over a few months and never once saw male customers. Wiz Note offered divination services and carried a variety of occult goods, including crystals, tarot cards, feng shui compasses, and amulets. The store was owned and managed by two women and was packed with female shoppers every time I visited. I often saw uniform-wearing schoolgirls inside rummaging through the tarot decks and occult goods that crowded the store shelves. Two women in their twenties who were seated at a very tiny round table where one was preparing to have a tarot card reading told me what they found most attractive about the shop. They liked that it was a welcoming space for women and that the all-female staff were always there to answer questions in a warm and kind manner. They also doubted that some of the items they found most intriguing or edgy, such as the deck of Gay Tarot cards, would ever be found in more "traditional" retail spaces.

New divination shops are always popping up in new locations. Within the Asakusa district in Tokyo are more than fifteen divination cafés and salons. Divination connoisseurs publish online articles ranking and evaluating them. In 2022 a new shop opened on one of the busy side streets next to the packed tourist shopping road that leads to Sensōji (figure 4). Core

Figure 4. Divination shop in Asakusa

Divination, which advertises itself as located in the "Asakusa powerspot," hosts a menu of services provided by an all-female stable of divination experts. In addition to tarot readings, they offer *magatama* therapy and pet divination. *Magatama* therapy is relatively new to the occult scene. It is a program created in 2015 that blends self-affirmation theory, New Age powerstone developments, and a strong dose of Japanese nationalism. The founder of *magatama* therapy, Itō Naomi, brands her program as a "pure Japanese therapy" that "originated in Japan by Japanese people" even though it is a creolized form of Chinese Taoist and American New Age concepts and rituals with an overlay of Shinto mythology. The occult hunter selects different-colored beads from an array that will then be used for the reading. The beautiful beads are named orgonite *magatama* and are amalgamations of crystals, resin, and metals. They are said to contain a supernatural power called orgone, a term coined in the United States in the 1930s.

A horoscope and powerstone salon I visited named ZyX (Zeikusu) was very elegant and New Age–like, on the fourth floor of a building in Shibuya. I read about it in a women's magazine, but it was difficult to find and not clearly marked. There was a *kamidana* (home Shinto altar) in the reception room on a cabinet. I was served tea in a delicate French porcelain cup while cool ambient music played in the background. I received a "geocentric horoscope" and a reading in which the provider, a young man I will call B-sensei, used a set of black dice. I was curious so reached for them to look more closely, but he grabbed them away and chastised me. This was one of the few divination shops where I encountered a male provider. (Mainly, I received tarot card readings from female divination providers.) The shop had never had a foreign client before, and he repeatedly asked how I knew about them. He took my birthdate and place of birth and then went into another room to enter the information into a computer in order to generate my horoscope chart. I could hear him and his officemates debating how to do it as their system was set up for people born in Japan. He returned and asked if Los Angeles was in the Pacific time zone, and when I said yes, he went back and finished setting up the chart. With the printed-out chart in hand, he proceeded to tell me about the strong points and weak points in my chart, using red ink to mark sections. Evidently, I was going to have good luck financially but not in the romance department. Before the reading I let him know that I was a scholar doing research on the divination business. Even so, at the end of the session I was given a small gift: a pink powerstone in a small red bag for good luck in romance. He tried to interest me in purchasing a powerstone bracelet but I declined. A week later B-sensei sent an email to invite me back for another reading, which I also declined.

There are so many divination stalls, booths, shops, and other venues for obtaining a reading that consumers value ratings and assessments. Published guidebooks to divination services have entered the publishing market. One was presented in a manga format by Kashiwagi (2013), who calls herself a "divination freak" (figure 5). Her interest led her to visit more than 150 divination providers in Japan and in other countries. She describes a range of divination shops and explains how reservations, payment, and the actual process of receiving a reading is conducted. In addition to traditional divination forms such as palmistry and tarot readings, she introduces a few unusual types such as psychometry divination (reading objects held in the hand) and "shrine appraisal," which helps one find the Shinto shrine that will offer lifetime protections. A few occult hunters posted negative reviews online because they found her style too cavalier and disrespectful. Her cover profile blurb affords some perspective on her stance: "I want to be praised even if I have to pay for it!" and "Divination is the heart's host club." Her words are a clue to a customer motivation found in much of the divination industry: women want to be able to center their attention on themselves and talk about themselves in a space where they will not be negatively evaluated for doing so.

Figure 5. Guide to divination providers

Divination Entertainment

Divination as a part of female entertainment is explicit at Namco Town, an indoor theme park complex in Ikebukuro, Tokyo (the name was changed in 2013, and some attractions have changed or been eliminated). It houses several discrete recreational areas along with alleys that zigzag through them. Most are food-oriented experiences, such as Gyōza Stadium, a laneway with retro-style dumpling stalls that sell famous potsticker types from around Japan. One distinct section is named Soothsayer Street. Here customers purchase divination forecasts in automated booths for ¥500, with a choice of eleven virtual experts in Chinese astrology, kabala, tarot, South Asian astrology, and other occult sciences. On visits I observed groups and pairs of women entering Soothsayer Street, where they first purchased tokens to use in one of the booths. The area is decorated in faux Arabian artifacts and drapery, with lamps and arabesque architectural bits scattered around. Each booth has a bench that might seat two or three people in front of it. I rarely saw a person enter Soothsayer Street alone, and men and boys seemed to enter only if accompanied by a female partner. My friends and I found it to be an enjoyable activity, and at the conclusion of the session, each booth yielded a sheet with forecasts printed on it that customers could take home.[1] One of the booths was dedicated to the famed Shinjuku Mother (Shinjuku no Haha), the nickname given to Kurihara Sumiko (1930–2019). She had provided palm readings, physiognomy, and nine-star astrology in Tokyo since the 1950s.[2] She claimed to have advised more than three million people! Kurihara was the subject of intense media attention, including an autobiography, a comic, and a TV drama. There is a manga anthology of vignettes in which Kurihara gives sage advice to people dealing with a messy office romance, a family interference, and a sweet but flawed husband with a gambling addiction (Bunkasha Komikkusu 2006). Kurihara was featured in a TV drama in commemoration of the fiftieth anniversary of her career (Fuji TV 2006). A young woman who paid for Kurihara's in-person divination service (she charged a flat fee of ¥5,000) told me that she felt more optimistic, uplifted, and happier after speaking with the warm and engaging Kurihara, regardless of how "real" or accurate the divination may have been. Younger women who cannot afford the actual service from Kurihara herself think the Namco Town booth falls in the realm of campy retro, yet they still believe that the game complex booth version is not only affordable, interactive, and fun but also less time-consuming and more comfortable to visit with friends. Asked if she would like to visit the real-life Shinjuku Mother instead of the video booth imposter, a young woman said, "It would be a little scary. And then there's such a long wait. It's a pain. Coming here is more convenient."

Divination is promoted as oversees tourism, with trips from Japan to Hong Kong, Taipei, and Shanghai. The tour companies pitch them as an opportunity to explore the birthplace of Chinese-style divination. For example, the Kinki Nippon Tourist Company advertised a visit to Taipei's teeming divination sector in its brochures, which promised to provide translators and guides for a safe and smooth experience. A popular destination is the Fortune Telling Street underground passage near Xingtian Temple in Taipei, Taiwan. Many of the divination providers post signs in Japanese announcing that they speak Japanese (L. Miller 2017a). It is not only historic Chinese divination that is used as a marketing device.

A number of divination businesspeople reference historical Japanese figures as part of their individualized services, often incorporating ancient costuming and ritual elements. How do the service providers modify or amplify characteristics of historic figures in order to make them effective for promoting contemporary divination efforts? I found wide variation in how they use the historic personage. Most often they are simply drawing inspiration from the past, perhaps symbolically through clothing, imagery, and text. This indexing of the historic figure may have different goals: to confer meanings of authenticity, Japanese identity, exoticness, or the magical. In a few cases, however, the occult entrepreneur claims a direct connection to the historic figure or their occult practices, either though family lineage or through supernatural means.

Selling Ancient Divination

Two figures from ancient history who appear often in the occult domain are Himiko (170–248 CE) and Abe no Seimei (921–1005). As mentioned before, Himiko was the paramount chief of the earliest Japanese polity, described only briefly in Chinese historical records. Because she was described as adept at magical arts, she appears often in occult domains. She is primarily a metaphor for female agency and innate magical abilities, alluding to occult practices that are associated with the celebrated shaman.

Some years ago, I was in Tokyo to meet and get readings from tarot readers. One day I went in search of someone who claimed in promotional materials that she exclusively used the seventeenth-century Tarot de Marseilles deck and had even studied with a master in Paris. While I was talking to her, another divination specialist who shared the office space joined us. She was dressed up in Yayoi-era clothing and said she conducted past life readings and other spiritual services during which she channeled the spirit of Himiko. She explained that she was simply continuing the occult craft associated with the celebrated Queen Himiko and was not herself a reincarnation of Himiko. However, there are those who promote Himiko in even more personal ways.

An unusual divination provider who goes by the name Hieda On Mayura maintains that Himiko was reborn in her body. She is the author of numerous divination books and articles. She began using the *bonji* Sanskrit "om" as a sort of middle name but now writes it in Japanese syllabic script. In her tweets, blogs, and advertising through internet divination sites, she usually uses the catch phrase "Himiko resurrected in our time." Hieda delivers divination readings in person, by phone, or over the internet, often using tarot cards. She prefers the tarot deck called Reikan Tarotto, or Inspirational Tarot. This version of tarot uses the same cards as conventional tarot, but the meanings are supplemented by the divination provider's inspiration. Hieda also claims to use a form of magic transmitted by Himiko that is called *kidō*. The term is found in the *Wei zhi* description of Himiko's ritual behavior. As Kidder (2007) notes, even though the characters used are literally for demon and path, we are not certain what the writers intended them to mean. It could simply be that anything outside what Wei historians considered normal ritual behavior was classified in this manner and not that it had reference to black magic or trafficking with demons. Hieda, however, does pull from the darker meaning of the term. She claims, for example: "Himiko's secret *kidō* has been handed down from ancient times—Please handle with care. . . . The power of *kidō* has been sealed away because of its terrifying power. I will use this immense power to lead people to happiness. How much pain are you in? I will release you from your suffering" (Hieda 2012, website).

One of her best-selling books is about how to deal with horrible men: *I'll Teach You the Way of Cursing a Difficult Guy or Obnoxious Boss* (Hieda 1994). Her self-presentation as well is almost always severe and unsmiling, as if she is channeling dark, angry spirits. When I first noticed her in 2017, she was dressed up as a *miko* shrine attendant or in Yayoi-era clothing. She gradually shifted to wearing vaguely South Asian garb. In recent years she has dramatically changed to nonbinary or male-coded fashion with short hair and black suits. She still claims to be the reincarnation of Himiko, however.

The Heian-era wizard named Abe no Seimei became a colossal hit among female fans after he became the romanticized subject of novels, manga, anime, feature films, and TV dramas beginning around 1990. Stories about Seimei are known from Japanese legend and history. Seimei was an occasional member of a guild of wizards that was an official part of the imperial court structure. Appropriations of Seimei proliferate within the occult goods and information industry, where his image is used to index hidden magic and the ancient. Seimei is intensely put to service in the divination book–publishing industry. For those who want to study how to become an accomplished wizard themselves—just like Seimei!—these manuals offer precise instructions on the types of spells and enchantments he is said to have used. One prolific producer of these occult manuals is Kuyōgi Shūkei.

Kuyōgi found the perfect formula for this genre: a slim book of instructions and directions accompanied by a cardboard box insert with objects consumers may assemble for their own occult play. They are packaged together in an attractive boxed set. The objects include things such as divination dice, *katashiro* paper effigies, cosmographic divination boards, and *reifu* Taoist paper charms that can be assembled, cut out, or unfolded. Kuyōgi's handsome book sets have titles such as *The Secret Wizard Abe no Seimei:"Spirit Helper" Divination* (Kuyōgi 2001), *Abe no Seimei's Secret Tricks: Writings on the Four Treasures and Tools of the Way of the Wizard for Spells and Incantations* (Kuyōgi 2002), and *The Abe no Seimei Codes: The Wizard's Craft, Circumvention of Directional Taboos and Charms for the Prevention of Bad Luck* (Kuyōgi 2003).[3] All these book sets are fairly well grounded in what we know historically about the complex and hybrid ritual practice called *onmyōdō*. Kuyōgi makes an effort to explain directional taboos (*katatagae*), use of *katashiro* paper effigies, Taoist *reifu* paper charms, the cosmograph board, feng shui compasses, and divination dice. At the same time, he also includes newly invented activities such as *shikigami* spirit helper cards. Beyond book publishing, a few contemporary occult entrepreneurs present themselves as modern-day *onmyōji*. Three I would like to introduce briefly are Obata Karindo, Ishida Chihiro, and Hashimoto Kyōmei.

Obata Karindo is active in the circuit of divination providers who travel around doing lectures and counseling sessions. His CD and DVD set contains methods such as using *reifu* paper charms and reciting ritual Shinto incantations (Obata 2010). For example, he suggests a particular chant that will help one smooth over relationships with others. Obata claims that by applying the wisdom of the past to our own lives, we will get positive results. In promotional materials for his workshops, he declares that clients will acquire the art of self-management as well as customer motivation from a real *onmyōji*. He says, "Get your motivation on the upswing and learn how to keep yourself and those around you happy and positive!" by using the wizard's techniques. In his workshops

Obata reconfigures Shinto mythology in a new fashion, in particular targeting people in the business sector, promising that these ancient teachings will help them get business results. He revamps the notion of the Three Sacred Treasures (Sanshu no Jingi), which are composed of a mirror, a sword, and a *magatama* bead. For today's office worker, Obata says that the sword represents the martial arts, the mirror represents rituals, exorcism, and prayers, and the *magatama* represents the use of magic and amulets. Other than the *reifu* Taoist paper charms, which date to at least the Asuka period and were part of the *onmyōji*'s hybrid mix of practice, there is not much in his book, CD, or other materials that can be linked to historic *onmyōdō*. Much of it appears to be warmed-over teachings from a modern-day martial arts studio and a Shinto incantation primer.

Ishida Chihiro also melds together common forms of modern divination and feng shui practice that are represented as lessons from an *onmyōji*. His book, *Invite Happiness with Wizard Techniques* (Ishida 2008), hinges on key words such as "practicality" and "anyone can do it." His simple and straightforward advice is meant to give readers a "happy charge." The book contains adorable drawings of samurai, everyday customs such as gift giving or the eating of red rice for celebration, and an explanation of the meaning of the Japanese pentagram, associated with Seimei. He also throws in a large red *reifu* paper charm for home protection. While it is a more pleasant and familiar mash-up than that offered by Obata, his book also has very little to do with *onmyōdō*.

Finally, there is Hashimoto Kyōmei (2016), who bills himself, with a knowing wink, as the Last Onmyōji. Hashimoto claims to be a son of a Shinto household and that he learned divination and exorcism from relatives who were *onmyōji* starting at the age of eight. He states: "I am today's *onmyōji* and always do fortune telling with the knowledge and statistics people of the past bestowed on us. As a descendant of a wizard guild, I will teach you how to live a great life by using statistics, which approaches everything scientifically and through understanding of nature." Hashimoto joins Obata and Ishida in delivering divination cosplay, modern forms of fortune telling dressed up in historic trappings. All three, despite claims to wizard family lineages or other avenues to *onmyōji* knowledge, nevertheless rely on the idioms and practices of the contemporary divination industry.

Although some divination entrepreneurs present their talents as ancient and legitimate, most occult hunters are informed consumers and are not dupes. Most do not claim to "believe" in the efficacy of any type of divination, even if they enjoy paying for it. Rather, they say that the divination events trigger new frameworks of possibilities. The tarot cards, Taoist *reifu,* and other ritualized forms and objects provide heuristic devices and are seen as inspirational tools for healing and guidance. For the most part, the entrepreneur's claims to legitimacy through posing as Himiko or modern-day *onmyōji* are recognized as obvious theatricality, appropriation, and playfulness by clients and customers. Because the domain is so flooded with comical or humorous forms of divination, these are merely additional ones appreciated for novelty and for the amusing exoticization of the ancient. The voices of occult hunters are strong, judgmental, and effective.

The majority of occult service shops, booths, and online collectives are not deliberately peddling forms of quackery. The extensive divination business category, which includes a broad menu of services and media, often provides customers with a safe space for introspection and self-talk, as well as a popular type of entertainment. Although there remain many free-ranging divination and occult providers who claim exaggerated or bogus facts about their provenance or skills, most members of the divination community try to prevent deliberate scams by promoting and hiring people who have been screened. For example, most of the online telephone and online divination services organize vetted providers into collectives with evocative names such as Tamayura, Dreamboat Annie, and Raphael. Customers offer feedback and evaluations online, and unfavorable ratings result in the elimination of the collectives' poorly regarded members.

CHAPTER 3

Tarot Cards

At a wood counter in Tokyo, an intent woman named Mizuki spread ten selections from a tarot deck into a Celtic cross layout, considered one of the most popular yet orthodox tarot reading styles. Mizuki-sensei told her client, a petitioner eager to know about her career prospects, that if she focused with a clear mind and confidence, she would continue to be financially successful. I participated in this divinatory event in 2008 with an old Japanese friend. It is not markedly unusual for a Japanese woman to receive a tarot card reading. What was unique was the location: it took place at a small bar in fashionable Roppongi amid glasses of wine and snacks. The owner of Tarot Bar Rosy, Inoue Yumiko, delivered both cocktails and tarot readings to a mainly female clientele. The bar (now closed) had only eight seats, and when it opened in 2007, Inoue hired several other "tarotists" (*tarotisuto,* Inoue's coinage) such as Mizuki-sensei to assist her with the business. This distinctive bar became so popular that customers were required to call to reserve readings weeks in advance.

Tarot readings are also delivered through encounters in divination shops, booths in malls and busy shopping areas, at festivals, at museum events, on tours, in cafés, and in other bars like Tarot Bar Rosy. Aficionados are also playing with tarot divination through computer games, iPhone and iPod applications, automated arcade booths, and online divination sites. Some occult hunters own six or more decks and are avaricious collectors of unique or particularly gorgeous cards. Love of the cards has spread beyond the objects to include other aspects of tarot culture. The best tarot readers, or perhaps those clever at promoting themselves, have become national celebrities. Several vocational schools offer courses and workshops on how to read and understand tarot cards. These opportunities for learning afford ordinary people an avenue for involvement in tarot culture. The imagery on the cards themselves might be customized for a Japanese viewer. In particular, the medieval European people and elements originally found on the cards are replaced with images from the world of Japanese art, history, and popular culture. These substitutions gloss over the gaps between worldviews or meld them into a new form, allowing the tarot entry into a different or hybrid metaphysical culture.

This chapter begins with a brief history of tarot cards to ground my discussion of card trends. It is followed by a description of discourse and norms connected to card readings, a brief description of tarot education and services, and a closer look at tarot aesthetics and themes. It ends with mention of other aspects of tarot culture, such as manga and literature.

Tarot History

The origin of tarot cards is unclear, with at least one improbable history asserting that they were used by the ancient Babylonians. It is more likely they began as simple playing cards that entered Europe from Islamic culture around the fourteenth century. The earliest tarot decks are fundamentally sets of playing cards with twenty-two supplemental symbolic picture cards. These have been traced to Italy in the fifteenth century. Using the cards for fortune telling was not well established until the 1700s with the creation of a literature containing arcane ascribed meanings. Most tarot decks are composed of seventy-eight cards. They are divided into two sets: the twenty-two major arcana (representing iconic principles or archetypes) and the fifty-six minor arcana suit cards. The tarot cards that emerged in Europe ultimately made their way to Japan. Euro-American tarot cards are most often the starting point for the amplifications or modifications we see in Japan. Tarot schools and readers are very particular about which decks they use and often name their preferred decks in promotional materials and on business cards.

It appears that tarot cards have been widely available in Japan at least since the 1930s, and for the decades up until the 1970s, they were part of a general fascination with the occult (the "occult boom" mentioned in the introduction). Writers such as Shibusawa (1961) delved into occult themes, contributing an influx of male adherents to tarot fandom. By the 1970s tarot appreciation shifted to realms outside male-oriented literary cultures. The expansion of women's and girl's magazines and manga, many of which featured tarot, played a role in carving out a niche among female readers. The critic Ōtsuka (1997) suggests that attraction to horror and tarot cards among female readers might derive from a desire to separate themselves from mainstream society through shared consumption of the fantastic and the occult.

Today most female tarot designers, readers, and devotees point to the fortune-telling magazine *My Birthday* as the starting point in their appreciation for the cards. The magazine, nicknamed *Maiba,* focused on young girls and teens and was published between 1979 and 2006. It frequently enclosed *furoku* supplementary gifts of punch-out tarot cards on strong card stock that readers could easily deploy. *My Birthday* provided guidelines on how to do card readings with friends. Famous tarot readers and card producers sometimes mention *Maiba* as the inspiration for their career paths (i.e., Bi and Umezawa 2004, 2). In 2012 the publisher released a nostalgia issue of *My Birthday* that included six insert pages of all seventy-eight tarot cards in beautiful color on heavy card stock (Jitsugyō no Nihonsha 2012; figure 6). Periodicals such as this, as well as other magazines, books, and manga, were significant factors in the expansion of tarot culture among girls and women.

An escalation in tarot enjoyment stimulated the creation of original and hybrid decks after 2000. New designs attract consumers and express a creative response to the customary concepts and meanings encoded in the cards. Thus, every year a range of new tarot are produced that express the various ways that people participate in the world of tarot, from serious pursuit to social play. Whether for amusement or for inquiry, perhaps half the decks sold in Japan are only composed of the twenty-two major arcana cards.

Figure 6. My Birthday magazine and gift insert cards

Card Discourse and Reading

Tarot cards may be used not only as predictions of the future but also as psychological tools for self-exploration. The person giving the card reading uses the images and symbols on the cards to address the questions or topics of concern to the occult hunter. Tarot symbols and images carry meaning, but the cards are physical objects that some readers say contain supernatural power. The energy of the cards is thought to be activated when they are handled and when they are the subject of directed focus. This power is made present not only from the images on the cards but also from the meanings they evoke in the person's consciousness. In his description of the general use of ritual objects, Eller (2007, 65) captures this aspect when he says, "Humans, concrete beings that we are, need something to talk to, to focus on, to hold and manipulate, and the symbols give us a 'hands-on' experience of the sacred."

A tarot reading is an intense space of interaction that connects the reader and the seeker through the physical object and its visual meanings. Sharing a focus establishes connections between the tarot, its handlers, and the supernatural realm. The cards go beyond their status as symbol vehicles and are seen as conduits through which supernatural essence or power is transmitted. Part of tarot instruction includes the primary rule that decks are personal objects and therefore should never be used by others. New decks need to be charged or enlivened. This entails keeping them close to the body and handling them repeatedly. Because cards are considered to be *shinsei* (sacred), those who handle them are expected to provide them with respect and care. For example, many tarot sensei urge the reader to wash her hands before touching them. One tarot specialist (Mūnpurinsesu Himiko 2008, 27) insists that if one card is missing from a deck, the reading must be ended. Some adherents suggest that cards be cleansed by placing them in moonlight for a few nights or placing them near incense or aromatherapy oils. This inauguration of sacred objects is found in other religious contexts elsewhere in Asia, such as rituals performed for new sutras or Buddhist statues (Kendall 2021).

Cards should be kept in a safe place, wrapped in a cloth or inserted into a small cloth case. Tarot sensei usually house their tarot in handmade pouches. Mizuki-sensei at Tarot Bar Rosy, for example, keeps her tarot in a blue velvet amulet bag with a pentagram embroidered on it. Teachers say that one should only read cards in a quiet location and never in a messy, jumbled room. One must ignore the telephone—if you answer the reading must end. There are countless methods for the shuffling and spread of tarot. The table used for tarot should be covered by a cloth to protect the cards and to contribute to the creation of a ritual space. I have seen many types of material used for this purpose, but velvet appears to be quite well-liked. Purple velour, red silk, and paisley materials also drape many tarot tables. Most tarot readers follow some general rules. For example, in an interview with the occult expert Izumi Ryūichi, who teaches courses for the Arcanum Seminars school located in Shibuya, he stated that it is important for the person reading the cards to clear the mind to "make their own frames of consciousness melt away" (Mizuhara 2011, 18). In addition to his widely popular tarot encyclopedia, Izumi (2004) also publishes and lectures on runes, numerology, and astrology.

To begin a reading, either the client or the reader uses both hands to shuffle the cards and then places them flat on the table. The cards are retrieved and put into a stack. With the left hand, the occult hunter might cut the deck into three piles. Some sensei said they do not want anyone touching their cards at all, so the procedure might be modified. Normally, the reader regroups the three piles and then places a hand on the stacked deck for a few minutes with closed eyes, clearing the mind before picking up and laying out the cards. The choice of one of the many possible card layouts hinges on the degree of time and insight determined beforehand. Layout types (such as Celtic Cross, Pentagram, Tree of Life, Timeline, Horoscope, and so on) are described in most easily accessible tarot guides. For example, to answer a query about romantic life one reader told me she prefers a five-card layout of the Pentagram spread.

Other accoutrements might be brought in to augment a reading. These might be beads, stones, crystal balls, bells, candles, and aromatherapy oils that are also placed on the table. A shop in Shibuya named Aquary occasionally hosted a few famous tarot sensei. It is a compact space, so they had a rotation system for the readers in residence. One was a celebrated tarot reader named Morpho who depends on a tuning fork and a rosary in her readings (Gyappu Japan 2010, 56). The manner in which Morpho commissions a variety of objects to enhance her readings is mirrored in other aspects of tarot culture. The world of tarot inspires the study of occult subjects and novel iconography, giving fans an avenue for displaying spiritual capital, including the choice of which accoutrements to add to their ritual spaces. For example, in *Spiritual Tarot,* writer Akatsuki (Akatsuki and Takano 2010) lists lucky colors and essential oils that may be associated with each tarot card, thus adding a further dimension to tarot mastery that fans can pursue as part of their study. Tarot may be studied in numerous ways, and media and schools with new offerings have arrived on the scene to meet the new demand.

Tarot Education

How occult hunters relate to tarot may depend on the paths they follow to learn and interpret its history and symbolism. In addition to guidebooks and websites, adult education courses became critical to the expansion and entrenchment of card divination practices. One of the notable aspects of tarot cards is the opportunity they have created for anyone to participate in occult activities, shifting the role of the card reader away from professionals to amateurs. With this shift, culture centers and schools increasingly offer tarot card lessons in their catalogue of adult education classes.

Some vocational schools specialize in training people to run their own divination businesses. The Tokyo Ekisen Gakuin in Setagaya offers courses on divination techniques and astrology. Another is Akademeia College, mentioned before, a business located in a modern office building where clients learn the fundamentals of a broad range of forecasting practices. Clients may take weeklong workshops or longer courses in order to learn a variety of divination types. The school also provides students with training in how to set up their own divination websites, stalls, booths, and shops. Together with other occult objects such as crystals, birth charts, feng shui compasses, and divination dice, tarot card photographs and drawings prominently adorn their booklets, brochures, and flyers. When I visited the school, I also noticed that several tarot decks were conspicuously displayed in cases near the registration desk. All the staff I encountered were young women wearing sedate business attire. At Akademeia College, tarot is taught at both introductory and master course levels.

The school groups together divination that uses objects, such as runes, compasses, and tarot, into a special curriculum. These forms of divination are attractive to clients because the seeker has a role in the process, unlike the zodiac birth chart that exists apart from the person. The tarot courses focus on various layouts and methods for reading, but they are limited to the study of the twenty-two major arcana cards. Teachers manipulate very large plastic placards of tarot (this school uses the Rider-Waite-Smith deck) that have magnetic backings, affixing them to a whiteboard in front of the class when discussing their iconography and layout. Students also do hands-on readings with the instructors, with other students serving as the querents. One of the tarot card instructors said she first received a book on divination as a small child and got her own deck of tarot cards at twelve years of age. Because so much of the instruction involves understanding the images on the cards, perhaps it is not surprising that another instructor's profile includes the fact that she was an art major at Nihon University.

The divination booths found in shopping malls usually offer tarot readings. The various tarot decks and ways of reading them are so well known and specialized that divination services often advertise by calling attention to the type of reading performed, including Inspiration Tarot (Reikan Tarotto), *I Ching* Tarot (Ekisen Tarotto), Spiritual Tarot (Supirichuaru Tarotto), Western Tarot (Seiyō Tarotto), and Eastern Tarot (Tōyō Tarotto). At a booth one might see groups of women approaching the activity as a type of light entertainment, while some customers present as clearheaded individuals seeking advice.

Tarot Symbolism and Themes

Regardless of the intent of their use, whether for entertainment or consultation, many decks created in Japan contain innovative and engaging imagery. Card devotees hunt through domestic and foreign history in order to resurrect antique visual elements that can be tweaked or recontextualized. For centuries the iconography of the tarot was essentially European, reflecting Jewish and Christian mysticism or the idea that even royalty, clergy, and other court nobility are subject to the laws of fate. Tarot in Japan reflects a deliberate adaptation or creolization process across both cultural and temporal borders. The medieval Europeans originally found on the cards are often purged or altered or mixed with images from the world of Japanese art, history, and popular culture. In looking at the variety of tarot available, it is clear that by recasting traditional tarot images into new visual idioms, tarot has successfully been able to take a place alongside other visual art forms such as manga. I would like to point out a few specific ways that artists and producers have been able to make tarot so appealing. Although the underlying allegorical meanings might remain, the images are often quite novel and stunning.

There is a staggering range of diversity in card themes and types. The card hunter's search has resulted in astonishingly innovative new motifs, such as the distinctive Particle Tarot (Izumi and Kumagai 2009). This deck was created by a designer named Kumagai Kan and Izumi Ryūichi, the tarot instructor at Arcanum Seminars mentioned above. I obtained the twenty-two major arcana cards as a cutout supplement (*furoku*) in a magazine. This deck pulls in Mesoamerican imagery that melds round shapes that resemble the putative Aztec calendar, gears, or modified Mayan glyphs with flowers, tentacle-shaped plants, and feathers. The card for Temperance features a figure with an abstract head simultaneously pouring liquids from two jars into a shallow bowl (figure 7; Izumi and Kumagai 2009). The ancient Mesoamerican theme of the imagery suits the occult nuances of tarot.

Figure 7. The Hermit and Temperance

Whether they are dreamily mysterious, such as the Particle Tarot, or intentionally playful, like the Hello Kitty Tarot discussed below, cards domesticate tarot symbolism by replacement with or in combination with animals and historical figures. Some are based on characters from popular culture, including Evangelion, Gundam, and the Sony cat mascot. Contrasting with the cutout magazine supplement tarot are hundreds of premium decks for purchase in shops, bookstores, and online. An example of deluxe tarot is a deck designed by the artist Kasai Ayumi (Kasai and Moon Princess Himiko 2002). Kasai is a popular manga artist who specializes in fantasy, Boys Love, erotic romance, and historical manga. Creating branded tarot is an important sideline for Kasai and other artists as a way to expand and maintain their fanbase. She uses saturated royal hues to depict novel scenes that meld both Asian and other elements. The tarot card for the Empress represents maternal nurturance and power, abundance, and a plentiful harvest. Most Euro-American decks depict a crowned woman wearing a sumptuous robe, holding a scepter, and seated on an opulently covered chair amid trees and growing plants. Kasai paints the Empress as a woman wearing the classic twelve-layered robes worn by court aristocracy during the Heian era (794–1185). However, instead of long black hair she has short red hair with bangs. She holds a sheaf of harvested rice and sits in a richly appointed room reminiscent of a twelfth-century scroll painting. Her card for the Hermit, which denotes introspection and isolation, is similarly modified to reflect an East Asian theme. The Euro-American deck normally depicts an elderly hooded man wearing the clothes of a monk. He holds a lantern aloft in one hand and carries a long staff in the other. Kasai replaces the image of the Hermit with one of a Buddhist monk holding a red lantern to illuminate the esoteric images before him. He is kneeling while contemplating a *bonji* Sanskrit graph (a writing system element) while a gorgeous Japanese scroll unfurls behind him (figure 7; Kasai and Moon Princess Himiko 2002).

A card from a unique tarot deck depicts a woman running down the street with a cute white puppy hanging onto her leg. She jogs along a magenta ground, a blue sky with a purple butterfly and bright sun suspended above. She is wearing pink panties, and a yellow top has slipped beneath her exposed breasts. The words "The Fool" are written below the scene in English. Without context it might be hard to recognize this as a card from a tarot deck. It was created by the writer Akatsuki Reika and the artist Aya Takano (2010). Takano garnered fame as the protégé of the artist Murakami Takashi and his Superflat movement. The tarot deck, named Spiritual Tarot, features thin, nude, or barely clothed women moving through magical tableaus filled with arcane signs and richly colored settings. On Euro-American cards the High Priestess card is typically depicted as the female Pope seated between two columns and wearing a papal or Egyptian crown. She holds an ancient text, normally a scroll that denotes secret wisdom. The card represents wisdom, spirituality, and insight. Takano's version of the High Priestess is a slim woman holding a book displaying unknown squiggly graphs (figure 8; Akatsuki and Takano 2010). She is accompanied by a lilac pony and a pink bunny. The drawing is both adorable and mystical.

An illustrator and tarot designer named Himiko Rose created an unusual deck with modern-looking people and scenes (Himiko Rōzu 2013). She incorporates new or additional symbols on the cards, such as gears, keys, stairs, and doors. Her tarot card for the Tower depicts two young women standing on either side of a dark tower. They are chained and clothed in high black boots, with black stockings and black garter belts, black shorts, and black crop tops. In contrast to this dark mood, the

Figure 8. The Empress and the High Priestess

Empress card looks like a young woman at her fifteenth-birthday quinceañera. She is wearing a puffy deep magenta and lace dress with her long hair flowing all around her (figure 8). In the foreground are three closed doors drifting on clouds. On her head is a glittering tiara, and a lock and a key dangle from one hand. According to Himiko Rose, the lock and key set is a symbol of fertility.

Cute tarot cards are common and widely loved. An example of the most recognized flavor of straight-up cute is a deck produced by the prolific card designer named Kagami Ryūji (2007). On one deck he used the early 1975 Sanrio characters Little Twin Stars. Little Twin Stars are a pair of siblings named Kiki and Rara. His Sparkling Love Tarot features the angelic siblings in scenes that have been cleansed of negative imagery. The Devil card, for example, presents the two in a visual story that denotes someone with a devilish intent: Rara mischievously tries to surprise Kiki by giving him a concealed cat in a box (figure 9). Instead of the towering horned satyr, a lecherous goat-man typically found on the traditional European tarot, this cute version lurches toward cute overload. Beloved characters from childhood strategically replace a foreign supernatural being. The card's original meaning of addiction to carnal pleasures and bondage to materialism has transformed into the idea of devilish prankery and intention to tease others or to shock them.

Many cards are intentionally humorous and playful. In Kagami's (2009) Hello Kitty Tarot deck is another version of the Devil (figure 9). It depicts Sanrio's famous Kitty with her paw covering her lower face as if embarrassed about the forbidden things she is thinking about—jewels, a doughnut, pudding, and candy, as revealed to us in a thought bubble. These images have popped into her head because the devil is tempting her. When one's heart is consumed with objects of desire, this is temptation. Anyone might identify with Kitty's encounter with the Devil and recognize her or his own fatal attractions too.

Figure 9. The Devil as Hello Kitty and the Devil as Little Twin Stars

While Japanese cute has often taken on a saccharine tone around the globe, we find that in Japan there has been an evolution and diversification in types of cuteness. For example, consider *guro kawaii* (grotesque cute), an aesthetic that reflects elements of both the adorable and the warped or weird. In the world of tarot, the grotesque cute aesthetic is celebrated in the imagery of numerous cards. The deck named Loveable Girl Skeleton Tarot by Hoshi and Satō (2013) is a fitting example. The two primary characters who populate the card imagery are a skeleton prince and a skeleton maid. The maid icon is derived from the enormous success of the maid café industry, where workers dress up in French maid outfits and serve coffee and mediocre food. The Hoshi and Satō (2013) card for the Magician depicts the skeleton maid wearing a black-and-white lace uniform and headdress (figure 10). On most Euro-American cards, this card is typically depicted as representing the ability and commitment needed for success. On an altar before him are the magical tools representing the four tarot suits and their associated meanings of earth, air, fire, and water. The skeleton maid retains the basic features of the card except for the character substitution. The

Figure 10. The World and the Magician

skeleton maid is a familiar shape in a cryptic spectacle, transforming the occult scene into the idioms of girl culture. The esoteric symbolism nods to foreign tarot imagery while adapting it to Japanese sensibilities.

Adaptation from European images to Japanese takes other forms too. Tarot devotees also use the deck as a canvas to explore symbolic meanings with images from Japanese history and religion. These new interpretive frames might retain the core archetypes of the cards or the symbolic meanings associated with them but recast the figures as those familiar to a Japanese audience. The producers and artists who make new cards study tarot lore and history and are therefore knowledgeable about the Christian-infused imagery and symbolism. Yet they also know that the esoteric references will not necessarily be meaningful or particularly attractive or interesting to their audience. Inserting native archetypes and symbols into the tarot milieu proves to be a shrewd and successful approach. It is ironic that a foreign form of divination now serves as a vehicle for a revived interest in Japanese history among young women.

Many decks that draw on figures from legends and folklore in Japan are available. Yasokawa's (2014) tarot uses well-known characters and images from native tales in its illustrations. Kintarō, a famous plump boy with superhuman strength, represents the card for Strength, while the card representing the Hierophant (also known as the Pope or the High Priest), is a statue of the Bodhisattva Jizō. A Buddhist deity is a clever substitution for a European religious practitioner. A different and more beautiful deck by Isaki (2008) uses deities and personages from one of the earliest written chronicles in Japan, the *Kojiki* (Records of Ancient Matters, compiled 711–712). Some of the substitutions are logical: The sun goddess Amaterasu for the Sun card; Tsukiyomi, the Deity of the Moon, for the Moon card; and Ninigi, Japan's first mythological emperor, for the Emperor card. Others are more idiosyncratic, such as Yamatohime for the Hermit. In the *Kojiki* account Yamatohime was commissioned by her father, Emperor Suinin (the eleventh emperor according to mythological history), to locate a suitable place for the enshrinement of Amaterasu. Starting out from the Yamato palace in Sakurai, she wandered around the region for twenty years before arriving at Ise, where she established the inner shrine dedicated to the sun goddess. The Hermit card represents a search for truth and wisdom; often it is a solitary quest. Yamatohime was the *saiō* (high priestess) of the Ise Jingū who never married. The card shows her as elderly and robed in the white and red clothing of the *miko* (shrine attendant). Despite the gender shift she represents the ultimate solitary quest.

Some substitutions of figures on the European tarot with Japanese historical or mythological figures are understandable. Two figures in particular, an ancient queen and a medieval wizard, often replace the Magician card and the High Priestess card, respectively. The artist Itateyama (2012) created her own tarot for an exhibit, and her card for the Magician is a handsome young Abe no Seimei holding a pentagram, the symbol most often associated with him. For the High Priestess, several artists substitute Himiko to address a card prototype meant to symbolize female religious authority. These tarot cards are usually intriguing and challenging. Yamamoto (2014) substitutes an image of a young Himiko in a provocative pose with her bare legs exposed for the High Priestess. The association of Himiko with magical power and expertise is so great that many tarot readers and writers have adopted her name as their own. Tarot creator Himiko Rose (Himiko Rōzu 2013) is bicultural and grew up in both the United States and Japan. She began creating tarot cards in Japan in 2003 and promotes her work in popular divination magazines. Another well-known divination expert uses the name Moon Princess Himiko, although she writes it with alternative characters. She has produced many tarot decks as well as a dictionary of Western astrology (Mūnpurinsesu Himiko 1989; Mūnpurinsesu Himiko 2010). By using Himiko in tarot card imagery or as part of the name for a tarot card creator, they substitute a well-known Japanese figure for an ancient European image, thus domesticating a foreign divination device. These logical substitutions serve as mediators between historical European tarot and the Japanese context.

Animals of the Major Arcana

There are many Japanese tarot decks in which the human figures depicted in the scenes of the major arcana are replaced with animals, most often cats. Feliform images in particular have a long history in Japanese visual culture. Zoomorphic images on tarot reflect a well-documented consumer aesthetic preference for cuteness, and the many appealing stylistic motifs also target a female audience. At the same time, the use of zoomorphic imagery is also a calculated move that goes beyond a concern for kawaii cute aesthetics. The animals working to expose the human condition on these cards are accomplishing more than simply appeasing a desire for adorableness. They do other image work as well, so we should be careful not to confound all zoomorphism with the aesthetic of cuteness.

The tarot set created by Bi Anjeri and illustrated by Umezawa Saki (2004) features charming animal drawings on all the cards. Bi wrote that she wanted to design a deck that was easy to understand and that would also help to alleviate worry by giving the user pleasant images with uplifting signs. This substitution strategy has the positive effect of presenting figures that are not racially marked, thus turning them into characters that anyone might identify with. The tarot card for the Empress, described above, normally shows a woman in a luxurious robe sitting in her garden. In this Japanese card, she is recast as a winged white dog wearing a pink crown with green jewels and holding a wand with a pink star. She is floating in the air above a cityscape with the sun and a rainbow in the sky with her. Animals standing in for humans ask viewers to insert themselves into the scene, thus giving them a grounded, personal handle on the tarot's meaning. Another example of an accessible zoomorphic tarot deck is Dayan's Tarot, which uses both animal and human characters to perform the esoteric scenes and poses (Kagami and Ikeda 2005). The cards are derived from Ikeda's books about a cat named Dayan and his compatriots who live in the fantasy village of Wachifield. In most Euro-American decks the card named the World depicts a nude woman, sometimes with a loose cloth draped around her body, suspended in the air in the middle of a green wreath. She glances to the left while holding a staff in each hand and is watched by four beings in each corner of the card (a lion, a bull, an eagle, and a human or angel). The World represents the meanings of completion of a cycle, fulfillment, and wholeness. In Dayan's Tarot the central figure of the naked woman is replaced with Dayan the cat holding two twigs crossed in front of his body. The four figures in the card's corners are replaced with vessels with the four elements of water, fire, wood, and air gushing from them (figure 10). A beloved figure preserves the original tarot meaning yet embeds it in the comforting familiarity of a book series known from childhood.

The deployment of animals as substitutes for humans should not be interpreted as simply catering to a cultural craving for the aesthetics of cuteness. It is a strategy found in other areas of popular culture that serves to allow wider identification with the figures and is also reflected in such things as public service posters, etiquette books, and regional mascots (L. Miller 2010). In the case of tarot, the replacement of medieval European queens, squires, popes, and hermits allows a different audience to identify more easily with the image. The animals strip the figures of ethnicity, nationality, and in some cases gender. These nonhuman characters beckon the Japanese girl or woman into a dialogue with a medieval foreign world or a newly formed intermediate world. They welcome Japanese people into the fold, where they join a sisterhood of tarot knowers and lovers. Animals representing human habits and traits invite the viewer to see themselves in this imagery, thus comprehending the tarot's lessons and meanings with less opposition. The card-maker's critique of humanity and her ideological aims in offering such critiques can also be made more easily when human foibles and faults are embodied in cute animal forms.

Tarot Culture

The allure of tarot led to the development of other types of divination cards. Outside Japan, card decks usually called "oracle cards," often linked to New Age cosmologies and philosophies, began to appear in the 1960s. Their purpose was not only to forecast the future but also for use as tools for meditation and reflection. Generally, fewer cards are found in these than in a tarot deck. These oracle cards have also become popular in Japan and reflect great innovation.

A well-known deck by Ōno (2008) features the earliest deities mentioned in written records in Japan. In an interview she said she wanted to create cards to enable self-discovery that resonate better for her Japanese fans, so she selected kami deities for her oracle card iconography (*Koiunreki* 2008). One of her cards depicts the deity Tsukuyomi, normally thought of as a male moon deity. In her deck, Tsukuyomi is transformed into a female deity who plays the flute against a dark night sky. A comparable idea is seen in oracle cards with different paintings of the Bodhisattva Kannon (Kusaba and Yayama 2010). Kannon represents mercy and compassion, and the idea is that the reader will shuffle the cards, select one, and use it as inspiration. The cards depict different versions of Kannon in a female aspect, painted in gorgeous color on glossy card stock.

Tarot scenes, ideas, and imagery surface in a range of cultural products, such as YouTube videos, games, and manga. There are light novels and manga that feature schoolgirls and their use of tarot (i.e., Nanae 2007; Himuro 2010). In a light novel for a female audience, the tarot reader dresses in Lolita subcultural fashion (Kunisawa 2016). Aimed at even younger girls is a series of spooky tales set in everyday locations and activities, such as game centers and the school bus. One volume in the collection is about a schoolgirl named Rina who buys a boxed tarot book and cards set at a secondhand bookstore. When she starts to play with the cards, she experiences odd occurrences (Kogure and Kunimatsu 2006).

The occult author Fujimori (2008) has written more than twenty books on divination, including a widely appreciated introduction to tarot. She collaborated on an old Nintendo game, Fujimori Midori's *Let's Tarot* (ASNetworks 2007). The game, with the subtitle *From Today On, You Too Can Be a Tarot Fortuneteller,* helps fans learn about the meanings and images on the cards, as well as how to shuffle and deal them. Tarot readings are occasionally offered at some maid cafés, such as the maid café chain Meidoriimin (Maiddream), with shops in Akihabara and elsewhere.[1]

A notable development among occult hunters is the increased consumption of tarot card culture. This interest promotes new opportunities for divination services, and fortune-telling experts offer extensive menus of card-reading services in a wide range of settings. A cursory examination of the cards themselves suggests that they are also objects that reach into the imagination through color, design, and symbolism. Tarot artists have been very successful in exploiting a spectrum of visual idioms in order to attract Japanese viewers and fans. Using established themes already circulating in mass culture brings a viewer into a visual relationship with foreign philosophical concepts. As we saw, in order to represent the concept of addiction to money, sex, food, and power, Euro-American decks often portrayed a human pair chained to a huge satyr. The Devil card in Japan, however, might represent this as a type of unhealthy or hedonistic temptation, especially additive cravings for food. In the Hello Kitty Tarot's Devil card, she dreams of fattening pudding and donuts. The Devil card in a deck by Kasai and Moon Princess Himiko (2002) is of a young man furtively eating a pomegranate. Such substitutions gloss over the gaps between Christian and Japanese worldviews, allowing the tarot entry into a different metaphysical culture. In order to avoid a foreign pictorial paradigm that indexes Christian concepts such as resurrection, sin, and salvation, Japanese artists have shown impressive creative and imaginative engagement that melds existing tarot protocol with new elements and meanings.

One role that divination cards assume is to prod the seeker toward self-reflection. Many women told me that tarot and other divination cards were the catalyst for them to make positive changes in their lives, opening their eyes to new directions or forcing them to face knowledge they intuitively possessed. They never claimed that they "believed" in the cards, only that they launched extended consideration of different potential paths and outcomes. Divination cards are a heuristic device, used as a tool for prediction, healing, and guidance. In his book on the uses of visual evidence for the study of religion, Morgan (1996, 4) wrote that "a gaze is a projection of conventions that enables certain possibilities of meaning, certain forms of experience, and certain relations among participants." The tarot is a go-between, an intermediary between two different philosophies or worldviews. We do not always find a smooth reconciliation of different cultural elements on the cards, and the imagery might leave someone puzzled or uncomfortable. Nevertheless, the power of the card imagery to traverse different time periods, cultural settings, and complex imagery is truly unique.

CHAPTER 4

Pilgrim Stamps

While in Nara I often visit the ancient temple Gangōji, located in the charming Naramachi district. One time while obtaining a special inscription in a dedicated pilgrim book, there was a woman waiting to do the same. The inscriptions are called *goshuin,* and they are usually beautifully written recognitions of a visit to a shrine or temple. She asked if I liked these ornate stamps, and I told her how much I appreciated their calligraphic beauty. She said she was doing something called a Naramachi Pilgrim Stamp Circuit. I had no idea what she meant. Some days later I found a guidebook at the train station bookstore titled *The Cute Nara Pilgrim Stamp Book* (Nishimura 2018, 21). It listed eight sites, including two at Gangōji, that are part of the Naramachi route. Unlike a few stamp collectors I witnessed during fieldwork, I doubt she was being a *goshuin* snob attempting to outshine a clueless foreigner with her knowledge. But it was not the first time I observed or met someone deeply invested in this cultural domain.

This chapter investigates the explosion of interest in pilgrim stamps and the little books in which they are collected. They are popular as religious material artifacts and as objects of aesthetic appreciation. Yagi (2015), a cultural anthropologist and folklore specialist, has written more than ten books on pilgrim stamp culture. The rediscovery of religious stamp art in recent decades points to issues of spiritual questing and connoisseurship primarily by female stamp hunters. According to one business source, in 2014 there were between five and ten times more women seeking pilgrim stamps than there were in 2004 (Nishiyama 2014). I am interested in the stamps because new social and cultural meanings are driving their collection beyond the original function of recording a visit to a shrine or temple. I often saw people who had received pilgrim stamps take photographs of the inscribed page in front of the shrine or temple. The selfies often appear on social media and in blogs.[1] The stamps also serve as an identity marker for shrines and temples. The religious institutions devote time to the aesthetics and branding of stamps because they offer an attractive keepsake of a visit and thus beckon visitors wanting to obtain their unique stamps. As awareness of the stamps escalated, commodification intensified to include the publication of hundreds of specialized guidebooks, stamp book tours, and even J-pop songs dedicated to these intriguing papers. Although the collection of stamps is popular among both female and male visitors to shrines and temples, the design of many new stamps and stamp books reflects feminized tastes. I provide many examples of *goshuin* because their diversity of styles and the evolution in the motif of obtaining a calligraphic memento is worthy of attention.

For more than a decade, a new term has been used to describe avid female fans of pilgrim stamps: *goshuin gāru,* or "pilgrim stamp girl." The term appears in blogs, books, and print media. In one essay on the trend, Horiuchi (2012) asks two hard-core *goshuin gāru* about the history of their collecting. Tomoko and Ayumi, both women in their thirties, discuss their favorite stamps and where they obtained them, as well as memorable experiences. Tomoko owns eight pilgrim stamp books, while Ayumi has five. Tomoko mentions that a calligrapher noticed how many stamps she had received and sweetly urged her to take good care of her book. Ayumi recalls the kindness shown to her when she lacked the proper small currency needed to offer and was allowed to receive a stamp anyway. There is a manga titled *Kamakura Pilgrim Stamp Girl* about a bored high school student who stumbles upon someone's lost pilgrim stamp book and locates the owner. Eventually, she herself becomes obsessed with collecting stamps (Goshirakawa 2019).

Before discussing these forms of material religious culture, I detour to describe Japanese writing and the history of pilgrim stamps. This is followed by a description of the customary structure of stamps and the various "house styles" that have evolved. The comparison of older stamps with newer ones, and the analysis of texts and fan sites, is supplemented with fieldwork done in Nara, Ise, Izumo, Kyoto, and Osaka in 2019 and in the Tokyo region in earlier years. Pilgrim stamp collection is tied to a surge in shrine and temple visits that followed the powerspot fad of the 2010s. The pilgrim stamp boom, unfortunately, has also engendered some unexpected debates and problems, discussed in the conclusion.

Writing

Scholars and scribes from the state of Paekche on the Korean Peninsula introduced the Chinese writing system to Japan during the fourth century. Although artifacts adorned with Chinese writing arrived from the continent in earlier centuries, it is believed that they were probably not understood by early Japanese. Over the following centuries, there were experiments in adapting the Chinese logographs, now called kanji. Eventually, two additional types of writing—syllabaries named katakana and hiragana—evolved from a few of the logographs to represent phonological elements, and these were used together with the borrowed Chinese characters. (A syllabary is a writing system in which each graph represents a phonological syllable.) Although the Japanese language could theoretically be written entirely in one of the syllabaries and the Chinese logographs discarded, this never happened because of their prestige value and role in the transmission of religion and statecraft. Another reason is that Chinese writing was borrowed together with its associated ties to the arts, especially that of calligraphy. A deep reverence for the antiquity and beauty of Chinese graphs walked hand in hand with writing from the start.

Pilgrim stamps and their collection reflect a continuing appreciation for calligraphy in many forms, from traditional to experimental. Discussing the art of calligraphy in the Chinese context, Barnhart (1972, 233) said that "the artistic effects of a work of calligraphy are fully apparent before one begins to read the characters or words." Appreciation for pilgrim stamps is also more than simply tapping into linguistic signification. Many stamp collectors are unable to decipher all of their calligraphic inscriptions, yet they are nevertheless highly valued for their aesthetic and symbolic characteristics.

History and Structure of Pilgrim Stamps

The murky origins of the custom of obtaining stamps and religious calligraphy during a visit to a shrine or temple opens the door to many theories. Some writers claim that the foundation for the concept might be traced to an eighth-century habit of providing patrons who commissioned hand-copied sutras with a written receipt. For example, nobles, private individuals, and community associations sponsored the copying of sutras by monks trained in the practice and received a receipt for their donations (Lowe 2017). Even so, I agree with Nishimura (2018, 90), who writes that the roots of pilgrim stamps are found in pilgrimages. We find the first evidence of bona fide pilgrim stamps from the Edo period (1603–1867). The earliest may be stamps associated with the pilgrimage to thirty-three temples throughout the Kansai region known as the Saigoku Kannon Pilgrimage (Saigoku Sanjūsansho). The pilgrim would have a record and a religious memento from each stop on the circuit. Because of the extreme travel restrictions imposed by the military dictatorship, pilgrim stamp records also proved they had legitimately been on a pilgrimage and provided evidence to show at the many barrier stations. Pilgrim stamps that begin to take the form of those we see today are found in collections of receipts for dedicated hand-copied sutras dating to around 1795.[2]

Early stamps did not include as much text or imagery as they currently display. At a Buddhist temple, they might have had simple vermilion stamps as evidence of a visit. Often the stamped image was of the wish-fulfilling jewel (*hōju no tama*), a peach-shaped orb regularly enclosed in a flaming nimbus. Another common image was the lotus, a core symbol representing transcendence and spiritual growth placed under the flaming jewel (Ruppert 2000). Over time the certification of the visit expanded to include handwritten calligraphic inscriptions of the name of the temple, the date of the visit, and other expressions (Nishimura 2018, 90). Today the stamp itself usually includes the location, the date of the visit, and the official name of the institution. The handwritten calligraphy in the center of the stamp might be a name, a mantra, or another brief saying. A typical layout is to write the date on the left side and the name of the shrine or temple in the center (sometimes replaced with a common saying, *hōhai*, or "offering of prayer," in the upper-right corner).

Pilgrim stamps and calligraphy can be placed on various surfaces. Common ones are a single sheet of paper, inside a dedicated stamp-collecting book, on a scroll, on the white jacket of a person on a pilgrimage, or on a square calligraphy board called *shikishi*. Early pilgrim stamp collectors used soft paper-covered notebooks in the four-leaf binding form. Beginning in the Taishō era (1912–1926), the use of accordion-style books with hard covers became popular and remains so today (figure 11). The two basic sizes for *goshuin-chō* (pilgrim stamp book) circulated today range from 110 × 160 millimeters for the smaller ones (4.33 × 6.3 inches) to 120 × 180 millimeters (4.72 × 7.09 inches) for the somewhat larger ones. Ōura (2019, 13), a writer who has published articles and books on unique aspects of religious culture, notes that the stamp books were larger in the past, around 5.8 × 8.3 inches. Most have around forty-four pages. There are exceptions, and pilgrim stamp collectors can take or make their own books or notebooks. In an antique shop, I found a softcover stamp notebook in the four-leaf binding style (figure 11). It had been used for the Saigoku Kannon Pilgrimage to thirty-three temples in the Kansai region. The pilgrim collected the stamps in 1987, yet the style of the calligraphy seems old-fashioned in the light of recent developments. At another antique store, I found a batch of loose unbound pages from another famous pilgrimage, the Shikoku Pilgrimage to eighty-eight temples.

Figure 11. Old and new pilgrim stamp books

A clerk at Loft, one of Japan's major household goods chain stores, was interviewed on television about a display of pilgrim books in a "*goshuin* corner" (Nagoya Broadcasting Network 2017). The clerk said they had around fifty types of stamp books and that the primary customers were female university students. In bookstores, at an airport shop, and in New Age boutiques, I saw many such displays of beautiful pilgrim stamp books. The close connection between the female consumer, the various occult pursuits such as divination and tarot, and interest in pilgrim stamp collecting struck me unexpectedly on a trip to visit Ise Jingū. After visiting the shrine, I wandered around in the nearby shopping district of Okage Yokochō, a recreation of an Edo-period townscape crammed with shops and eateries. One of the boutiques sold incense, lotions, candles, and other merchandise for the discriminating female traveler, and on a table lay a selection of beautiful pilgrim stamp books. One had a cover that I recognized as the same one found on a divination card representing the deity Amaterasu by the artist Ōno Yuriko (2008). Ōno, an established creator of oracle card decks popular among female divination enthusiasts, had also designed a range of pilgrim stamp books. Another store that specializes in making and selling pilgrim stamp books, named Horiihokku (Hollyhock), opened in Matsusaka in Mie Prefecture. It also has an online store and a branch shop in Ise. In addition to hundreds of pilgrim stamp books, it carries book covers, special books just for the Shikoku pilgrimages, book bags, bead or tassel bookmarks, kits to make your own stamp book, and other related goods for the selective stamp hunter. An article on increased interest in getting one's own personalized stamp book with an original cover design links it to young people such as the subculture of female history aficionados (Kisha Ichi-go 2018).

The elaboration of calligraphy styles is seen in stamps from Kasuga Taisha in Nara. I received one in 1990 and one in 2019 and upon comparing them see that the "house style" of calligraphy has changed somewhat. The early one lacks force, while the newer one has a posture of intensity. I obtained my first pilgrim stamp book in 1985 and looking through it today am struck by its somewhat stodgy uniformity. Only a few stamps stand out as unique. In contrast, pilgrim stamp art in recent years reflects a re-enchantment with calligraphy and a broader interest in opportunities to locate novel or beautiful stamps. A comparison of other stamps from decades ago to those offered today demonstrates increased attention to aesthetics and branding.

The stamping and calligraphy are provided by a *miko* shrine attendant, a priest, a part-time worker, or a volunteer. They cost between ¥300 and ¥1,000 for each stamp. Blank pilgrim stamp books cost between ¥1,000 to ¥4,000. The books can be purchased at many shrines and temples and at stationery stores and other shops. One of the more impressive trends is to offer single sheets of preprinted stamps on colorful paper, called *kakioki* (already written). These prestamped and preprinted papers may later be pasted into one's stamp book. They are often duplicated in color with designs or touches such as sparkly elements that are difficult if not impossible to include on individual stamps done in real time. Some of the papers are intended to look like precious mulberry paper made with flecks of gold or silver, although they generally fall short of that goal. Collectors might gather many of these loose-page *kakioki* and put them in clear files or scrapbook albums.

Obtaining a Pilgrim Stamp

Staff at shrines complain about the bad manners of the *goshuin* hunters who insist that their pilgrim books be stamped on demand. For example, Iwatsutsukowake Jinja (2020) in Fukushima posted a very long discussion of manners on their Facebook page expressing irritation at visitors who treat the shrine like a souvenir shop and interrupt the shrine workers engaged in other duties. The basic rules for both shrines and temples are to attend to the following points (Ōura 2019, 20–24; Morimoto et al. 2019; Nishimura 2018, 96–101): pay your respects to resident deities before requesting a pilgrim stamp, open the page of your pilgrim stamp book to where you want the stamp placed, do not put nonreligious commemorative stamps from castles or other sites in your stamp book, do not tell the calligrapher how you want an inscription written, and remember that you are receiving the *goshuin* as a certificate of your worship—it is not something you are "buying." A few sites have rules about receiving only one type of inscription per visit. Although it is not required, after years of using the same pilgrim stamp book for both temples and shrines I switched to two separate books. Some of the temples that are part of the Nichiren sect of Buddhism have specific rules about pilgrim stamps and stamp books. Instead of a regular *goshuin,* one will often receive a type of stamp called *goshudai,* which is the title of the *Lotus Sūtra* (*Namu myōhō rengekyō*). This is stretched down the center of the paper, and sometimes the splayed characters are described by female occult hunters as *hige moji* (facial hair characters). A few temples are persnickety and refuse pilgrim stamp books that are not specifically dedicated for Nichiren temples. Most Jōdo Shinshū Buddhist temples are not interested in providing pilgrim stamps at all.

House Style, Cute Stamps, and Novel Stamps

The expressive styles now seen in pilgrim stamp production entice occult hunters who value beauty and novelty. The profusion of new ways of writing them is impressive given the stylistic restraint imposed by the size of the paper. The art of the *goshuin* forces the writing into a small rectangular shape. They manifest new aesthetic tastes and a renewed appreciation for calligraphy styles. The stamp's worth does not reside in its denotational meaning because most people are unable to read all the graphs selected for inscription. Rather, it is cherished for its beauty and proof of participating in pilgrim stamp culture.

Calligraphers rely upon at least six fundamental written styles that developed in China and later entered Japan. The main script styles range from antique forms based on the earliest writing (early seal *kōkotsubun* and formal seal *tensho*), to forms used for official documents that are the basis of most fonts (clerical script *reisho* and standard script *kaisho*), to those that are flowing (running *gyōsho* and cursive *sōsho*). Early stamp inscriptions were most often written in clerical script and standard script for legibility, but all possible styles and beyond became popular with the stamp boom.

Schoolchildren are expected to master iconic graph styles through writing practice (called *shūji*). It is taught with the aim of producing uniform characters with balanced strokes. Once they have learned the basics, they may advance to calligraphy training (*shodō*), writing that is an artistic expression. At least since the postwar era, calligraphy has been considered an expected cultural attainment for middle-class women, so it is not surprising that most fans of *goshuin* calligraphy art today are female. Calligraphy artists experiment in various media, including film (Nornes 2021). Beginning in the early 1990s, a new type of calligraphy called "performance calligraphy" was popularized and adopted as a notable aspect of female culture. It is a team event that combines large-scale calligraphy writing with dance and music and was highlighted in the film *Calligraphy Girls* (Inomata 2010). This may have been one trend that contributed to a new interest in stamp collecting.[3] A prominent calligrapher named Takeda Sōun has also helped to renew interest in calligraphy among younger people. With youthful long hair, often clad in the comfortable attire worn by Zen monks, Takeda added excitement and relevance to the art of calligraphy through publishing more than fifteen accessible books in addition to numerous workshops, exhibitions, and blogs. More than the mechanics of script styles, he teaches others to attend to the flow of writing, the versatility of the brushstrokes, and ways to insert emotion into graphs by paying attention to the density of the ink (Takeda 2005). Many of the popular *goshuin* reflect his thinking.

The priests, shrine attendants, part-time workers, or volunteers who write the inscriptions have training in basic calligraphy (*shodō*), but additionally, they must master the predetermined style created for the shrine or temple. I call this the "house style." The house style represents a calligraphic marriage of aesthetics and evidence of having visited a temple or shrine. It includes the expected information such as date, center inscription, location, and institution stamp yet also allows for some calligraphy experimentation. The calligraphers do not use an exemplar model to copy from as they write, yet no matter who does the actual inscription, the writing looks more or less the same. Obviously, temples and shrines try to ensure that only those trained in the "house style" provide the calligraphy.

Temples and shrines take great care in visualizing the way their stamps appear as a unit. They want viewers, even unconsciously, to make connections or see the gestalt of it. There may be efforts at resonance between the shrine's profile and the calligraphy style or other visual elements. Character strokes that involve some iconicity are found in a stamp I obtained in 1985 from Takedera in Saitama Prefecture. The stamp featured characters for the temple's name, literally "Bamboo Temple," with thin, watery ink and elongated brushstrokes that resemble grassy bamboo stalks. Another example of a stamp that reflects appreciation for the gestalt effect is from the Nigatsu-dō, a temple attached to the Tōdaij in Nara (figure 12). "Tōdaiji" is written in the top-left corner in thin writing that looks as if an ant stepped into the ink and walked over the page. All the calligraphy is delicate yet is dancing energetically. The hairlike writing of the temple name and the date in a cursive style lacks backbone, yet the delicate brushwork intertwined with exaggerated upticks from vertical strokes and curvy horizontal strokes lends a jaunty air. The center inscription, *Kannon-riki* (The Power of Kannon), is executed in extremely leggy brush strokes that cover a red-ink stamp of the Flaming Jewel with a special Sanskrit graph at its center. A friend thought the combination suggested "red fire, black smoke."[4] The force of this inscription contained in the small space of the page is very satisfying and pleasant. This exciting new style contrasts with older stamps for Nigatsu-dō, which display the center column of characters in regular script style, with thick brush strokes. Another example is from Tsumakirishima Jinja in Miyazaki, a place associated with many interesting spiritual energy themes. On its grounds is an ancient cedar tree that resembles a dragon, and at times the stamp incorporates dragon

Figure 12. Nigatsu-dō pilgrim stamp

imagery. The standard script calligraphy is very sharp and angular and looks almost as if it were written with a European-style calligraphy pen.

A special type of writing used for Sanskrit words, mantra, and sutras was borrowed from India. It is called the Siddham script, or *bonji* in Japanese, and it looks very different from Japanese syllabic writing or Chinese characters. *Bonji* is usually written with a special type of stiff brush. Many Buddhist temples incorporate these graphs into their stamps, even though most people are unable to read them. Calligraphy using *bonji* is esteemed for its connection to the roots of Buddhism, a symbolic function that takes precedence over the unlikely possibility of reading or pronouncing them. For example, a stamp from Zenjōji in Tokyo features a very large center *bonji* for Fudō Myōō (Acala Vidyārāja), which is read *kān* or *kānmān* (figure 13). Zenjōji is a small temple run by a couple in what looks like a converted shop. The writing on the pilgrim stamp is executed using a rubber stamp. Stamp hunters appreciate the novelty of the writing. A few said, "I personally like *goshuin* with Sanskrit characters," and "The *goshuin* with the Sanskrit character is nice, it's so wonderful that you will feel the weight as soon as you receive it." Others complain that because a ready-made rubber stamp is used it is not worth going out of the way to obtain it.

Figure 13. Zenjōji pilgrim stamp

Jindai Moji (Script of the Age of the Deities) is the term used for the different sets of artificially created syllabaries that replaced the regular syllabic characters with fantastical graphs. Japanese nationalists invented these script sets after the great antiquity of the Chinese writing system was established through archaeological discoveries of written artifacts dating to the Shang dynasty (1600 BCE–1045 BCE). Jindai Moji, they claimed, predate all Chinese writing but had been lost to history. More than a dozen varieties of such presumed indigenous Japanese scripts are extant, and all have been firmly debunked as counterfeits. Nevertheless, they continue to hold a fascination in popular media such as manga and games and are still revered in some religious settings. There are guides to reading and learning the squiggly and ornate sets. Harada (2008) offers a lighthearted manual illustrating dozens of script sets and practice sheets, while Maruyama (2019) claims that because the graphs have strong energy, one may improve their luck and power simply by tracing them. His book includes pages of tracing guides. A pilgrim stamp from Hirata Jinja in Tokyo uses a version of one of the fake substitute syllabaries named Izumo Moji (figure 14). The enshrined deity is theologian Hirata Atsutane (1776–1843), a prolific scholar who believed that the Jindai Moji

Figure 14. Hirata Jinja pilgrim stamp

were the earliest writing system. The use of this occult cryptograph links the stamp to Hirata and his promotion of the bogus graphs. The squiggly inscription on the Hirata Jinja stamp is meant to be read as *kamunagara* or *kannagara,* which the shrine explains means "Leave the will of the deities as is, without artificial intervention" (Hirata Jinja 2022). The saying may have been derived from a similar one in the *Man'yōshū,* the late eighth-century poetry compilation.

Many pilgrim stamps are tinged with the cute kawaii aesthetic. This cute aesthetic is pervasive in all aspects of Japanese culture, including religious artifacts (Miller and Stevens 2021). One of the priests at Wakeoe Jinja in Nagoya, a woman named Kaneko Reika, visited many other shrines around the country to learn what popular cute mechanisms were used to attract followers and incorporated them into her revisions of shrine imagery. She designed an adorable mascot named Bekki-chan and also revised Wakeoe Jinja's pilgrim stamp style and monthly design rotation (there is a new stamp each month). She used her media shrewdness to promote the shrine on YouTube, Twitter, Facebook, and a blog. In an interview she admitted that her father, the head priest, as well as other parishioners were opposed to her efforts but eventually saw that they helped to draw many visitors (Tokai Television Broadcasting 2021).[5] The cute style of stamp is perfectly embodied in a stamp from Wakeoe Jinja. It was created in December 2021 to herald the impending new year. A popular New Year's custom is to eat a bowl of buckwheat noodles called *toshikoshi* soba (literally "year-crossing" soba) to symbolize longevity and good fortune. The stamp featured the shrine's mascot, Bekki-chan, together with a tiger who was the Chinese zodiac animal for 2022. In a cheerful scene, Bekki gleefully slurps a huge mouthful of soba noodles while the tiger bites into a piece of shrimp tempura, a common topping for the noodle dish. Wakeoe Jinja was featured in a television news story about the stamp boom (Nagoya Broadcasting Network 2017). In interviews with women who got stamps there, one said that "they are colorful and are super beautiful when you look closely, so I wanted to come here no matter what." Another added that "somehow they feel like an artistic Report Card Five they are so well done" (in school students receive a grade from one to five, with five as the top grade).

One special pilgrim stamp from Darumaji in Ōji appeals to female visitors. On the temple grounds is a statue of a dog who is purportedly the beloved attendant of the semi-mythological hero Shōtoku Taishi (574–622). According to legend, Shōtoku's dog Yukimaru had the ability to understand human speech and could read Buddhist sutras. In the precincts is a stone statue of the dog that was erected there during the Edo period. The town of Ōji capitalized on the legend by creating the snow-white dog mascot in 2013, and afterward his popularity soared.[6] Darumaji (2022) began offering the charming Yukimaru pilgrim stamp in 2018. The white dog is dressed as a Nara-era court noble in an *eboshi* cap and carries the ceremonial baton of office that we often see in illustrations of Shōtoku (figure 15). Covering the image is a red-ink paw stamp. The name of the temple is written on the left in simple syllabic script, which is rare to see on pilgrim stamps. Perhaps it would be easier for other dogs to read? The shrine welcomes dogs who are with human companions. When I visited Darumaji, numerous female visitors in its precincts exclaimed in delight over the cute Yukimaru statue and the pilgrim stamp.

Other aesthetics in addition to cuteness are also fashionable. Some of the most detailed and beautifully executed artistic stamps are created by Daishōin, a Shingon Buddhist temple nestled at the base of Mount Mise in Miyajima. In addition to the usual black-ink calligraphy stamps, they periodically create special paper-cut pilgrim stamps as separate *kakioki* insets. The Japanese art of papercutting is called *kirie* (literally, "cut picture") and has a history dating to the seventh century. The dainty papercuts at Daishōin

Figure 15. Darumaji pilgrim stamp

are finely executed in great detail. One of my favorites commemorates a visit by the Dalai Lama and his attendant monks in 2006 to celebrate the twelve-hundredth year of the temple's founding. The visiting Tibetans created an enormous sand mandala that remains in one of the temple's great halls. A flowery, ornate papercut pilgrim stamp of the mandala was released as a limited edition on black or peacock-blue paper and quickly sold out (*Hiroshima keizai shinbun* 2021). The papercut stamp concept evolved into an elaborate version at Kumano Kōtai Jinja in Nagano: they offer a three-dimensional paper-cutting *goshuin* with a tree that pops up from the flat surface of the paper (sometimes called sliceform *kirigami* among English-language crafters).[7]

Newspapers and broadcast news channels in Japan have noticed that artistic pilgrim stamp inscriptions are attracting visitors. A priest at Kannon-ji in Tsushima appeared in mainstream news because of his artistic talent in illustrating the pilgrim stamp books (Hara 2018). Hasegawa Yu likes drawing manga and transferred that interest to depictions of Buddhist supernatural beings and other religious imagery. He draws two-page spreads with thick black ink, sprinkles of ink dust, and seriated brushes that give a dreamy yet forceful quality to his creations. So many visitors thronged the temple for his art that it set up an advance registration system.

Some of the most delightful art *goshuin* are made by the priest-artist at Soga Jinja in Omitama City, Ibaraki Prefecture. Two of the enshrined deities walked straight out of the earliest legends—Amaterasu's brother Susanoo and one of his wives Kushinadahime, whom he rescued from a monster. The shrine offers regular pilgrim stamps, but to entice children one of the priests began to draw elaborate manga-like illustrations that became a hit among visitors of all ages, especially women. He also invented a special script style using a brush pen (*Ibaraki shinbun dōga nyūzu* 2020). The script is rococo and ornate. This shrine's stamp has often been voted the best in the country.[8] Although he is not using Jindai Moji graphs, his invented style looks as if it was modeled after the fabricated syllabary substitution set called Izumo Moji. The writing has an uprightness yet playful quality with its curly strokes, and while the filigree style is unconventional, it is rich with a stylized archaic effect. The stamp in figure 16 was created in December 2021 to commemorate the deity Susanoo. The shrine periodically posts photos of seasonal pilgrim stamps on Facebook, and comments from page visitors always reflect appreciation. On one occasion an admirer named Miwako SJ wrote that the stamp reflected a favorite motif and that he or she would "love to frame it and display it" (Soga Jinja 2023).

Figure 16. Soga Jinja pilgrim stamp

A disruptive aspect of some pilgrim stamps results when the calligrapher adds an extra red touristic stamp after completing the inscriptions. These are not the unique name or location stamps but rather stamps that advertise participation in local circuit routes or civic boosterism efforts. For example, in looking at the stamp I received at Yakushiji in 2019 it seems that the red stamp at the top left detracts from an otherwise pleasing composition (figure 17). The extraneous stamp commemorates a relatively new pilgrimage route created in 1989 named Saigoku Yakushi Shjūku Reijō. It is for forty-nine sites in western Japan dedicated to Yakushi Nyorai, the Medicine Buddha. The center calligraphy is Nyoirin Kannon (Bodhisattva of Compassion with the Wish-Granting Jewel). The inscription is forceful, with dramatic energy in its saturated brushing. The fat strokes are well ordered, with a solid backbone. It retains inner tensile strength even with thick, wild strokes. But three red stamps, especially the one at the top left, add too many visual elements. In contrast the stamp on the right facing page from Murōji is busy yet not overwhelmingly so. Nicknamed Nyonin Kōya, "Women's Mt. Kōya," it is located in the mountains of Uda city in Nara Prefecture. The modulating brushstrokes are in flight, and although many graphs are crammed into the space, the calligraphy retains plasticity. It is fleshy in some areas and sinewy in others.

An elaborate pilgrim stamp offering is the Augmented Reality cell phone app from Momiji Hachimangū in Fukuoka.[9] Once you obtain the *goshuin* and the app from the shrine, you hold your phone camera over the stamp, and four animated figures rise out of the stamp book page in succession while court music plays in the background. The first to appear is a priest who waves a purification wand and chants while red autumn leaves drift down the screen. When he departs, a new whirl of movement turns into the armored figure of the legendary Empress Jingū, one of the enshrined deities there. She is holding a baby and is venerated there as a protector of safe childbirth. Jingū performs some maneuvers with a spear (still holding the baby!) and paces across the pilgrim book page. When you tap "Next Deity," another twirling figure appears, this time her son Emperor Ōjin riding a white horse. The horse neighs and gallops around the page, and Ōjin performs mounted archery. The last figure to appear is Ōjin's son, Prince Uji no Wakiiratsuko, who is known as a deity of schooling, learning, and employment. According to legend, the first scribes from the state of Paekche on the Korean Peninsula, Achiki and Wani, were

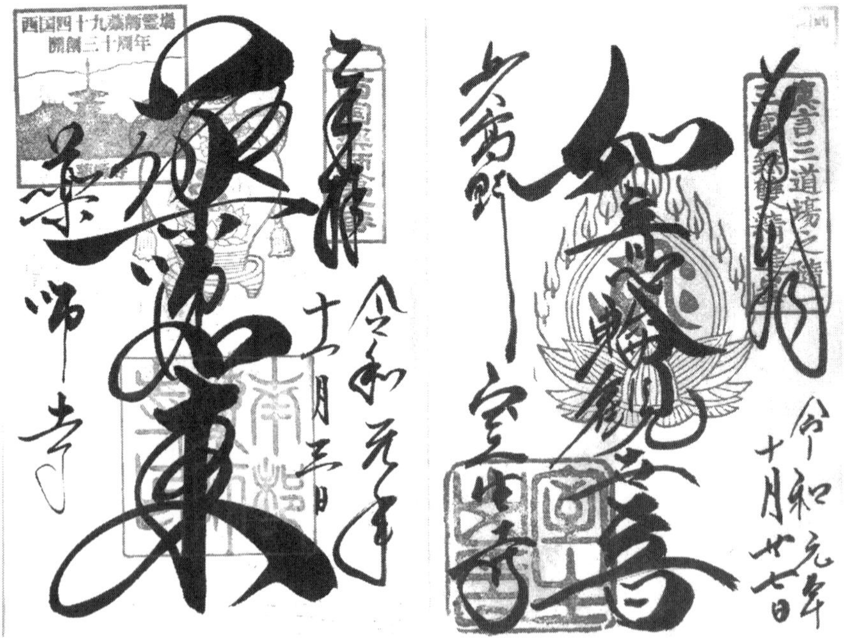

Figure 17. Yakushiji and Murōji pilgrim stamps

tutors to the prince and fostered his love of literacy. He is seen walking around while writing with a brush. At any time one can tap the bottom to reach a screen with background information on each figure. The combination of a stamp with animation and music deflects attention away from the elegance and innovation of the script forms that are normally the focus of attention, yet this innovation has its own charm.

Commodification

In 2019 national and international news excitedly described the presentation of an automaton bodhisattva named Mindar at Kōdaiji in Kyoto. The robot was modeled after an androgynous bodhisattva, Kannon. One may download a special pilgrim stamp featuring a silhouette drawing of Mindar from the temple website for ¥300. It is not a particularly fine stamp, but it links to efforts to reach a younger generation. Even so, it indicates a type of marketing produced by most shrines and temples. As part of the local tourism campaign, the town of Amakusa in Kumamoto Prefecture created a *goshuin* set of three stamps from a temple, a shrine, and a church (*Jiji News* 2019). The stamps are from the Shinto shrine Sakitsu Suwa Jinja, the Zen Buddhist temple Fuoken, and the Sakitsu Catholic Church. The Sakitsu church *goshuin* has a variant of the cross patonce symbol in red ink and the words "God is love" in black Japanese calligraphy.

Pilgrim stamp hunting became commodified in tandem with the powerspot boom, which entailed visiting sacred places to gather spiritual energy. Tourism associations, railway corporations, and the travel industry all offer stamp-related tours and guides. A roundup of online magazine articles covers some of the main trends in the boom (*Rurubi* 2021). It points out that the visual elements collectors value most are stamps with animals and stamps with motifs such as novel writing elements. The number of *goshuin* pilgrimage walking tours has increased, and the range of pilgrim stamp books to select from has expanded to include more beautiful and unique ones. When thinking about the craze for pilgrim stamp collecting, one writer said, "The point of having it is not to get as many as possible, but to have stamps from the temples and shrines you want to visit" (Ōura 2019, 25). Perhaps an interest in curated visits is partly what drove the creation of themed pilgrimage circuits to obtain stamps that are organized around a specific area or linked to a historic personage. In addition, some recent circuit stamp tours reflect sharp thinking by civic leaders, tourism agencies, and railway companies. In 2019 Keihan Railway offered a spectrum of seasonal tours, and one was the Blue Maple Pilgrim

Stamp Pilgrimage around Kyoto. The pilgrim can enjoy viewing the fall leaves while collecting beautiful pilgrim stamps.

A robust instance of themed circuit pilgrimage for *goshuin* is connected to the historic figure of Shōtoku Taishi mentioned above, who is credited with the early promotion of Buddhism (Nishimura 2018). The route includes six of the first temples established in the Kansai region that are linked to him (Tachibanadera, Asukadera, Kōkenji, Hōryūji, Chūgūji, Hōrinji, Hōkiji). Excluding a few of the temples (especially Hōryūji and its close neighbor Chūgūji), the others on the route are not on the top destination lists for visitors to Nara because they are not easy to access and are not well known. Another history pilgrim circuit that is especially fashionable with women is dedicated to a historical figure named Chūjō-hime (747–775). She was born into an eighth-century aristocratic family and took religious vows at Taimadera. While there she observed the miraculous making of a woven mandala tapestry, a visual and symbolic representation of Buddhist concepts and figures. The famed Taima Mandala, created around 763, represents the Buddhist Pure Land and today remains at the temple, although stored away from view. Chūjō-hime became a folk heroine through centuries of plays, folktales, films, and other forms of popular culture. The pilgrim on the Chūjō-hime tour visits Taimadera and its subtemples (Nishimura 2018).

Massive media attention to the popularity of pilgrim stamp collecting inspired other novel uses of the format.[10] The toy-maker Toys Cabin created miniature pilgrim stamp books, sold in vending machines, called Gashapon (figure 11). A few buyers of the tiny books, which measure around five by seven centimeters, began taking them to temples and shrines to get actual pilgrim stamps. This irritated many priests, yet by 2022 at least fifteen shrines and temples were offering their own mini-*goshuin*. These were usually prestamped. An exception is the Hōshuin in Shiba Park in Tokyo, where you can get miniature pilgrim stamp books in addition to regular-sized books. These are endearingly named Mame Goshuin-chō, "Bean Pilgrim Stamp Book." Another interesting evolution of the concept was the creation of stamps called *gojōin* that commemorate visits to Japan's castles. There are more than nine guidebooks or magazines on how to collect stamps at castles. One of the earliest included a hundred castle stamps from all over the country (Gakushū Kenkyūsha Plus 2019). Fans are warned to never have the stamp placed in the same book used for regular *goshuin* for shrines and temples. Because castles charge an entry fee, advertising the existence of special stamps has garnered even more revenue, and now more than three hundred castles are associated with the trend. The stamps are distributed at the museum shops found at the sites or even at nearby tourist information centers.[11]

An electronic rock duo named the Idol Formerly Known as Ladybaby (2016) produced a song about obsessive female pilgrim stamp nerds. The lyrics are a strange mixture of religious allusions, but the diversity of designs and the beauty of the calligraphy found in the stamp books is mentioned. The music video of the song is a jarring mash-up of tropes of piety and Japaneseness (Tada 2016). Perhaps the reason the singers in some scenes dressed up as Shinto shrine attendants and pranced around in front of Buddhist imagery was to convey the idea of both venues as sites for collecting stamps. Whatever one's opinion of the video, the high-end video production highlights how pilgrim stamp collecting changed from being a subdued religious activity to a status as a prominent feature of mass culture.

During the early days of the COVID-19 pandemic, a visitor posted images of the cute pilgrim stamps found at temples with the message "If we visit each one of them, putting our hands together, the coronavirus turmoil will surely end someday, and peaceful days will come again" (Sakamoto 2020). The pandemic led many shrines and temples to begin providing a selection of prestamped sheets (*kakioki*) by mail. Elsewhere, because of staffing shortages, some offer the "Do it yourself *goshuin.*" They leave individual small rectangle pages and ask visitors to stamp them on their own, while others have ready-made *kakioki* available. The tiny hilltop Hiyoriyama Sumiyoshi Jinja in Niigata usually leaves prestamped pages and other items in a cabinet and asks visitors to offer the right amount of money for what they take. When a pilgrim stamp collector named Watanabe (2020) visited another location, he tweeted, "What! They do self-service at Samezu Hachiman Jinja!" Watanabe is something of a *goshuin* fanatic, with a YouTube channel, a Facebook page, an Instagram account, and a blog site about his collecting. He claims not to have a driver's license so does all his hunting by train, bus, or on foot. He was not pleased with the self-stamp method.

Not all those who visit are on their best behavior, and some shrines and temples become exasperated with obnoxious conduct. The Izumo Shrine Sagami branch in Kanagawa Prefecture finally decided to halt supplying pilgrim stamps for a month after the *miko* shrine attendant quit after receiving verbal abuse from visitors (*Kanazawa shinbun* 2020). She was the only person available to do the calligraphy in its "house style." The shrine posted a large sign asking visitors to observe better manners. Similarly, during the massive Sanja Festival held at the Asakusa Jinja in

Tokyo, crowds in 2019 were unpleasant and intimidated the *miko* shrine attendants and priests. Pushy crowds treated the shrine like a service industry and complained, "We are the customers here." The shrine said there had been too much rudeness and bullying, with visitors wanting the pilgrim stamp on demand, so they discontinued offering special stamps (Andō 2019). Another controversy that developed was internet auctions for *goshuin* and pilgrim stamp books sold at exorbitant prices. When the journalist Nagano Tsuyoshi (2017) did an online search for these auctions, he found more than one thousand listings. In one case the bid for a single pilgrim stamp book containing twenty-three stamps sold for ¥100,000.[12]

Scholars of Japanese religion often ask questions about how certain behaviors or beliefs, including pilgrim stamp collecting, qualify as religion or as something else, such as "spirituality" (i.e., Fujiwara 2019). However, from an anthropological perspective any behavior or ritual activity related to the supernatural world might qualify as religion. Horie (2018), for example, suggests that collectors of pilgrim stamps feel they are creating a tie to the resident deities where they obtain the stamp, ties that can be renewed long after they leave the sacred place. I am not as concerned with questions about what people "believe" about *goshuin* or whether collecting stamps fits some theological definition of religion. Pilgrim stamp artists have met the challenge of the confined space for the writing and have used interest in stamp collecting as an avenue for creative expression. I found that the stamps are valued as inventive or beautiful material religious items that are also reminders of shrine and temple visits. They are mementos of a sacred place that the person visited. Their writing, which often extends beyond its referential meaning, is valued for its own sake.

CHAPTER 5

Taoist Paper Talismans

When I lived in the Kansai area of Japan in the late 1970s, a friend showed me a mysterious slip of paper. She told me it was a protective charm her grandmother had given her. The elongated and seemingly disordered red-ink writing was unlike anything I had ever seen. Later I learned that it was a *reifu,* a type of talisman that displays its own genre of oddly shaped Chinese graphs (writing elements) and pseudo-script. Historically, *reifu*

Figure 18. Reifu on manga cover

were prepared according to procedures passed down through oral transmission between religious practitioners and their adepts and kept secret from public view. Today *reifu* are a common feature of popular culture about wizards and the occult. An example is found on the cover of an anthology of stories and manga about yin-yang masters (wizards called *onmyōji*), with *reifu* charms floating around the sorcerer (figure 18; Rigia 2003). No longer secret, *reifu* are a symbolic device and celebrated emblem of the supernatural.

In this chapter I trace the history of the *reifu* paper talisman and highlight some of the ways they are being created and used in contemporary Japan. A change in the technology of *reifu* production has moved their manufacture out of the hands of ritual specialists and into a range of easily accessible public domains. Egalitarian access to *reifu* through reproduction in books, magazines, manga, and the internet has shifted control and distribution away from a religious context into new realms. Even so, *reifu* obtained through specialists or from sacred locations retain some esteem. I will explore how *reifu* have been resurrected from their status as a marginal, semisecret writing practice to become a widely known symbol of the magical in popular culture, as well as a device easily obtainable for those interested in its religious power. This chapter contributes to the scholarly literature on written material objects in their own right and offers an analysis of the materiality of writing and language, domains explored in edited volumes by Fleming and Mann (2014) and Cavanaugh and Shankar (2017). Some questions about *reifu* of the past are difficult to answer because of their blurred history and the former secrecy of their production. For example, one historian asked me about the precise provenance of *reifu*, wondering if primary sources provide clues to their place and time of production. As a transnational form of Taoist magic that is materialized within the small borders of the written slip, the historic *reifu* itself was primarily embedded in ritual practice rather than codified within historic materials. To answer the historian's question, there is not much archival information on when or where historic *reifu* were made and "charged" with supernatural energy.

What happens when esoteric, specialist knowledge becomes egalitarian, and the embodied object of this knowledge is commodified and promiscuously disseminated? The *reifu*'s distinctive pictographic signs and warped graphs taunt viewers with their unreadability and intricacy. While intentionally cryptic, the way that *reifu* are used today in popular culture allows great latitude in playing with the original structure and configurations. Of course, people messing around with their scripts is nothing new. Take the case of the young women who created a novel writing style called *gyaru moji* (girl characters). It is a basic substitution system composed of graphs from other writing systems, mathematical and other typographic symbols, mixed with deconstructed Chinese characters and Japanese syllabic graphs to create a mash-up that is not readable for most Japanese (Miller 2011a). Yet, unlike these graphs from girls' culture, the representation of paper talismans in contemporary manga and anime is sometimes perplexing. Most often the media-embedded *reifu* do not faithfully represent the genre. Even so, it is remarkable that artifacts that were once part of a semisecret writing practice are taking center stage as symbols of the occult in mainstream popular culture.

I will explore the new uses and understandings of these seemingly impenetrable slips of paper using examples from multiple sources, including books, manga, magazines, and visits to related Shinto shrines. One primary interest I have is in the material or visual traits seen on *reifu*, as well as their new uses and meanings. Thus, ethnographic attitudes are of less interest than the shifts in imagery and consumption. I look at *reifu* from a few different perspectives, beginning with a short overview of their history and a review of orthodox *reifu* structure. Prior to looking at how they are used today in media, I highlight a unique shrine that has strong links to *reifu*. This is followed by a discussion of how access to and the spread of *reifu* diversified due to the efforts of occult entrepreneurs. Finally, some of the appropriations and patterns of *reifu* use in popular culture are mentioned. Although *reifu* are common in popular media directed toward both female and male consumers, their particular appeal to women is seen in many female-oriented books, manga, and magazine articles. Contemporary popular culture artists and divination enthusiasts often copy or create *reifu* without regard for their origin as ritual implements, recasting them as objects that serve entirely symbolic functions.

History of *Reifu*

The earliest East Asian talismans written in an esoteric script were found in third-century Han dynasty tombs in China (Robson 2008). By the sixth century, talismans had assumed recognizable, systematic forms. They were inscribed on paper and fabric, engraved on wood, or even written on the body. These charms most likely originated as tools used by folk sorcerers and were borrowed by Taoist priests and later by Buddhist miracle workers who adopted them as their own ritual implements.

Buddhologists and scholars of Taoism are not in agreement about which group first manufactured the paper talisman. Called *fu* in Chinese, they are found in both noncanonical Buddhist sutras as well as Taoist scriptures. A few scholars insist that all religions, including Taoism and

Shinto, owe their very existence to Buddhism. They point out that Taoism formalized itself by writing down its principles and precepts in order to become established as a legitimate religion in response to Buddhism. However, research by Mollier (2009) looked beyond these doctrinal disputes to the material objects and practices that surfaced in texts. She studied the interactions between Buddhism and Taoism and how they shaped each other. She discovered that most often the Buddhist writers reframed indigenous (mainly Taoist) apocrypha rituals and texts (Mollier 2009, 6). She compared early texts side by side and found that the plagiarist's cut-and-paste method dates to at least the Tang period (618–907 CE). In short, many Buddhist texts with *fu* in them are flagrant pirating of Taoist writings. She uncovered instances of identical "scriptural doppelgänger" in which the same material was presented in both Taoist and Buddhist frames, usually in cases in which the Taoist texts have earlier dates (Mollier 2009, 10). The texts present the visual forms of *fu* and name the issues they are meant to address, but they do not describe how they are launched or energized during rituals. This debate is beyond the scope of this chapter, but this scholarship supports the view that *reifu* in Japan were primarily taken from borrowed Taoist arcana.

The manner in which *reifu* entered Japan is also a subject of much conjecture. Some scholars believe the deity Chintaku Reifu Shin was transmitted to Japan during the reign of the Female Emperor Suiko, who lived between 554 and 628 (Nikaidō 2015, 117). The earliest texts containing Taoist material arrived along with Buddhist priests and scribes, as part of a general library of Chinese classics and divination books. The Taoist concept of yin-yang appeared in the Yamato court at least by the time of its first recorded mention in the year 671 (R. Miller 1979). A later administrative structure based on the Chinese model of state organization was established during the rule of Emperor Tenmu (673–686 CE). It included a formal department of yin-yang (*onmyōryō*) that was charged with divination activities. The department's court magicians who were responsible for regulating divination were exposed to Taoist texts, which had a great influence on the seventh-century syncretic system called *onmyōdo*. Japanese *reifu* have long been associated with *onmyōdō*, and especially with the *onmyōji* (wizard) named Abe no Seimei (921–1005 CE). We know about Seimei and his magical talents from folktales such as the late Heian collection *Konjaku monogatari-shū* (Ury 1985). In these compilations he uses his remarkable ability to command goblins, channel spirits, and predict the future to rescue court nobles and to protect the capital (to some extent, I believe that the current interest in *reifu* can partly be traced back to popular culture fascination with Abe no Seimei.) Taoism as a religion, however, never took root in Japan and was actively discouraged as part of official state policy (Yoshida 2006, 152). Even so, Taoist ideas, omen theology, and deities continued to be found in popular folk religions or were recast and nativized in established religions.[1] For instance, two of Japan's popular Shichifukujin (Seven Deities of Good Fortune) are derived from the Chinese Taoist tradition, and the Taoist deity for the Big Dipper was recast as the Buddhist bodhisattva Myōken. When the professors of yin-yang borrowed *reifu,* it was a conventional art with existing norms for how they should be constructed and put into ritual service. Their appropriations did not deviate much from the Chinese models, and even today the Japanese *reifu* and Chinese *fu* used by orthodox religious specialists look more or less similar, with some minor differences.

Reifu Structure

The mixture of elements found on *reifu* charmingly entices us with anthropomorphic images, schema of stars, and malformed Chinese characters. An excellent analysis of the graphic elements and structure of *reifu* was presented by Drexler (1994). She describes the altering of graphs through abbreviation, doubling, layering, elongation, and other means and also details the way characters were combined with other imagery. *Reifu* may have images that look vaguely like stick-figure demons or animals. Some exhibit a dance of spider legs and insect bodies combined with distended characters. For example, a *reifu* requesting work and business improvement sports a bug-like image with written characters for supernatural demons (figure 19; Kuyōgi 2002, insert gift).

Some scholars propose that the zoological and entomological graphs on *reifu* arose due to high regard for the pictograms found in Shang oracle bone script (1200–1050 BCE). Mollier (2009, 20) thinks that the writing found on *reifu* is intended to activate the metaphysical value attributed to this archaic writing, as well as the belief that characters hold an innate vitality. Whatever their origin or inspiration, *reifu* look primordial, with an occult aura and graphic novelty.

Reifu codes can be understood by practitioners but not by laypeople without assistance or guidebooks. Some, as in the demon graphs in figure 19, may display characters that represent concepts but are not supposed to be read as specific morphemes or sounds. *Reifu* allude to meanings, but they do not encode spoken language even though spoken incantations might be associated with them during rituals. Gestalt imagery dominates *reifu,* while linguistically meaningful graphs become secondary or irrelevant. Numerous other examples abound of languages or scripts that people are unable to

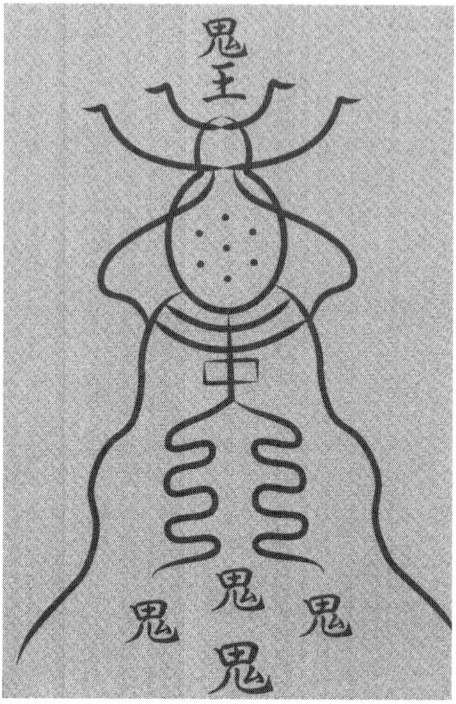

Figure 19. Bug-like *reifu*

read or pronounce being used in religious or cultural settings. Tambiah (1968, 179) noted that "in ritual, language appears to be used in ways that violate the communication function." The unreadable, disproportional characters on *reifu* claim authority through their esoteric nature, as well as their opacity to nonspecialists. It is notable that the incorporation of Japanese syllabic graphs, phonological scripts accessible to readers, is nonexistent on conventional religious *reifu*.

Elements within some *reifu* begin life as normal Chinese characters such as those seen in calligraphy, but within the small space of the paper slip they became distorted or jumbled. Characters on *reifu* occasionally reflect an orientalizing impulse, by which I mean an effort to exoticize or highlight their esoteric thrust. We see, for instance, stroke augmentation. Take the character for "day," normally written with four strokes. In the domain of *reifu*, the day character might be written with five or more busy strokes. In addition, there is no effort to place the graphs into a uniform square space, as is commonplace in writing that is linguistically meaningful. In everyday writing, characters are chambered into the same imagined box regardless of their simplicity or complexity. On *reifu,* the space might be extended, as multiple characters are layered into it. Some look as if they have been stacked on top of each other or contain graphs imbricated into other graphs. *Reifu* reject the aesthetic principles that govern standard calligraphy and writing. Although normal writing aims for balance, *reifu* may be stretched in unusual directions.

Despite the oddly shaped writing, there is still structure in most *reifu.* We often detect a head, a body, a belly, and feet or legs. Normally, at the feet section of the talisman a specific Taoist guild would insert their own graphs as identification. However, these leg graphs are not found on most Japanese *reifu.* Another difference today is that in China and Taiwan they are written in black and red ink on yellow paper, while in Japan they are written on all sorts of papers in different ink colors. In all other respects *reifu* art in Japan, Taiwan, and China is strikingly similar. Cosmological star elements are another common feature incorporated into the *reifu,* usually banded at its top section (figure 20).

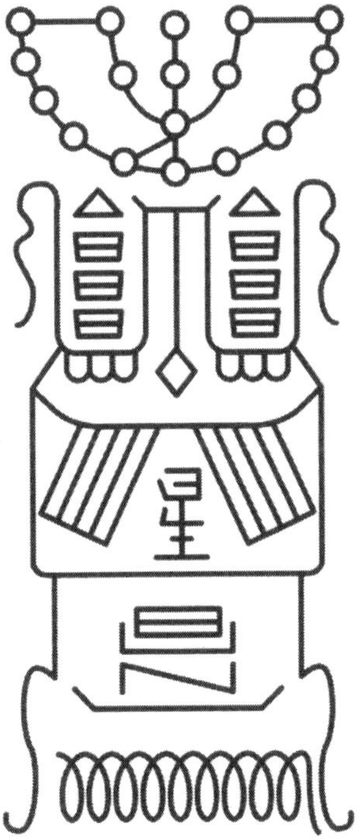

Figure 20. Reifu with cosmological elements (*Kaiunchō* 2012)

Big Dipper veneration is found throughout East Asia and in all religious traditions. In Japan it surfaces in calendars, almanacs, and other writing and imagery from the earliest contact with mainland culture. Northern Dipper (Hokuto Shichisei) star veneration evolved into various forms, such as the worship of Myōken Bosatsu in Buddhism (Nikaido 2015). According to Mollier (2009, 172), Myōken began as a Taoist Big Dipper figure who was later combined with Buddhism during the Tang dynasty. *The Sutra of the Big Dipper for Prolonging Life* (Běidǒu qīxīng yánmìng jīng), which she refers to as a "pseudo-sutra," was a Buddhist appropriation based on a Taoist prototype. Veneration of the deity Myōken entered Japan at least by the seventh century, carried by immigrants from the Korean Peninsula.[2] In Japan it developed into a syncretic blend of Buddhism, Taoism, Onmyōdō, and local kami deity cults. Myōken personifies the deity of the Big Dipper as well as the Little Dipper and the Pole Star. Within Onmyōdō, the deity Myōken became known as Chintaku Reifu Shin.

A famous collection of seventy-two *reifu* within one chart is called the Taijō Shinsen Chintaku Reifu (figure 21; Talismans of the Most High Divine Immortals for Protecting the Home). Homes positioned poorly in terms of feng shui are thought to be protected with this famous chart. Ōmiya (2007a, 132) devotes effort to explaining the efficacy and use of the Taijō Shinsen Chintaku Reifu, including a ritual prayer to recite in front of where it is hung, and includes an attractive yellow insert printed on good card stock. Intrigued by this type of *reifu* bundle, I decided to visit a notable shrine in the Kansai region with links to this *reifu* chart.

A Mountain Star Shrine

A shrine in Katano city in Osaka Prefecture named Hoshida Myōken-Gū (also known as Komatsu Jinja) venerates a version of the Taijō Shinsen Chintaku Reifu. I visited the shrine to learn more about its connection to *reifu*. The Myōken cult was always syncretic, a mash-up that the current priests enthusiastically embrace. The shrine links its founding to a story about the great Buddhist master Kūkai (774–835), who purportedly recommended a shrine be established after three meteorites fell in the vicinity in July of 816. One of the meteorites fell somewhere near where the shrine was built. A cleft in the side of the mountain is claimed by some to be where it made impact. One woodblock print of the shrine gives a sense of the steep and winding paths required to reach the main building near the top (Ritō 1801). Images and drawings of the mountain with its various shrines and points of interest are very popular today and are found in

Figure 21. Taijō Shinsen Chintaku Reifu, Hoshida Myōken-Gū (partial view of 72 *reifu*)

posters and on signboards on the shrine's grounds. The embroidered cover of one of the pilgrim stamp books depicts the mountain and its shrine. A young male priest I spoke to was eager to explain the intertwining worship of a celestial deity known by different names in different traditions. He made it clear that the shrine equates the enshrined principal Shinto deity Ame no Minakanushi no Mikoto with both the Buddhist bodhisattva Hokushin Myōken and the Onmyōdō deity Taijō Shinsen Chintaku Reifu Shin. After the forced separation of Buddhism and Shintoism in the Meiji period (1868–1912), shrines commonly replaced the deity Myōken with the Shinto counterpart Ame no Minakanushi. Although the shrine is officially dedicated to this deity, the other versions of the deity continue to be cheerfully recognized.

The extensive grounds of the shrine are spread over part of Osaka's Mount Myōken (numerous mountains or hills throughout the country have this name). Originally, they covered a larger area, but part of the mountain was transformed into a residential development. In addition to the main shrine are numerous small grottos and subshrines dedicated to more than sixteen Buddhist and Shinto deities, including Fudō Myōō, Toyotomi Inari, and Seiryū Daimyōjin. Walking up a few hundred steps to the primary worship hall, I experienced the precincts as lush and dank, smelling of rotted foliage and mildew. Unlike a shrine such as Ise Jingū, with its clean spaces, elegant trees, and pristine wood structures, the complex at Hoshida Myōken-Gū was busy and dense. The main worship hall and shrine office were rather small and contributed to overstimulation, with many things to look at, such as a giant zodiac compass on the ceiling (representing protection from all directions). On the grounds was an interactive signboard for visitors, asking "Do you know what your Guardian Star is?" The table contained birth years and Chinese zodiac

Table 6. Stars and Chinese zodiac correspondences

Donrōshō	Rat
Komonshō	Ox and Pig
Rokuzonshō	Tiger and Dog
Monkyokushō	Rabbit and Rooster
Renchōshō	Dragon, Monkey
Mugokushō	Snake and Sheep
Hagunshō	Horse

animals to determine one of seven possibilities. There is a primary star sign and a secondary one based on gender. For example, a snake year person born in the year Shōwa 28 (1953) will be assigned the star named Mugokushō (Mizar). Here are the stars and their Chinese zodiac correspondences in table 6 (the list is also in Arichi 2006, 199).

Reifu amulets for each of the twelve Chinese zodiac signs were available at the shrine office, and I obtained a package of two dedicated to those born in the Year of the Snake (figure 22; Sukeno 2013). Their guardian star is Mugokushō and their secondary star if they are female is Donrōshō (also known as Tonrōshō or Dubhe).

The priest clearly loved his work, and when I asked about the shrine's connection to Onmyōdō, he hurried to a desk behind him and, rummaging around, found a book to use for explanation. When I decided to invest in obtaining a copy of the Taijō Shinsen Chintaku Reifu, he packaged it carefully in tubing and wrapping paper, apparently pleased that a foreigner valued it. It is based on a woodblock print made in 1856 (figure 21).

There were very few visitors when I was there in early November. However, during special events and festivals the shrine is packed with pilgrims. One can see numerous advertising posters and local news items

Figure 22. Reifu amulet for the Year of the Snake

about happenings at the shrine, especially the Tanabata Matsuri (Tanabata Festival, July 7) and the Hoshikudai-sai (Descending Stars Festival, July 23), which both draw enormous crowds.[3]

I visited two other shrines at which Chintaku Reifu Shin was the enshrined deity. One was the tiny Chintaku Reifu Jinja in Nara. It was no more than the size of a one-car garage nestled in a residential neighborhood, with no visitors around and closed up both times I visited. The other was a subshrine located on the grounds of a Zen Buddhist temple named Kanga-an. The subshrine for Chintaku Reifu Shin was originally established during the Heian era in order to protect the Imperial Palace. In 1671 it was moved to the precincts of Kanga-an, a very unique temple. The current woman head priest, who was not very friendly when I visited with a Japanese friend in the afternoon, opened a vegan restaurant and bar in rooms near the altar. She charged a fee for us to sit on tatami and watch a short video. Guests at the bar have complained on various internet forums about the prices at the Kanga-an bar.

How to Use *Reifu*

Reifu address many functions, which can be grouped into two main categories, either therapeutic or exorcistic ends, although there is much overlap. The prophylactic *reifu* are used for therapeutic aid, cures, drawing in good energy, or attracting power. The exorcism *reifu* are for the removal of bad energy, to protect from evil and to guard against accidents, misfortunes, and "demons, government officials, and other robbers" (Robson 2008, 147). It is interesting that the first category of prophylactic *reifu* is rarely found in Japanese popular culture such as manga and anime, where the focus is on chasing away demons and monsters. It should be mentioned that *reifu* are not the same thing as *ofuda. Ofuda* are pieces of wood or paper that usually have the name of the shrine, temple, or deity written on them, so the writing, unlike that on *reifu,* carries linguistic meaning. *Ofuda* can be obtained at both Buddhist temples and Shinto shrines and are meant to be placed in a household altar. Some might also have signs or other graphs on them. If the *ofuda* is from a Buddhist temple, it may have some writing in the revered *bonji* Siddham script. *Bonji* has been valued as authentically tied to Buddhist roots, so even if nonspecialists cannot read the graphs, they still cherish them (Stevens 1995). After being sacralized *ofuda* are thought to contain the essence of the deity.[4] In contrast, *reifu* do not usually contain deity essence but rather are thought to be "charged" with spiritual energy by the specialist who makes it. The techno-religious specialist must "open up the *reifu*." The charged writing and imagery on *reifu* communicate with the spirits and deities who will carry out the work intended. Many young Japanese and foreign fans of manga and anime incorrectly use the term *ofuda* to refer to *reifu*. Ordinarily, *reifu* would be placed somewhere on one's body or in the home to attract good energy, addressing the prophylactic function. New *reifu* manuals show exactly what to do with *reifu* and how to make them. Many say that *reifu* may be burned and the ashes placed in a river, or even mixed with water and ingested for best protection. (Ingesting the ashes of charms is not unique to China or Japan.) Ōmiya (2007a, 20–21) recommends that men carry it on the left side of the body, while women should do so on the right. *Reifu* may also be placed inside purses or business card cases. He also offers some admonishments as well: Do not show others, do not fold it, do not staple it, do not tack it up. Similar to other items such as business cards, folding or modifying a *reifu* is a sign of disrespect. In addition, folding, stapling, or punching holes in it might damage or siphon off its energy.

In the past, some people found *reifu* slightly creepy. I recall asking friends in the late 1970s about them and getting a standard answer along the lines of "They are just superstition," uttered in a manner that did not invite continuing discussion. Old-fashioned *reifu* are not cute like many other material artifacts from religious contexts. Cute religious objects are admired in books with titles such as *I'm Happy I Got to Know Japan's Lucky Charms* (C. Hirota 2008). Books like this contain adorable drawings or photographs of hundreds of items but rarely are *reifu* celebrated in their pages. One exception is found in *The Cute Amulets of Japan* (Nihon Juyohin Kenkyūkai 2005, 41), which mentions the *reifu* found at Hoshida Myōken-Gū, discussed above. Perhaps one outcome of the recent promotion and visible presence of *reifu* in popular culture is that they have lost some of their aura as uncanny artifacts that should be hidden and not talked about.

Reifu Production

For centuries *reifu* have been prepared according to procedures passed down through oral transmission between masters and their students. Different sects might have hidden or unusual ways to interpret them. In China, each Taoist guild had its own techniques for teaching and drawing *reifu*, so the imagery would be specific within a school. There was also a concern with maintaining secrecy, and those in possession of *reifu* were instructed to keep them hidden from others (Robson 2008, 154). Yet today we find *reifu* in many new contexts, from trade books that contain *reifu* inventories of charm types to popular manga and anime. *Reifu* are also distributed in divination magazines as insert supplement gifts (*furoku*). An example are ones ready to tear out from the divination magazine *Kaiunchō* (2012). They were a sheet of four large, gorgeous, double-sided *reifu* printed with rich, colorful origami-design paper on the back and the *reifu* framed on the front.

Hundreds of inexpensive manuals that allow one to easily trace the entwined graphs and variform images are available. The recent publication of *reifu* manuals can be viewed as something the scholars Stark and Bainbridge (1987) described for other situations: religious entrepreneurism as part of innovation and response to cultural change. We find religious entrepreneurs who create niche identities and careers based on their knowledge of *reifu*. One of the most prolific entrepreneurs is Ōmiya Shirō, who describes himself as a master of an archaic form of Shinto. He claims to have rigorously studied the ancient texts, theology, aikido, and wide-ranging esoterica, with the aim of restoring time-honored pathways. Among his dozens of books is an anthology of *reifu* (Ōmiya 2011), and in another guide he provides information and practice sheets for tracing *reifu* (Ōmiya 2007b). Occasionally, he delivers ready-made *reifu* that can simply be cut out of the book and put to immediate use (Ōmiya 2013).

Some new types of *reifu* address modern problems. There are *reifu* to help one get beautiful hair and to protect a pet's health, as well as other modern concerns. An example is a *reifu* for Japanese who travel oversees to use for protection against getting bamboozled. The description mentions that it is especially useful when buying Cartier, Tiffany, and Bulgari jewelry for men. This *reifu* will ensure that one gets the real thing and not a fake (Ōmiya 2007a, 105). Another writer named Nakayama Hideaki pens several blog sites on which he also sells *reifu* made to order. He appears to run his online business out of a studio in Utsunomiya (Tochigi Prefecture). He reported that with the increase in pollen, he received a few requests to make *reifu* to prevent hay fever, so he created a stacked one that has a few recognizable "day" graphic elements on it (Nakayama 2019). Several female entrepreneurs also provide *reifu* services. A woman who promoted herself as the Onmyōji Miko sold beautiful calligraphy *reifu* for a steep price. Most other online *reifu* outfits charge less than ¥2,000 for one handmade *reifu*, but at her Tōgenin Kanaeya Shop a *reifu* encased in a cedar box and accompanied by fifty grams of pure salt sold for ¥18,000. Another entrepreneur is Matsu Rika-sensei, who promotes herself as a *miko* medium (*reinōsha*) and will create individualized large, beautiful *reifu* for purchase. These female entrepreneurs have several blog sites and advertise on numerous divination and esoteric websites.[5]

New Reifu

Entrepreneurs such as Ōmiya, the Onmyōji Miko, Matsu-sensei, and others refurbish and update *reifu* for contemporary anxieties while retaining their ordinary appearance. They do not veer too far away from old-fashioned *reifu*. However, *reifu* in other domains of contemporary culture have not retained their integrity. Once a culturally specific magical technology, they have shifted to become cultural signifiers that anyone at all may use to indicate a supernatural arena. Ancient *reifu* never included Japanese graphs from either of the kana syllabaries, or other script elements. But the rules have changed, and now any writing, scribbling, or decoration is acceptable. In *Twin Star Exorcists*, a manga series on young wizards by Sukeno (2013), the *reifu* display an unusual appearance. They became a favorite of fans who created versions with angular and flame-like graphs (figure 23; Sukeno 2018; Kuse 2015). These Gothic-style *reifu* have been sold as souvenirs at anime conventions and on T-shirts available from Amazon. Not everyone appreciates this *reifu* style mutiny. One critic is quite dismissive: "These bogus wizard spirit writing amulets are

Figure 23. Fan *reifu* based on *Twin Star Exorcists*

awful. The talisman of the Twelve Heavenly Generals from the manga Twin Star Exorcists by Sukeno Yoshiaki are being sold online as 'genuine talismans'" (Shōmoji Fudōdō 2023).

Popular culture *reifu* are not simply forms of entrepreneurism; they are historical appropriations that draw on the principles of abstraction to signify. Even so, such *reifu* complicate simple notions about religious or historical appropriation. The writing found on new *reifu* are used for symbolic and decorative purposes. Years ago, on a visit to the Namco Town indoor entertainment complex in Ikebukuro, I saw oddly drawn *reifu* tacked onto a post near the entryway to a section on famous divination providers. They were used to signal that a zone for the supernatural was in the vicinity. *Reifu* decorate other mundane objects, such as T-shirts, and artistic art in limited-edition music CDs, such as *Music for Onmyōji* (Eno and Schwalm 2002). Because the *reifu* in Japan were based on Taoist versions, those that incorporate script elements not based on Chinese characters are notable deviations. The writing found on some new versions is *bonji,* the imported Siddham script mentioned above. Although often seen on Buddhist *ofuda* and *omamori* amulets, this script is not associated with *reifu.*[6] But this has not deterred contemporary culture producers.

An example is found in a Nintendo DS video game about some ostracized ninja in a small village (Ninja Studio 2006). The *reifu* they use are envisioned as weapons for "*reifu* battle." The main character, Izuna, explains that one can use other weapons but that "doing battle using *reifu* is nice and easy." *Reifu* in the game enable fire attacks and teleportation and will also boost the efficacy of traditional weapons. On the official game website, fans may freely download four colorful *reifu* featuring Izuna and another character named Shino. One of the *reifu* has a *bonji* character on it below an interesting mash-up of the characters for "demon" and "woman" (Ninja Studio 2006). In a manga series by Kuse (2015), the *reifu* look as if they have *bonji* script on them. Set in the Edo period, the female *onmyōji* wizard Shima always wears a kimono, sometimes with the sash tied in front in courtesan style. In one scene she holds a folded *reifu* (not good!) while streamers mimicking the *reifu* with reversed fake *bonji* on them swirl around, mirroring the flowing sleeves of another female character. Among the reference books on *reifu* in my library, I do not find any with *bonji* on them. For example, of the 118 *reifu* in one collection (Ōmiya 2007a) and the 60 in another guide (Ōmiya 2007b), not one has *bonji* on it. Although *reifu* like these are innovative and enticing, they do not conform to normative expectations.

The *Reifu* Pose and My *Reifu*

Fans of manga and anime have latched onto the *reifu* as a way to indicate the supernatural and the occult. In thinking about recent representations, I see two trends I have labeled *Reifu* Pose and My *Reifu*. The *Reifu* Pose is a type of patterned stance in which the character holds one or more *reifu* in front of their body. In My *Reifu* there is no concern with reproducing *reifu* imagery along customary lines; rather, it is adorned with individualized graphic elements.

The *Reifu* Pose is often found when culture producers depict *reifu* as a direct tool for exorcism. Centuries ago, *reifu* would have served as written instructions to deities or spirits to conduct the exorcism on behalf of the human practitioner. The ritual specialist would instruct the supernatural realm in how to address the problem at hand. There is no historical description of Taoist priests or *onmyōji* running after demons with *reifu*, yet this has become a dominant image in popular culture today. In excavating this trope, I found one of its early expressions in an anime series from 2006 named Shōnen Onmyōji (Mori 2006). The series, based on a light novel, is about a character named Masahiro, who is the fictional grandson of the great wizard Abe no Seimei. In episode six Masahiro chases after a demon named Wanyūdō (Firewheel), who appears as a flaming oxcart wheel with a bald monk's face in the center. As he is chasing after the demon Wanyūdō, he has a *reifu* clutched between his fingers. The image of an *onmyōji* or other character wielding a *reifu* has become a dominant motif in popular culture.[7] In the case of manga covers, wizards, witches, *miko,* and others are pictured aggressively holding them out as a signal that the subject matter inside relates to the supernatural. The cover of a manga featuring a female wizard shows her holding a *reifu* that bears the Taoist yin-yang symbol (figure 24; Nanao 2017).

In manga in which the characters never use *reifu* in the narratives, they, too, might be brandishing them on covers. Two amateur fan manga (*dōjinshi,* or self-published) with *reifu* on the covers contain no *reifu* on the pages inside (figure 25). These manga are no more than ten pages long. In other manga and anime, both amateur and professional, the character is fortified with handfuls of *reifu.* If one *reifu* will repel evil, imagine what several can accomplish.

A transnational aspect should also be noted. Many scholars have traced the spread of Japanese popular culture, such as TV dramas (Iwabuchi 2004) and print club photos (Miller 2017a), to other parts of Asia. Silvio (2019) illustrates how the Japanese aesthetic of kawaii (cute) was adopted in Taiwan and reflected in things such as the design of deity figurines. In contrast, it

Figure 24. Reifu on manga covers

Figure 25. Reifu on amateur manga covers

seems that the Reifu Pose may have been adopted into Japan from Hong Kong fantasy and martial arts cinema in which actors often perform it.

The other theme is My *Reifu,* which is my term for *reifu* that are self-styled or individualized with unique symbols that have nothing to do with traditional forms. They are iconic shorthand for magic or the supernatural. Drawing on the logic of abstraction, My *Reifu* isolate certain properties or obliquely suggest expected elements. Because *reifu* are no longer exclusive to ritual specialists trained in their construction and interpretation, we see many changes in their appearance and function. Such changes could mean they are no longer *reifu* but rather *reifu*-like signs or signifiers. New ones move beyond esteem for Chinese characters, transforming them into lines, dots, or squiggles that fill the space merely to signify the esoteric writing.[8] The archaizing mode that characterized centuries of *reifu*-making is muted or eliminated. An example is a drawing of Abe no Seimei in a manga in which he holds a *reifu* with nothing on it but a pentagram (Hayami and Koyanagi 2003). The pentagram does double duty in comics and anime about Abe no Seimei, representing both him and his magical skills. A slip of paper bearing a pentagram is sufficient to represent Seimei's very own *reifu.*

One radically simplified *reifu* that illustrates the process of simplification is found in a card collection game named *Valkyrie Crusade.* One of the thousands of cards features a character called Onmyōji (Mynet Inc. 2014). The *reifu* held between her fingers depicts a bunny and a heart, with some squiggly lines underneath (figure 26). It presents a shift from a talismanic assault on bad energy to a cute symbol. The weight of the motif is simple and tamed. These easily understood *reifu* now serve straightforward purposes.

Some popular culture *reifu* are pictorial commodities that have vacated any immediate referential connection to the religious world of the Taoist talisman. Odd script, squiggly lines, curly shapes, and abstract icons are sufficient for the slip of paper to indicate their *reifu*-ness. The massive flourishing of *reifu* and *reifu*-like objects widens their exposure, and to some extent, anime and manga have normalized such versions. One might ask whether this will contribute to *reifu* longevity and expansion?

While some fans and artists see them as inspiration and seek out their history and meanings, others restrict their interest to the symbolic value of the *reifu* papers and thus feel free to substitute any writing or images on them. In addition, as mentioned before, many fans misidentify *reifu* as the *ofuda* written religious charm, further diluting the essence and depth of *reifu.* Rather than serving as one of the many devices in the wizard tool kit, the *reifu* is often just an iconic shorthand for the occult. Originally based in Taoism, Onmyōdo, and folk religion, they are now a

Figure 26. Bunny and heart *reifu* (Mynet Inc. 2014)

commonplace sign that alerts us to the occult domain. These slips of paper dressed in their authority of weighty writing played a role in divination and occult domains and now have found an audience among popular culture fans.

Despite the flourishing of *reifu*-like art and the use of pseudo-*reifu* in a broad secular context, it is also true that *reifu* as a technique of magical practice has not disappeared. Part of the longevity of *reifu,* with their aura of celestial calligraphy, is that the esoteric functions remain tied to a body of semisecret knowledge. Although that knowledge has become easily available, the expansion in accessibility has not led to *reifu*'s demise. One would think *reifu* should have disappeared by now, yet their tenacity indicates that people continue to imagine the possibility of *reifu* protection or intervention in assisting in their own fate or that of their family. In addition, the defamiliarized Chinese characters and the archaic aesthetic keep people interested in them as material religion. In popular culture there has been an evolution of *reifu:* Demonic characters shift to parasitic writing of any type, including formerly excluded scripts such as Japanese kana and Buddhist *bonji,* and finally to *reifu* that merely display simple symbols such as pentagrams or heart shapes. Even so, the deracinated *reifu* never fully dislodge the power or status of original ones.

My trip to Hoshida Myōken-Gū was a reminder of the possibility of both cultural longevity and renewal. The head priest Sasaki Hisahiro had been a white-collar worker until he was in his thirties. He and his wife decided to rehabilitate the dilapidated shrine and spent decades clearing the debris and repairing the grounds that cover nearly seven-and-a-half acres of mountain (Tamagawa 2021). Hoshida Myōken-Gū was transformed from a worn-down and hard-to-reach shrine into a popular local destination and a place to enjoy festivals such as the Tanabata Matsuri. The globally poplar anime *Your Name* (Shinkai 2016) contains a narrative that includes a meteorite that lands on a fictional town. One unlikely folk theory is that the anime tale was derived from the legend at Hoshida Myōken-Gū, and the resulting influx of fans is partly why the shrine has seen better fortunes in recent years. Although commoditized on the shrine's amulets and through copies of the Taijō Shinsen Chintaku Reifu, *reifu* are nevertheless linked to this specific shrine and an understanding of their history and original function. I experienced satisfaction that, along with other visitors, my hunt for *reifu* had led me there. I am optimistic that *reifu* will continue to appeal to different audiences through both traditional and innovative methods and that they will endure as a writing artifact that is part of cultural life.

CHAPTER 6

Votive Tablets and Amulets

An unusual restaurant named Kigandō in Tokyo once welcomed customers into a space that felt like a step back in time. The hobbyist owners had covered the deep maroon walls of the dimly lit eatery with hundreds of antique votive plaques, called *ema.* These small pieces of wood are intended to be left at shrines and temples with petitions to the deities written on them. When I visited Kigandō with friends in 2005, it was crammed with *ema* of different types and sizes.[1] The couple had opened it as a type of pub in 1977. They claim to have amassed more than seven thousand *ema* of various types, accumulating them for everything humans worry about—good relationships, safe childbirth, business success, recovery from illness, and more. Although Hada Nagako became interested in the artifacts after getting married, her partner Hada Yūto began collecting them as a young man. There were some with horses, Ebisu (a Shinto member of the Seven Lucky Deities), snakes, and female figures expressing breast milk.[2] The shrine theme in the pub was mirrored in some of the offerings to guests as well, such as lottery fortunes (*omikuji*) that were given to each customer. Their collection tells us that in addition to serving as material religion, *ema* are a type of art that is admired and analyzed.[3] The restaurant is a secular space that is home to thousands of objects from sacred spaces, blurring those boundaries.

In this chapter I focus on the *ema* votives and good luck amulets called *omamori,* as material objects that open a pathway for exploring the meanings of the supernatural. As Morgan (2012, 89) said: "Human interactions with spirits, ancestors, gods, and other forces unfolds in and around things." Historical accounts, myths, local gazettes, and religious exegesis all provide tantalizing descriptions of folk practices, divination activities, and religious rituals involving objects. Today consumers and producers of material artifacts have a rich storehouse of cultural memory at hand to appropriate. These objects confer spiritual capital. They function as souvenirs of pilgrimages and visits. They act as conduits to the supernatural.

They allow great creative expression and experimentation. Occult hunters visit shrines and temples for multiple reasons, and thus obtaining *ema* and *omamori* extends beyond seeking help or protection. Seeking them out is not necessarily linked to worries about relationships, childbirth, health, or a career. Many people go to shrines and temples as a relaxing activity in its own right, to walk through a beautiful space and to enjoy some time away from everyday life. While there, they may obtain *ema, omamori,* and other items. In some cases, visits are stimulated by a desire to obtain one of the cute or unusual items described in tourist magazines and books on lucky objects. Increasingly, these objects are designed with the aesthetics and tastes of the female visitor in mind.

There is a danger of overinterpretation when decoding the meanings of objects found in other cultures. Keesing (2012) notes that observers occasionally attribute superfluous cosmology or cultural schemata to others when the people they describe are simply using metaphors. Even so, it is possible to infer the significance of particular items given their ubiquity or location in sacred contexts. The surfacing of *omamori* and *ema* in contemporary anime, manga, promotional activities, and other secular contexts also makes them worthy of notice. The biographies of *ema* and *omamori* are significant because they reflect creative and expansive uses of things once cordoned off as sacred. *Omamori* and *ema* replicas and imagery are used in secular contexts but retain an aura of the supernatural, the special, or the enchanted. They often present more positive features and imagery than in the past.

As with my discussion elsewhere in this book, my aim is not to determine if people believe in the efficacy of *omamori* and *ema.* The study of religious artifacts does not align well with the usual scholarly perspectives that focus on issues of doctrine and individual belief. The problem of trying to make "belief" a central point about religious objects is apparent in Silvio's (2019) work on deity toys in Taiwan. The people she spoke to have a range of feelings and attitudes about religious objects and are generally open to different types of intersubjective engagement with them. Following the work of Reader and Tanabe (1998) and Kasulis (2004), my goal is to look at *omamori* and *ema* as legitimate aspects of culture that illustrate the theme of ritual practice rather than belief. I also reject descriptions of *ema* and *omamori* in the manner described by one scholar as aspects of "superstition" or as the "products of a primitive religion" (Ashikaga 1954, 33).

Extending analyses provided by earlier scholarship, this chapter looks at the playful creativity that often reflects feminized and popular culture aesthetics, as well as the secular uses of *ema* and *omamori* as part of a continuum of appreciation and enjoyment of their forms and symbolism. I begin with *ema* and review their history, the types of written messages we find on them, and some innovative uses of their forms. I then turn my attention to *omamori* amulets, including form and construction, styling and secular uses of the shape as a symbol of good luck, and some notable innovations. Finally, I link both *ema* and *omamori* to global cultural identity.

Ema History

Ema comprise two main categories: large commissioned types and much smaller ones for everyday visitors. Both types of *ema* were originally square or rectangular, but over time many shapes have evolved. The large types are called *o-ema* and take the form of detailed paintings on slabs of wood that donors paid artists to execute.[4] These large painted panels were produced by professional painters or craftspeople and usually hung in specially designated pavilions or other dedicated areas. The large *ema* depict themes related to the enshrined deity or to the miracle legends of the shrine or temple. An example is the painting of the court wizard Abe no Seimei conducting an exorcism ritual that hangs in the Seimei Jinja in Kyoto. It is a scene adapted from *Fudō riyaku engi emaki* (Illustrated Handscroll of Benefits from Fudō), dated between 1333 and 1392.

The small *ema,* about the size of a boxed candy named Pocky, are those most people imagine when the term is used. Initially, they were individually painted wood plaques sold at stalls near temples and shrines. People on pilgrimage would obtain *ema* prior to arrival at the temple or shrine. Woodblock-printed books dating from the Edo period (1603–1868) provided ideas for *ema* painters or served as catalogs for patrons to select desired patterns. An early book of samples is the 1749 *Pattern Book of Valor Ema* (Snow 2010, 42). An unusual *ema* sourcebook with six hand-painted designs includes one with an octopus (Toshitsugu Tanaka 1918, 7). The word for "octopus" is *tako.* A homonym is the word for "wart," so this would be intended for people worried about skin ailments (figure 27). Even today *ema* employ such visual puzzles or inferred meanings.

Until the fifteenth century, most *ema* depicted horses. The name literally means "horse picture," and it is theorized that they were first made as substitutes for the known practice of offering horses as gifts to shrines during the Nara era (710–794). However, Snow (2010) traces both the earliest visual representations of large *ema* as well as other types and notes small ones depicting horses dating back to the Asuka period (538–710). Researchers at the Okayama University Archaeological Research Center

Figure 27. Octopus votive plaque design

announced in 2013 that they had discovered the two oldest *ema,* dating to the second half of the eighth century (Okayama University e-Bulletin 2013). The very simple drawings on the small pieces of wood depict a cow and a monkey leading a horse.

For at least four decades, some shrines have been displaying enormous votive plaques called *dai ema* (huge *ema*) during the New Year period. These usually depict an animal from the borrowed Chinese zodiac that commemorates the current year, and they are typically painted in a cute cartoonish style. Several shrines take credit for initiating the *dai ema* fad. In a news item about the huge *ema* painted for the Sōsha Jinja in Akita City, it was stated that the custom of unveiling these huge *ema* for the New Year began in 1990 (*Kahoku shinpō* 2016).

Today most Shinto shrines provide small *ema,* and many Buddhist temples do as well. They are ritually burned each year. Anyone may obtain one at the shrine or temple office (the *juyosho*) for ¥500 to ¥1000. They are no longer individually painted but rather mass produced off-site and delivered to designated shrines and temples. Decorated *ema* are incredibly diverse and imaginative, and most locations offer more than one design. Each shrine and temple commissions its own designs, which are usually related to a resident deity or a symbol tied to its origin story. They may be drawings of a buddha, bodhisattva, Shinto deity, or other iconic or famous character, such as Daruma (the Japanese name for the Buddhist saint Bodhidharma in the form of a paper-mache figure) or Hello Kitty. The drawings could also represent themes of good luck, health, fertility, or safe travel. Some encode rebus wordplay, such as the octopus *ema* seen in figure 27 or symbols of the shrine such as deer, a pentagram, or wisteria. The visitor writes messages of gratitude or requests for assistance on the blank side (the back) and then hangs the little plaque on the dedicated stand for the deities to see. The next section considers a few of these messages.

Writing *Ema*

The written petitions on *ema* have been affectionately called "letters to *kamisama* (the deities)" (C. Hirota 2008, 42). Scholars and collectors have found these messages to be ethnographically instructive. Holtom (1938) examined twenty-eight *ema* inscriptions and DeSmet and Reader (2017) devoted an entire book to one subset of *ema,* those related to health issues. Reader (1991) collected and analyzed hundreds of *ema* writings that reveal a spectrum of anxieties and culturally specific concerns. When he examined *ema* from around two decades ago, he found many that were heartbreaking, asking the deities to intercede in the illness of loved ones. There were also hopeful tablets asking for help in finding a marriage partner, not being betrayed by a partner, receiving positive prospects for the future, passing university exams, or getting pregnant. Similar *ema* are still found today, like these recent ones from various shrines with the following sentiments written on them (my translations):

> I hope a healthy and bright baby will be born.
> I hope I can live together with a splendid person.
> I hope I am not betrayed this year.
> I hope I can debut as a manga artist.
> I hope to pass the university entrance exams.
> Everyone passes! Fight!

I have seen some in recent years that might be interpreted as irreverent or trivializing, such as these:

> I hope my room will become clean.
> I hope all five SMAP members do a live show [SMAP is a former boy band].

The *ema* messaging seen above might be a sign that the medium is currently being accessed and exploited by a younger group of people. As they age, of course, those worried about pop groups and clean rooms will face more difficult life challenges. The concept of writing wishes for the future is appealing, and the *ema* format has been adopted in secular contexts. *Ema* were featured in an issue of the former girls' magazine *egg* (2007b). *egg* was a street magazine for the *gyaru* (girl) subculture that spanned around twenty years, published between 1995 and 2014. Eleven *egg* models wrote messages on *ema* for the new year, including the following:

> The fulfillment of my dreams.
> Live a more enjoyable life.
> I've got to become an adult.

Elsewhere in the same issue of *egg* (2007a) is a drawing of a young woman at a shrine holding an *ema*. It is an illustration for a regular feature of the magazine in which readers share their sexual escapades. The writing on the *ema* states, "Let it happen to be able to have sex that feels good." *Ema* found hanging in shrines that allude to sex or romance with actors or J-pop idols are not unusual. I have seen *ema* at the Seimei Jinja in Kyoto that expressed a desire for male beauties who resemble the manga and film representations of the historic Seimei. Irreverent *ema* inscriptions in both sacred and secular contexts illustrate playful and optimistic attitudes.

There are other precedents for understanding *ema* as serving multiple functions extending beyond individual petitions offered to deities. It is not only the deities who read *ema*. It is clear that human visitors are an additional audience. This was beautifully described in the analysis of wartime soldier *ema*. Robertson (2008, 68) examined these rare votives and paintings that at times suggest divergent meanings and perhaps occasional resistance to officialdom: "Like popular culture itself, the soldier *ema* genre was a complex dialectic of resistance and acceptance, refusal and capitulation—a dialectic manifested in the polysemous readings of the various motifs we have analyzed." Anderson (2002) found that the *ema* discovered at two sites were active objects of commentary and debate during the late Edo and early Meiji eras. The tablets related to the Female Emperor Jingū and reflected political sentiments about the Japanese invasion of Korea. His detailed study looked at the *ema* in shrines in Fukuoka and Yamaguchi Prefectures, including transcriptions of *ema* messages. Anderson evaluated *ema* as a type of community communication in which political debates were shared among common people. Both studies by Robertson and Anderson draw attention to how *ema* may play roles that are not centered on the individual and that link to broader contexts of local thinking about political and historical events.

Ema Art

I visited the temple Gangōji in Nara on a misty day when the crows were noisy. There is a small museum in the precents with a glass case displaying every *ema* the temple has offered since it began to do so in 1959. As I was chatting to the museum assistant about them, she mentioned the few still available from the last fifty years that one could obtain for ¥200. She fetched some shopping bags from a closet and searched through them until she found the earliest one for the zodiac animal I inquired about, the Year of the Snake. The designs for the *ema* in the earlier decades were prosaic, but beginning in the late 2000s, many became cute and manga-like, especially those made for the New Year that feature the animals of the Chinese zodiac. *Ema* at other temples and shrines show a similar historic trajectory from orthodox to cute. During the Edo period, visitors would purchase their *ema* at shops in the vicinity, write their messages, and leave them on the grounds of the shrine or temple. Since the postwar era, the revenue these institutions have received by providing their own special *ema* to visitors has been greatly valued. They now offer a menu of designs and are eager to attract younger petitioners with cute or fashionable images.

On a visit to Tokyo's Kanda Myōjin, I admired the display of *ema.* They are hung on a designated stand called *ema-kake.* As I examined the plaques, an elderly woman sweeping leaves came over and told me that another *ema* stand further along might interest me as well. I went to the area she indicated and discovered a dizzying array of *ema* bearing incredible art by the petitioners on the reverse side where one usually writes a simple message. The promiscuous display depicted colorful characters and scenes from the world of anime, manga, and video games. These fan *ema* have become a source of pride and care for the shrine, which has benefited from a massive increase in visitors from the nearby Akihabara district, known as a destination for popular culture fans. Once the district became a core geek destination, its proximity to Kanda Myōjin provided a steady stream of fans to the shrine as well.

Eventually, Kanda Myōjin became a fan pilgrimage site, an activity fans named *seichi junrei,* which means "holy pilgrimage." These are real-life locations included in manga, anime, and games that now attract visitors and pilgrims. Not to pass up a good opportunity, in 2014 Kanda Myōjin commissioned a special *ema* featuring a character who appeals to this crowd (figure 28). The character, Nozomi, is from a media empire named Love Live RAIBU School Idol Project. It is a media mix of CDs, anime, manga, and video games beloved by women about a group of schoolgirls. The character Nozomi works part-time as a shrine attendant (*miko*) at Kanda Myōjin. Fans love visiting a place linked to her—she may be fictional, but the shrine is real.

Another trend in *ema* production is to link famous figures from the world of sports to specific shrines and temples. For example, fans of figure skater Hanyū Yuzuru, wildly popular after his blast through several world records, began visiting Yuzuruha Jinja, a shrine in Kobe with a similar name. The shrine has been deluged with mostly female fans of the skater after he stopped there in 2010. Fan pilgrimage increased after Hanyū became an Olympic medalist in 2014 and 2018. The shrine's priest Sawada Masayasu noticed that of the five to six thousand *ema* left during 2018, 70 percent were dedicated to the skater (*Nikan Sports* 2018). Many of these fan *ema* feature amateur drawings or even photos of Hanyū glued to

Figure 28. Kanda Myōjin votive plaques

them. The *ema* often ask the deities to protect him from injuries or to help him heal quickly from them.[5]

In addition to *ema* commemorating characters from the world of manga and anime, a new fashion in votive-making transforms the experience of obtaining one into something more interactive. These are *ema* that invite the petitioner to fill in or complete the drawing on the front of the wood plaque. At Kasuga Taisha in Nara, an ancient shrine famous for its sacred tame deer, we find a type of *ema* that allows one to draw in the deer's face. People are creative with these, adding sunglasses, bows, freckles, and long eyelashes (figure 29). Kasuga Taisha has often been at the forefront of creating adorable *ema* and other sacred objects that appeal to young and female visitors. At a different shrine, dogs get the same treatment: Jingi Taisha in Itō City provides *ema* in the shape of a dog. People visit the shrine with their dogs, draw in details such as ears and noses, and write wishes for or on behalf of their canine friends.[6]

Daikakuji, a Buddhist temple in Kyoto, has a record of creating unique *ema*. In one case they used a famous rebus for the *Heart Sutra* (*Hannya shingyō* in Japanese) on it. A rebus is a puzzle that substitutes pictures for words, and a number of rebus versions of the Heart Sutra were created for the illiterate in earlier centuries (Eubanks 2013). In 2019 Daikakuji offered a clever *ema* with a Chinese character that could be punched out of the thin wood and left in a tray for wish fulfillment (figure 30). It was called the *wazawai otoshi ema* (*ema* for dropping disaster). The petitioner writes a

Figure 29. Deer votive plaques, Kasuga Taisha

wish on the *ema,* punches out the graph for "disaster" (*wazawai*), and drops it into the tray in front of a small Fudō Myōō image. Fudō-sama will then take away the problem. As one Kyoto blogger wrote, "A number of 'disaster' Chinese characters had fallen before Fudō-sama. This is strangely surreal, and I'm intrigued (haha). It's one of the things to make one chuckle, part of Daikakiji's charm" (Burarinko 2020). These various interactive *ema* transform the petitioning into an enjoyable activity.

The existence of draw-the-face *ema,* puzzle *ema,* and popular culture *ema* tells us that they are valued for their humor and novelty and for affording an avenue for emotional expression. Thousands of books and magazines are dedicated to the study of their imagery. Centuries before the votive collection bar mentioned above, Edo-period connoisseurs collected *ema* and wrote about their art. The *ema* available today normally feature cheerful motifs and images. Many depict Chinese zodiac animals rendered to reflect kawaii cute aesthetics or pleasing images of people or objects associated with the shrine or temple. In contrast, historical collections of *ema* from earlier centuries noticeably include numerous types of negative imagery. In Iwai's (2007) collection are many examples of *ema* targeting disease and divorce. *Ema* for people wanting a divorce often depict an estranged couple with their backs to each other. These are a general type for those wanting to cut ties with friends, family, coworkers, and

Figure 30. Puzzle votive plaque, Daikakuji

others. A type of *ema* never seen today is the *mabiki ema* (infanticide votive plaque) common during the Edo period. Drixler (2013) used documents, scrolls, and *mabiki ema* to document the cultural history of infanticide. Although people today might leave written messages on *ema* that indicate despair in unfortunate circumstances, the *ema* pictures themselves usually reflect positivity and hope.

Current events and interests inspire new paths of entrance to the world of material religion. When Russia invaded and occupied parts of Ukraine in 2022, Enoshima Jinja began offering a new *ema* design with sunflowers that referenced a film partly set in Ukraine. The proceeds were donated to the Ukrainian ambassador in Tokyo (Kamoshida 2022).[7] A traditional card game based on an anthology of poems compiled in the eleventh century was featured in *Chihayafuru,* a film about a high school club devoted to the game (Koizumi 2016). Ōmi Jingū near Kyoto became a pilgrimage destination for young people because it hosts annual competitions of the card game and was the location for scenes in the film. Ōmi Jingū now offers a beautiful *ema* depicting two women playing the card game (figure 31).

Figure 31. Ōmi Jingū votive plaque

Rather than view *ema* with anime and manga characters as spiritual kitsch, perhaps we should consider them to be the contemporary version of Edo-era *ema* that similarly relied on popularly circulating imagery and symbolism. They depend on meanings that the viewers of the images bring with them. The *ema* may be left in the temple or shrine compound or else taken home as a good luck memento. Another much-loved object is taken away by the visitor, the amulet called *omamori*.

Omamori Amulets

When describing the contact situation between West Africans and Portuguese in the colonial era, Latour (2010, 5) had this to say about the Europeans' denigration and condemnation of non-Christian religious practice: "We see one group of people covered with amulets scoffing at another group of people covered with amulets." Each year, undergraduate students at my American university ask me why Japanese "believe" in "weird" things like *omamori* amulets. Their stance always puzzles me. They do not ask such questions about Saint Christopher medals or crucifixes worn around the neck. I do not consider scarabs, hamza, ankh, devotional scapulars, crosses, *omamori*, or any other protective object to be forms of "superstition." Amulets are found universally among all human groups and should be categorized as a normal aspect of material religion. Over the course of knowing people in Japan since 1972, the most common thing I have heard people say is that although they do not know if *omamori* actually work to confer good luck, it is nevertheless worth getting one at vulnerable times just in case (my poker-playing father said this was "hedging your bet"). Especially for potential inauspicious years called *yakudoshi*, friends said things such as "Maybe it will help? I don't know but anyway. . ." In addition, people often said that because *omamori* are pretty and cute they are nice to have as an accessory, they are attractive gifts to give to others, and they are evidence of a visit to a sacred place so they are valuable in that regard.

Omamori have been expertly analyzed by Reader and Tanabe (1998) in their study of the way that religious institutions provide spiritual benefits to a population that consistently claims to not be religious. Amulets are cast in the idiom of borrowing supernatural power from the shrine or temple. The power-endowed amulets are gifted from the deities, and therefore the visitor is only submitting renumeration money for them. When the object has worn out, when it has run out of sacred juice, it should be returned for ritual disposal (burning). Old *omamori* do not need to be taken back to the same shrine or temple where they were obtained, although the Shinto objects go back to shrines, and Buddhist objects are returned to temples. A few angry blogs and online chats about *omamori* tell us that not all occult hunters and players are aware of the norms for visitation to sacred places. Concerned, Meiji Jingū in Tokyo prints instructions for care of the *omamori* and *ofuda* (household talismans) on the paper bags in which they are wrapped.

What is inside an *omamori?* They might contain the name of the shrine or temple, a prayer or incantation written on a slim piece of paper, wood, or silk, or a visual image related to the story of a resident deity or other enshrined supernatural being. If from a Buddhist temple, it could be part of a sutra. The paper, wood, or silk slip might be wrapped in paper before it is placed in the brocade pouch. Opening the amulet will release its supernatural power, nullifying it. Although they know they should not do so, some people open the amulet pouch out of curiosity. Many blog posts show photos of *omamori* innards strewn on a table. A popular blogger wondering what is inside *omamori* posted an exposé on the "shocking contents" (Ōsumi 2015). He cut open five from different shrines or temples and posted photos and comments of what he discovered. He expressed disappointment that so many of them are simple slips of balsa wood or paper. One with a color-printed image of the Bodhisattva Jizō excited him a little, but he thought the last *omamori* he opened, from Hanazono Jinja in Shinjuku, was surprising because it contained tiny gold metal charms of male and female genitalia.[8] The shrine houses the deity Inari, associated with fertility and success.

In online blogs people post about their displeasure when they obtain *omamori* and votive plaques and the *miko* (shrine attendant) does not say, "Thank you." Although all shrines and Buddhist temples operate as businesses, they are also unique spaces of worship, public good, and historical significance. They do not like to present their activities as a form of commerce. Guides and manners books for shrines and temples caution visitors never to ask to "buy" *omamori* and never to treat the *miko* or temple employee as shop clerks. One is expected to use forms of speech that mean "I will receive it." A powerspot guidebook, for example, dedicates two pages to the cultural conventions adhering to *omamori,* stressing that one is not "buying" them (Nagakubo 2012, 19–20). Some institutions deem handing over money for entrance or purchase of amulets or other goods as a type of ceremony fee (*hatsuhō-ryō*).

Omamori Production

Before the 1950s, *omamori* provided by the shrines and temples merely took the form of a written text or visual images without being swathed in material (Swanger and Takayama 1981, 240). People carried them home and made their own protective pouches from strips of old kimono and obi sashes. Today the process of making *omamori,* from design, textile creation, sewing, and assembly, is generally outsourced and not done within the shrine or temple grounds. When Reader and Tanabe (1998, 222) studied *omamori* production, they noted that the religious goods wholesale companies that made them would visit the temple or shrine with big catalogs of *omamori* from which priests or other staff could select. But now there might be as many as three different corporations involved in the supply chain, including various aspects of *omamori* design, production, and packaging. Because of the critical economic role played by providing goods to visitors, shrines and temples have had to treat the design and production of *omamori* as worthy of great thought and innovation. To appeal to younger people and women, they have turned to outside companies for assistance.

One of these companies, Kowa Display Co., specializes in corporate design, planning, and promotion. Their company slogan is "We turn our customer's important image into reality." One of their areas of specialization is working with shrines and temples on *omamori* concepts and design (En Tenshoku 2017). The company makes an appointment with the shrine or temple and visits to learn about its history and special traits. The corporate amulet designer then begins working out prototypes, usually with the idea that it will be women whom they need to attract as consumers. Once they have a prototype, they revisit the shrine or temple and discuss any needed modifications. The design process takes one to six months. Kowa holds monthly in-house planning meetings where they exchange ideas and observations about trends. They talk about the type of *omamori* they see women carrying around, especially young office workers, and news about powerspot pilgrimages.

A separate company will produce the cloth and sew it into the desired shape. Some of the celebrated Nishijin weavers in Kyoto have turned their skills to *omamor*i making. Nishijin is an area in the northwest part of central Kyoto famous for its many kimono and other weaving workshops and stores. Several types of Nishijin brocade are produced, and the art form was designated as a national traditional craft in 1976. However, because fewer people buy or wear kimono, the Nishijin workshops transitioned into digital weaving and other types of textiles. Hall (2020) provides historical and ethnographic accounts of the business, tracing how the Kyoto dyeing and weaving industries have managed to stay afloat after a period of economic distress. Companies, craft guilds, and individual artisans have been willing not only to transition to new types of production but to invest in innovative ways to use traditional fabrics and designs. One is a company named Kyoto Hosei, which opened in 1974 and has around five thousand shrine and temple customers. They make twenty million *omamori* amulets per year, which are not handwoven but made by machine-operated looms and a digital-weaving process. Hikita Satoshi, president of the company, says his philosophy is "to contribute to the happiness of the people of the world through making amulets" (Kyōto Iju Keikaku 2016). Yet another company will manufacture the paper or plastic bags that the *omamori* and other goods are placed in before being handed over to the shrine or temple visitor. Some shrines buy mass quantities of blank paper bags and stamp them with their name and logo. Others, such as Seimei Jinja in Kyoto, invest in well-made custom-printed bags. Their bags, clearly produced off-site, are shiny white and display a red pentagram and the name of the shrine.

Shrines and temples have such an infallible sense of what young visitors desire that I imagine more than a few professional amulet production designers are involved. Perhaps they also hire coolhunters, people who track trends and motifs. The creative designs now found on *omamori* are seen in a published collection titled *The Cute Amulets of Japan* (Nihon Juyohin Kenkyūkai 2005). The small book describes hundreds of *omamori* as well as maps to each location where the reader may obtain them. Included are some with Namazu-san, the giant catfish that guards against earthquakes, and *omamori* in the shape of small books for success in school. Kanda Myōjin offers one in the shape of a computer circuit board that will help prevent laptop and desktop system crashes.

The Adorable Protective Pouch

Omamori come in a spectacular variety of types, from simple cloth bags embroidered with the name of the shrine to multicolored pouches with little charms dangling from them. The packaging apparatus most often consists of a brocade pouch folded at the top and fastened with a fancy white knot drawn through holes at the top. Shrines and temples offer a large selection of the amulets. For example, Kanda Myōjin in Tokyo offers sixty different *omamori* (Kanda Myōjin Kanshō 2008, 82). The Nihon Daiichi Kumano Jinja (2006) in Okayama Prefecture is famous for its website that offers fifty-seven amulets for specific bodily ailments and symptoms in addition to the usual *omamori* for business success, relationships, and scholarship. A priest at the shrine created a paper *omamori* to reassure people worried about the COVID-19 pandemic. His *omamori* design included the mythological tripodal crow (*yatagarasu*) that is a symbol of the shrine. He planned to distribute ten thousand of the good luck paper amulets for free (Mitsuyuki Satō 2020).

I am charmed by the way a writer named Hirota Chieko (2008) presents *omamori* in a book targeting a female readership. She has published several small paperbacks about Japanese holidays, festivals, annual observances, and unique items, all illustrated with delicate and appealing images. While at times verging on nationalistic nostalgia for fading tradition, her work is nevertheless sincere and insightful. In her book *I'm Happy I Got to Know Japan's Lucky Charms,* she offers comments about many auspicious things, including *omamori,* noted for their great variety: "After all, it is the Japan of multitudinous *kami*" (*yaoyorozu no kami,* "eight million kami; C. Hirota 2008, 62). She also mentions the problem of young Japanese not knowing manners when they obtain amulets at shrines.

Books with cute illustrations of *omamori* like those discussed above are an interesting contrast to older books on religious culture, such as guidebooks to shrines and temples. Books published since the 2000s highlight the visual appeal of material religion. Old-style guides like *Guidebook to Supplications at Temples and Shrines* (Shinbutsu Goriyaku Kenkyūkai 1989) mention *omamori* as part of the experience of visiting particular temples or shrines for various issues, but their appearance is not the main attraction. The guide does not contain photos or drawings of *omamori.* Now, however, the style of *omamori* is critical to its appeal to occult hunters who want beautiful or novel objects to take home.

Omamori Styling

The many attractive features and possibilities for *omamori* position them as available for extensive appropriation. But if the "*omamori* is given power by the *kami-sama*" (Kanda Myōjin Kanshō 2008, 82), what is the purpose of creating or producing them outside a religious context? Because *omamori* obtained at shrines and temples have been imbued with supernatural power not only through written or visual means but also via rituals of spiritual conveyance conducted by specialists, secular *omamori* are unable to grant the same type of protective supernatural essence. Nevertheless, nonreligious *omamori* continue to be widely produced and circulated. The secular *omamori* operate as symbols that denote good fortune. *Omamori*-like items have value in other ways as well. They present a motif borrowed for stationery design and are popular on fan websites.

Some producers make it clear that these are not sacred by naming them "*omamori*-like" (*omamori-fu*) or "*omamori*-style" (*omamori-gata*). For example, Adventure World in Wakayama is an enormous combo-theme park that encompasses a zoo, aquarium, and safari experience. One of the main attractions are the pandas who live in their Panda Land section. The Adventure World gift shop sells *omamori*-like cell phone straps in pairs to promote love and affection. Each bright pink amulet features a mother and baby panda and the words "Happy Panda Family, Adventure World" stitched in English on it.

A friend told me he often saw secular *omamori* cell phone straps sold in musical instrument shops and sheet music shops. These are a type known as *ongaku omamori* (music amulets). One style is made of black cloth with white music notes and the English word "music" stitched in gold thread. Gold charms for various instruments, such as the flute, saxophone, or piano, are also attached. The music lover's "cute mini *omamori*-type straps" are made by a company named Southern DS Create (2016). The company specializes in goods for high school clubs. They have *omamori* for martial arts, baseball, soccer, ballet, and so on. These secular *omamori* come with small cards to be inserted before presenting them as gifts. They suggest giving them to people before exams or auditions. Thus, even a secular *omamori* is used as a good luck object. We might think of nonreligious *omamori* as functioning as a framing device. The amulet elevates the character or theme, making it special.

It is not always easy to distinguish at a glance between secular *omamori* and the consecrated ones obtained from a shrine or temple. Secular amulets often have themes from popular culture, such as manga characters or famous animals. Examples are found in figure 32. The Tora-san amulet was sold at the Katsushika Shibamata Tora-san Museum in Tokyo. The museum commemorates a much-loved figure in Japanese cinema, the character from the long-running series of films *It's Tough Being a Man* (Y. Yamada 1969). Kuruma Torajiro, nicknamed Tora-san, works different sketchy jobs, from itinerant peddler to fortune teller. Although some shrines and temples do offer amulets for pets, the dog amulet named *wanko omamori* (doggie amulet) was purchased at a stationery store. Another is an elegant amulet made of beautifully woven material with a gold *magatama* floating against blue clouds. It is part of a set of secular amulets named "Izumo pattern" produced for the agate and semiprecious stone seller Anahita Stones (2023).

At the same time, shrines and temples occasionally offer amulets with secular imagery. Sanrio contracted with several shrines to use Hello Kitty on official religious *omamori*. She is popular at the Tenjin Shrines on the "success in studies" amulets (figure 33). The shrines hope to appeal not only to children but to female visitors, who continue to love the cat character into adulthood. Three featuring Hello Kitty are from the Yushima

Figure 32. Secular amulets: Tora-san, dog, Izumo pattern

Tenman-gū in Tokyo, one of the many Shinto shrines dedicated to the deity of scholarship. On one Kitty-chan wears a Heian-era court costume.[9] A cute deer amulet is offered at Kasuga Taisha, and beckoning cats are on the amulet from Imado Jinja, where they represent the resident deity couple Izanami and Izanagi.

Several companies will make *omamori* to order for individuals. A printing company in Osaka named Sunrise Publications (Sanraizu Paburikēshon, n.d.) has been specializing in reproducing amateur self-published manga for a few decades and has realized that fans would also pay to have *omamori* made of beloved characters. Sunrise will also make individualized *omamori* to order. The customer sends them the image and text, and it is printed on polyester. Fans and shops like to give these out as gifts and souvenirs commemorating events. Outside Japan, fans are also making their own *omamori*. The *Ynao Otaku Blog* is written by a native English speaker and is mainly about anime and costume play. One post on "Make Your Own *Omamori*" gave step-by-step instructions. The blogger

Figure 33. Shrine amulets: Hello Kitty, deer, beckoning cat

used some gingham fabric (*Ynao Otaku Blog* 2014).[10] There are also several YouTube tutorials in English, such as one called "Omamori Charm Workshop" (Ka-Pya! Sisters 2014). Ka-Pya is the name for a fan arts group that provides workshops at the Anime Revolution conventions (called AniRevo) held in Vancouver, Canada. They have held Omamori Charm Workshops since 2014.

Omamori are encased in a pouch intended to protect. Now the packaging itself with its iconic white ornamental knot is sufficient to serve as a sign of good luck, and thus even secular *omamori* will hold a talisman-like function. In this sense the continuum between sacred and secular *omamori* might merely represent approval by a religious institution. Occult hunters desire material evidence of their visits to shrines and temples, but they also appreciate related objects and media obtained outside sacred spaces. At times the official religious outlet for obtaining *omamori* and other religious objects fails to satisfy. This was the case at Seimei Jinja (L. Miller

2008a). Troops of Abe no Seimei fans left the shrine's narrow parcel of land hungry for more merchandise associated with the ancient wizard. While other famous temples and shrines might have cafés, souvenir shops, and other touristic destinations nearby, Seimei Jinja at the start of the boom had only a gas station and a wide modern roadway. A nearby resident who had a small tie shop revamped it as an Onmyōji Goods store to snare the throngs of visitors who were traipsing around the area. A few occult hunters told me they liked the secular *omamori* found in the shop more than the sacred ones they could obtain at the shrine.

Omamori-Like Goods

A friend in Kanazawa received a card from her sister that had a small piece of origami paper folded into the shape of an *omamori,* including a string drawn through a hole punched into it. The object was not intended to denote an *omamori* from any specific place or be for any specific type of petition, such as asking for success in school or romance. It was therefore functioning as an icon of itself. The card was just a basic greeting not related to any special event, and the *omamori* theme was meant to convey general auspicious good vibes. Like the cutout red hearts and cupids that denote Valentine's Day on any object, including stationery, the *omamori* image is a stand-in for auspiciousness.[11] In stationery shops and online stores, a variety of *omamori* letter sets and message cards are available. Gift cards shaped like the *omamori* pouch allow a letter or note to be inserted. I once saw one in a shop that was decorated with tiny Daruma (a round paper-mache figure of Bodhidharma) and had the English loanword "fight" printed on it. The package explained its use: "For sending messages with important feelings or to cheer someone up, use this cute *omamori*-type card!" In this context "fight" means something like "do your best," so this item is for starting a new life, exams, or sports competitions.

A designer named Inoue Aya created a whimsical multipurpose fabric pouch that is modeled after a traditional *omamori.* The pouch is open at the top and is the perfect size to slip a cell phone into. These are named Omamori Pokke (from the English loanword "pocket") and are made of modern fabrics with soft padding inside. Inoue did not want her new concept to look too much like a real *omamori,* however: "The *omamori* amulet is related to Shintoism or shrine, and if I make the *omamori* design too directly connected to an *omamori* amulet it will be too easy to evoke mysterious and ghostly feelings. So, I want to avoid it becoming too religious" (Owada 2013). Omamori Pokke reminds us of the attraction of having a pretty material object to hold in the hands. A good example to return to next is the unique *omamori* provided by a Buddhist temple in Tokyo. Its creation of a new type of religious *omamori* combines the themes of aesthetically attractive material with individuality.

Authentic *Omamori* for Each Person

Perhaps the most brilliant innovation in religious *omamori* was devised by (or for?) a Nichiren sect Buddhist temple named Ikegami Jissōji. In this evolution of amulet styling, the individual takes center stage, and it becomes highly personalized. The new item was named Omamo and was introduced in 2016 via a superb advertising blitz that included a video describing the new form (Sheepme 2015). The promotional video for Omamo was created by one of the top advertising agencies in Tokyo, I&S BBDO. The company eventually received an award from the Ad Stars international advertising festival for its design and branding of Omamo. One news site introduced Omamo with the headline "Cute!!!! A made to order *omamori* that matches your worry!" (*Shirabē* 2016).

The video opens with scenes of a monk named Sakai Chiko explaining the idea behind these new *omamori*. Sakai says he thought established amulet categories were not sufficiently helping people with modern worries and concerns. He created a menu of conventional symbols and patterns to represent different concepts. Many are time-honored patterns known to most women because they are commonly found on fabrics for curtains, cotton hand towels, *yukata* (cotton kimono), and other textiles. A popular design is the beloved arrow motif (*yagasuri*), which was used over centuries for many textiles. The arrow is used within Shinto and Buddhist tradition to represent the repelling of evil. Omamo gives the arrow motif the meaning "to ward off evil spirits and to shoot down targets." A design composed of rows of waves forming a fan-shaped pattern (*seigaiha*) suggests a wish for continued tranquility and calmness. A few of the designs are from the world of the occult: the Aries symbol from the Western zodiac and the pentagram from the world of the Japanese wizard.

In the Omamo scheme, two designs are combined to yield a more specific application to a person's issue. In the case of a woman who complained about a lackluster sex life, Sakai combined material with a gourd pattern (fertility and sexuality) with one showing fireworks to yield "spark love." A transgender person desiring to increase her cuteness is given an *omamori* design that combines seven different flower symbols to yield the meaning of "transcendental cuteness" (*chōzetsu kawaii*).[12] Omamo's symbol system eerily resembles the extremely popular made-up classification systems that have been ubiquitous in women's magazines and books since at least the 1980s. These short, entertaining personality quizzes, called *shinri tesuto,* literally "psychology tests," might be on anything, such as party personality types, mothering types, or boyfriend personality types (L. Miller 1997a). The Omamo system draws on these folk categories of personality. The petitioner visits the website, fills out a form with the concern, and sends it and the remittance amount to the temple. According to the website, Sakai himself picks the two designs that address the petitioner's problem. He will also conduct the necessary prayers to sanctify the charms.

The stated goal of the advertising surrounding Omamo is that these new-style *omamori* will better meet the spiritual needs of people today. Another unstated purpose can only be called robust commodification. The temple's hiring of a top-notch advertising agency to create an award-winning campaign that includes a stunning video, one with erotic undercurrents, hints at deeper plotting behind Omamo. The monk Sakai, putative creator of the Omamo concept, is tall, fit, and handsome. It might be ungenerous to think it, but perhaps Sakai was not, after all, the genius behind Omamo. Maybe a group of middle-aged priests, together with the advertising agency staff, came up with just the right skillful means to entice people to contribute to their temple. One can imagine the advertising people asking the temple to "send us your best *ikemen* (hunk) monk!" for the video.

Omamo is a triumph of both social and aesthetic timeliness. The focus on the individual (me!) is perfectly crafted for the younger generations of affluent but damaged seekers. The website name for the service even has "me" in it. The design features as well are precisely hip: a festive palette of magenta, guava, yellow, and aqua against a crisp white background. The Omamo is "cute" (kawaii) according to many of those who have blogged about it. Despite all the effort, the playfulness, the intense marketing, and the pop colors, there is one flaw related to Omamo: it moves the focus away from visiting the temple to merely looking it up online. One unchanging attraction about *omamori* is that they are proof that one has visited a shrine or temple. Religious *omamori* are not simply testimonials to amelioration efforts or proof of a pilgrimage or visit. They are an ontological link to a deity and the power they confer.

Omamo eventually collaborated with the globally famous cosmetics company Clinique for a short-term and unexpected alliance. For a few months in 2018, the cosmetics giant teamed up with Omamo to create the Pink Charm Maker promotional effort. The customer would first buy the new Clinique Moisture Surge line of skin lotions and gels that, according to ad copy, "are like a skin care *omamori* for the skin." As a gift the customer could use the Omamo site to create a digital *omamori* composed of two pink-colored designs. It was suggested that the digital image be used as cell phone wallpaper or included in text messages to others. By piggybacking on the *omamori* motif, Clinique capitalized on the concept of self-care that Omamo promoted and also implicitly the magical powers of their skin-care products.

The beautiful and unique *omamori,* many with intriguing backstories or captivating visual imagery, have sparked a global demand for them outside Japan. One internet company named Omamori.com World Co. ships them worldwide for a substantial markup. For example, the love and romance *omamori* from Kitano Tenmangū is ¥700 at the shrine, but it is ¥2,400 from this outfit. With shipping added the *omamori* cost dramatically increases. This company also claims that the items are "totally handmade by artisans in Japan," although they are actually produced through digital machine weaving (Omamori.com World Co., n.d.). Before the pandemic, the majority of tourists visiting Japan were from China. In 2022 most were from South Korea, Taiwan, and Vietnam (Imahashi 2023). This company hosts their internet business in English, so they are targeting a smaller group of visitors. In addition, *omamori* amulets may not be particularly exotic for people from Asia. Perhaps international tourists from Europe and the US return home wishing they had gathered more of the beautiful pouches as novel souvenirs and so are willing to pay the exorbitant prices. Many fans of games, anime, and manga outside Japan may be introduced to *omamori* through those media.[13] It might be that fans wish to have one of the artifacts in hand to more closely connect them to their fantasy worlds.[14] In addition, possession of these culturally specific items confers cultural capital on Japan enthusiasts.

Because of their long history and beautiful and unique presentations, *omamori* and *ema* are often linked to a sense of Japanese cultural identity. Books such as *Things Japanese: Everyday Objects of Exceptional Beauty and Significance* (Bornoff and Freeman 2014) include beautiful photographs and descriptions of both objects. Museums in Japan and in foreign countries host collections of *ema* as folk art, with special exhibitions, events, and lectures. In 2018, for example, the Yamazaki Memorial Hall Historical Museum in Tokyo hosted an exhibition of *ema* with dogs on them. In some settings, *ema* votive plaques outside Japan are incorporated into interactive events as both a form of entertainment and as an activity symbolic of Japanese culture. At a joint Japanese-government-sponsored exhibition held in Paris in 2018, one of the event halls was devoted to manga and anime, and an imitation *ema* station was set up for visitors to write on *ema*-shaped papers. Instead of petitions to the deities, visitors drew manga characters or wrote messages such as "It was fun" (Miyamoto 2019). Both *ema* and *omamori* have proven to be objects of interest and awareness outside Japan. Similar to the way visits to Yuzuruha Jinja increased dramatically after its connection to the skater Hanyū Yuzuru, sports celebrities associated with particular *omamori* might spur increased requests for them. While in Australia for a tournament, tennis star Osaka Naomi carried a bag that had an *omamori* dangling from it. Fans zeroed in on the design and inferred that it was from Shirasaki Hachimangū in Yamaguchi Prefecture. Fans swamped the shrine, demanding a type of *omamori* called *hisshō* (determined to win). Within days four thousand *omamori* were provided from the shrine's online service, and eight hundred were obtained by visitors (Terashima 2021).

The talent for inventing new connections between sacred things and nonsacred imagery and objects tells us that people are creatively searching for ways to tap into supernatural power. Even people who claim not to be religious expend energy looking for good luck through artifacts such as *ema* and *omamori*. They use these artifacts to enable the performance of imagination and as a pathway for transcending the mundane world and the daily grind. Both *ema* and *omamori* have retained their enchantment over time and are valued, whether sacred or secular. They are notable because their spiritual capital continues to be linked to popular tastes and interests, casting them as desired objects for occult hunters.

CHAPTER 7

Precious Curved Beads

Fifteen years ago I was wandering among the stores in the Asakusabashi section of Tokyo nicknamed Bead Town, and inside one shop were tables set up with baskets of beads, charms, and phone straps. One basket contained hundreds of curved beads called *magatama,* which took me aback. I had read about them and their mythology in the 1970s while an undergraduate student studying Japanese history. *Magatama* were recognized as a unique artifact associated with ancient rulership and religion, but it was the first time I had seen one outside of a museum display case. These days, *magatama* are easily available in shops everywhere and are often found on amulets available at shrines. Their popularity soared, no doubt fueled by the rise in supernatural and occult themes in mass culture. Occult hunters desired them, media fans wanted them, and their historic and mythological associations proved to be irresistible. Initially, I thought the *magatama* were primarily a way for female occult enthusiasts to symbolize female power or a basic marketing device. I mistakenly assumed that contemporary people did not have a deep connection to the ancient bead.

In this chapter I review the *magatama*'s presence in the archaeological record and the texts of the past to illustrate why an ancient artifact is so tempting today. Looking closely at *magatama* allows us to see what aspects of their career are most enticing and why the crescent stone has so noticeably made a reappearance. Beyond uses of *magatama* in religious settings, they are part of the divination and spiritual goods market and are found in diverse forms of popular culture. *Magatama* are polysemic, reflecting different interests and meanings for culture producers and users. They are transformed into edible weapons in anime, while their enduring connection to female shamanism remains. A famous *magatama,* to be discussed below, is part of the three imperial insignia stored away from public view. The current ubiquity of *magatama* asks that we examine their history, uses, and meanings more closely. Unlike the situation in most Euro-American countries, where items like the Christian cross are not often used in profane or humorous settings (Madonna and Mapplethorpe notwithstanding), *magatama* are found in a surprising range of secular contexts.

Paine (2013, 114) made a good case for the claim that "objects have unique power to speak to people, and do so on a quite different level to words, or even to images." I think *magatama* are excellent messengers. They may act as agents of the past that pull our minds centuries back in time. They serve as a bridge between eras and cosmologies. Although this luniform symbol of ancient Japan has slightly changed through time, evolving from a rounder, less elegant droplet to a more defined one with a pointed tail, its essential meaning as a supernatural artifact remains. Perhaps the shape of *magatama* provokes subconscious associations. Their antiquity offers an unexhausted resource for contemporary people interested in drawing on their iconography.

A *magatama* derives its meanings from the network of associations assigned to it: ancientness, mysteriousness, shamanism, and imperial authority. A *magatama* is able to symbolize divination, protection, authority, female power, local identity, or spiritual energy. Unlike questions that arise concerning objects or entities associated with some other religious imagery (for example, why the fox is associated with the deity Inari), the link between *magatama* and all these meanings seems logical or reasonable. Not everyone knows exactly what a *magatama* was used for, but nearly everyone in Japan can name one on sight. I once heard a young man in a museum say about a clay figurine from the Kofun era (300–538 CE): "Oh look, that clay figure [haniwa] is wearing a *magatama* necklace." The shape is easily identifiable, and using the *magatama* to denote the mystical, the magical, and the ancient is common.

Following the trail of *magatama* meanings and uses, I first thought that after navigating through their archaeological traces and linking them to the relevant mythology, I could finally address the current stage of history where they operate as shrine gimmicks and popular objects among occult hunters. But I was mistaken. In 2019 I visited two different shrines with similar names: Tamatsukuri Inari Jinja in Osaka and Tamatsukuriyu Jinja in the resort town of Tamatsukuri Onsen. The visit to the latter, a shrine dedicated to a deity of *magatama* and to a *magatama* bead-making workshop nearby, returned me to the beginning. For some people, *magatama* continue as objects that have been "ensouled" or contain a spiritual essence just as they did when they began their journey through time.

The Birth of *Magatama*

For most of Japan's history, *magatama* were never just baubles worn for adornment. They also carried intense cultural meaning and served ritual functions. They appear in numerous stories in ancient mythology in which their mojo is commemorated. The historical significance of *magatama* is noted by nearly all scholars of ancient Japan, who comment on their unusual shape (figure 34). The tiny artifact has made an indelible mark.

The paisley-shaped bead elicits a spectrum of responses. When I posted a photo of *magatama* to Facebook, a friend said, "They look like fetuses!" There are countless theories about the origin of the intriguing half-moon shape. They are said to have evolved from animal teeth used for decoration, from the borrowed Chinese yin-yang symbol (called *taikyokuzu* in Japanese), or else from the practice of reusing half of a disc-shaped ornament for the ear (from the Jōmon period, called *ketsu*). Some people think they are abstract representations of the shapes of the moon, fish, fishhooks, human kidneys, or embryos. A theory that is not often mentioned is that the *magatama* became a powerful ritual object because of homophone association. *Tama* may mean the spirit or soul, but it is the same sound as the word for "jewel" or "bead." Because the *tama* spirit was thought to occasionally assume physical form, there was a displacement of *tama*/spirit onto *tama*/beads (Collins 1997, 57). By the time writing came to Japan in the fifth century, the *magatama* had become a prestige item valued for itself without drawing on any primitive meanings.

Archaeologists have unearthed *magatama* carved from many different materials and in a range of colors. They were made of jasper, quartz, steatite, agate, talc, and other materials. The most valuable were made of a type of green jade. There are two types of jade. One is the more famous nephrite, the stone known from Mayan artifacts and Navajo squash blossom necklaces. The other is jadeite, a gemstone native to Japan, California, Kazakhstan, Russia, New Zealand, Central America, Canada, Myanmar, and China. Oddly, the occurrence of jadeite in Japan faded into obscurity after the Nara period. *Magatama* carved from jadeite date from seven thousand years ago in the later part of the Jōmon era (14,000–300 BCE). These *magatama* look more bent and less tapered than their later shape. One scholar asserts that jadeite found in Jōmon sites in Itoigawa, Niigata, are the oldest documented human use of this type of jade (Miyajima 2017). For most of the Jōmon era, *magatama* are found along with other common objects and tools within household settings. It was not until the late Jōmon that they turned up in burial sites. The *magatama* found in late Jōmon graves are smaller and more varied in shape (Nishimura 2018, 105). Over time they became high-status objects almost exclusively found in tombs and ritual settings. Many researchers believe that the ancestors of the Jōmon people likely entered the Japanese islands from Siberia via Sakhalin and Hokkaido. This population was later swamped by a series of immigrations from the Korean peninsula by a people now labeled the Yayoi. It is not clear how or if the *magatama* was transmitted from the Jōmon people to the Yayoi cultural group. Did Yayoi bring their own *magatama* tradition with them, or did they appropriate it from the Jōmon people? Curved beads have been found in early archaeological sites in Korea as well. Called *gobeunok* or *gogok,* they are a slightly different shape than the iconic Kofun-era Japanese *magatama* because they are less pointed at the end. They resemble the primitive *magatama* found at Jōmon sites in Japan. However, *gogok* appear centuries after Japan's Jōmon *magatama.* Perhaps they are one of the few cultural items that spread from Japan to the continent, unlike the majority of cultural innovations. Some of the most notable examples of *goguk* dangle from elaborate crowns excavated from Silla Kingdom tombs dating to the second half of the fifth century.

From the late Yayoi period (300 BCE–250 CE), Itoigawa in Niigata served as one center of *magatama* production and widespread trade. Initially,

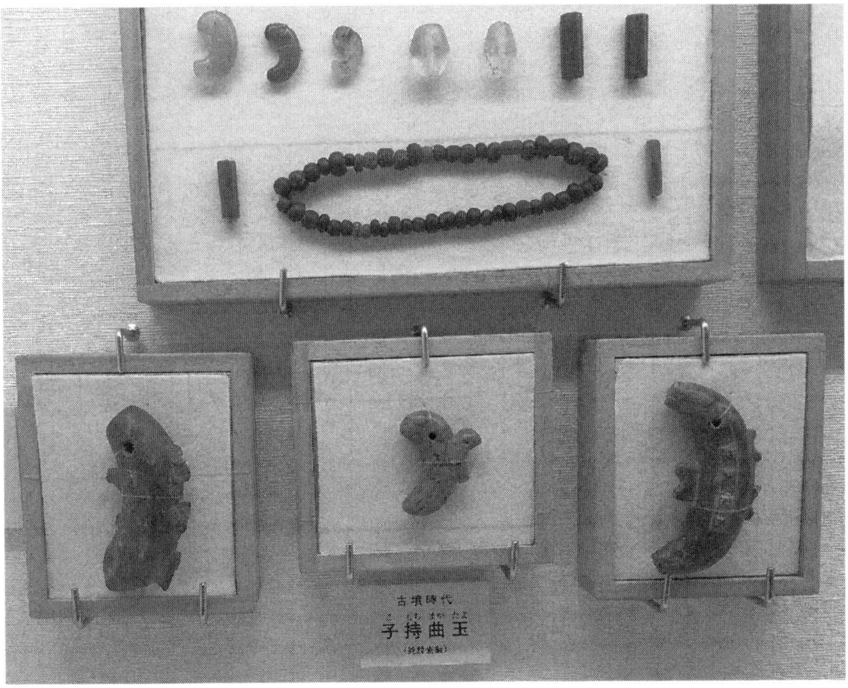

Figure 34. Parent-and-child *magatama,* Tamatsukuri Shiryōkan

workshops using jadeite were located only in Itoigawa, but later the jadeite was sent to other workshops in western Japan. There was a jewel-making production site at Kaminoshō near Miwa station in Sakurai (Nara), and remains of stones from all steps of the process, from chunks to finished beads, as well as cutting and grinding tools, have been excavated. Yayoi-era lapidary workshops for fashioning *magatama* out of agate were also located in Izumo.

In addition to the iconic comma-shaped bead are zoomorphic ones that resemble birds, fish, or animals (Umehara 1965). There is another type called clove-head *magatama* (*chōjigashira magatma*), characterized by cut grooves in its side. An interesting iteration was the piggyback *magatama* named *komochi magatama*. These are *magatama* with smaller baby projections mounted on them.

Magatama are most closely associated with the Kofun era (ca. 300–538 CE). The period is named after the enormous mounded earth tombs that mark the transition to a stratified society and the consolidation of regional power. Today there are more than 160,000 known *kofun*, the majority of which are located in the Kansai region. The tombs are notable for ritual earthenware objects called haniwa. Haniwa burial mound figures range from simple cylinders to more elaborate sculpted figures that represent humans, animals, houses, boats, weapons, and tools. They were placed on top of or around the exterior of the tomb mounds. There are various theories about the functions served by haniwa. Perhaps they accompanied or protected the dead or marked the perimeter of the tomb, served as a sort of retaining wall, or embodied the souls of people and animals. Many of these clay death dolls represented female shamans wearing necklaces with *magatama* beads. An exquisite example is a Kofun-era earthenware haniwa in the Asian Art Museum of San Francisco (figure 35). It is a female shaman wearing a flat hat and a necklace holding at least four large *magatama*.

An escalation in bead production took place from the middle of the Kofun era (Kidder 2007, 105). A system of occupational guilds was established and included bead engineers such as the Tamazukuri-be (Bead-Making Guild). The "sculptors of ornamental minerals" (Brinkley 1902, 92) were located at several sites. There were workshops throughout the Nara region, in Furu near Isonokami Shrine in Tenri city, Sogachō in Kashihara, and Miwa in Sakurai (Barnes 2001).[1] The existence of districts named Tamatsukuri (Bead-Making) in Osaka and the Izumo region in Shimane Prefecture indicates that hereditary bead-making craftspeople were in those locations as well. Some sites have large caches of the beads. An excavation of one Kofun-era site in Sakai City yielded 725 *magatama* (Kidder 2007, 108). This was the Katonboyama Kofun, a mound tomb dug

Figure 35. Haniwa shaman, Asian Art Museum, San Francisco (Wikimedia)

up in 1949 and then destroyed because of development. It was a smaller satellite tomb of a larger one named Gobyōyama and was packed with many *magatama* and other ritual items, suggesting that the hoarder may have been a type of administrator for religious goods.

As mentioned, one location in Japan that uses the place-name Tamatsukuri is in Shimane Prefecture. The stones used to make *magatama* were quarried from nearby Mount Kasen, an onshore volcano. Archaeologists found up to thirty *magatama*-making villages in the vicinity of the mountain. From 200 CE to around 400 CE, Mount Kasen produced agate, jasper, and occasionally rock crystal. Unlike the famed Itoigawa area of Niigata, Mount Kasen does not produce jade, nephrite, or jadeite. This former *magatama* production site is now recast as the Izumo Tamatsukuri Historic Park in the resort town of Tamatsukuri Onsen on Miyagaki Hill. It is one of the largest archeological excavations of a Kofun-era *magatama*-making site. Many *magatama* in various stages of manufacture from unfinished or broken beads, as well as polishing wheels and iron-drilling tools, were recovered. There is an identifiable "Izumo-style *magatama*," which is plump green agate with rounded rather than tapered tails. Other types of tubular beads, such as one called *kudatama*, were also manufactured at the site. The hot spring here was well known during the Heian period (ca. 794–1185). The renowned author Sei Shōnagon listed three famous hot springs in her masterpiece *The Pillow Book* (*Makura no sōshi*): "As for hot springs, Nanakuri no yu, Arima no yu, Tamatsukuri no yu" (Nanakuri no yu is now called Sakakibara Onsen).[2] Today this is a beloved quote that nearly all the inns and hotels include in an exaggerated manner in their promotional materials, even though almost all modern versions of the work do not include this short list. I visited Tamatsukuri Onsen to explore the meanings and uses of *magatama* today and discuss this at the end of this chapter.

Another symbol is called the wish-fulfilling jewel (*hōju-no-tama*). It looks like an onion, or a peach, and is a symbolic element on Buddhist statues, on votive plaques, on architectural features, and in mandalas. The wish-fulfilling jewel is also associated with one type of Shinto shrine, those dedicated to Inari, a deity who protects agricultural cultivation and aids fecundity, as well as general business success. At Inari shrines the wish-fulfilling jewel appears clenched in the jaws or under the paws of the fox, Inari's messenger. It is noteworthy that at one particular Inari shrine the wish-fulfilling jewel is replaced with the *magatama*. This is the Tamatsukuri Inari Jinja in the Tamatsukuri district in Osaka. According to Smyers (1999, 23), it was thought to have originally been a shrine founded by Emperor Suinin in 12 BCE, and the deity worshipped then was Shitateru Hime. Today the main deity enshrined is Ukanomitama, the deity of abundant harvest and food who is viewed as a manifestation of Inari. I wanted to visit the shrine in Osaka for two reasons: to view a statue of the fox messenger for Inari who wears a *magatama* necklace and to look inside the Tamatsukuri Shiryōkan, a small museum dedicated to *magatama* artifacts that is located on the shrine grounds.

I made a reservation to visit Tamatsukuri Inari Jinja and its museum weeks in advance and went there on the scheduled day. It was raining hard, and after walking from the train station and getting lost a few times, I was somewhat drenched when I knocked on the closed-up shrine office. The priest named Suzuki who finally came to open it explained that he did not think I would show up because of the wretched weather. We chatted for a little, and he mentioned a daughter living in my hometown of Los Angeles. I obtained an amulet (figure 36), and he threw in a few gratis *magatama* stickers before leading me over to the museum. The *magatama* museum is a beige-colored structure fashioned in the style of a Yayoi-era storehouse with its trademark flared roof. The top of the building has five logs laid at a right angle to the roof ridge (called *katsuogi*). Today this decorative architectural feature is associated exclusively with Shinto shrines. After unlocking it, Suzuki told me to take my time and to let him know when I was leaving so he could lock it up again. The museum was small but the focus on *magatama* was impressive. There were *komochi* parent-and-child *magatama* and a gigantic one fashioned from red, green, and white stones. Some *magatama* were rare, such as a gold-tipped one. There was a replica of a haniwa clay figurine of a female shaman wearing a *magatama* necklace. There were tools such as stones used for grinding and polishing and Kofun-era bronze mirrors and ritual spear blades (*dōhoko*). I was surprised to see a replica of a fifth-century crown from the Silla Kingdom on what is now the Korean peninsula, gold with many small *gogok* beads dangling from it. The Silla artifact was included to illustrate a shared *magatama* culture.[3] Most curators, enthusiasts, and those such as

Figure 36. Shrine *magatama,* Kanda Myōjin, Tamatsukuriyu Jinja, Tamatsukuri Inari Jinja, and Ise Jingū Geikū

the shrine's priests embrace the appearance of the bead in multiple archaeological contexts, from the various ancient states located in what we now call Japan or Korea. *Magatama* also caught the attention of other foreign visitors to Japan in the nineteenth century.

Early European and American antiquarians of Japan described a relic called *magatama-tsubo* (*magatama* vessel). The image of a pot containing nothing but *magatama* is intriguing and alludes to their abundance. An Austrian collector of Japanese ethnographic artifacts claimed that the term was given to all pottery: "The Japanese have given to every vessel of antiquity the general name of 'Magatama Tsubo' or 'pot for curved Jewels,' because these curious stone ornaments have sometimes been found in vessels which have been dug out from graves" (von Siebold 1879, 9). This obscure name for ancient pots caught on for a few decades and appeared in European and American catalogues of antiquities.[4] The Japanese writer Kanda (1884) also used it in reports on ancient objects but with a decidedly negative view of its ritual contents. These references to bead pots are fascinating, although I have never seen the term today in the writings of archaeologists or historians. References to the role of *magatama* in mythology, on the other hand, are plentiful.

Magatama in Mythology and Legend

The connection between *magatama*, shamanism, and other religious activity is found in the earliest texts written in Japan. They play a role in numerous episodes of the first native mythological histories. The two accounts are the *Kojiki* (Records of Ancient Matters, 712 CE) and the *Nihon shoki* (Chronicles of Japan, 720 CE). Both relate origin stories intended to validate the Yamato clan's right to rulership. *Magatama* became an integral part of an ensemble known as the Three Sacred Treasures (Sanshu no jingi), a ritual set composed of a mirror, sword, and curved bead that are the insignia of imperial rule and legitimacy. Many origin stories concern Amaterasu Ōmikami, the Yamato clan deity known as the paramount deity, the sun goddess. In one episode, Amaterasu and her pesky, badly behaving brother Susanoo agree to a challenge between them to determine who can produce the greatest number of deities. She wears *magatama* together with male battle garb when facing off with her brother. He eats all her *magatama*! And then from his mouth "spew[s] out a misty spray from which deities were born" (Hardacre 2016, 52). While he crushes her *magatama* in his mouth and vomits out five new male deities, she in turn eats his sword and produces three female deities from her breath. Amaterasu claims that she ultimately won the battle because her *magatama* were more productive. In another famous episode, Amaterasu has shut herself into a cave after Susanoo commits polluting acts. Because her retreat has deprived the world of sunlight, the other deities attempt various enticements to lure her out from the cave (see Aoyama 2018). A deity named Tamanoya no Mikoto is asked to create *magatama* to decorate a five-hundred-branch sakaki tree placed outside her hiding place in order to persuade her to exit the cave. A mirror is added to the display in the hopes that her own magnificent reflection will dazzle and draw her out. Today Tamanoya is known as the deity of *magatama*.[5]

Imagine a legendary *magatama* bead that has its own name. Perhaps the most famous role of *magatama* in mythology is in the story of the heavenly descent and the peopling of Japan. Amaterasu's grandson Ninigi is sent to Earth entrusted with the Three Sacred Treasures. In some versions Ninigi is accompanied on his descent to Earth by the deity Tamanoya or by members of the Tamanoya-be (Jewel-Maker Clan; Hardacre 2016, 59). Each of the treasures is a named entity with its own history and current place of residence. They are shrouded in mystery, closely guarded, and never displayed in public. The mirror, sword, and *magatama* are each stored in different locations. The mirror named Yata no Kagami (literally "eight hand widths," therefore large) is enshrined at Ise Jingū, the primary shrine dedicated to Amaterasu.[6] The sword is named Kusanagi no Tsurugi, and it is held at the Atsuta Shrine in Nagoya. The sword has a murky history in legend and oral history.[7] The sacred *magatama* is named Yasakani no Magatama and is stored in the Imperial Palace in Tokyo. It is unclear whether it is a single curved bead or a necklace with one or more beads strung on it. The Yasakani no Magatama is used in the ascension ceremony for each new emperor. The most recent ritual employment of the relic occurred in 2019 during the enthronement ceremony for Naruhito. He was presented with the imperial regalia on platforms in front of him as proof of his ascension to the throne (*Kyodo News* 2019a). The concept of three divine imperial heirlooms dates from the Kofun period.

The *magatama* is also associated with a few notable female figures from mythology and prehistory and with the production of jadeite deposits. For unknown reasons knowledge about early quarrying of jadeite in Itoigawa disappeared after the Nara period. It was not rediscovered until a poet and literary critic named Sōma Gyofū (1883–1950) suggested that the precious stone must be native to the area. Sōma, an Itoigawa native, was well aware of the legends surrounding a local folk legend. Her name was Nunakawa-hime, and she is known as the shaman of Koshi (Kidder 2007, 140). Koshi (its historic name) is the place in Itoigawa where jadeite was quarried. There are various tales about Nunakawa in the *Kojiki* chronicle as well as in regional gazettes (*fudoki*) that recorded official information, oral accounts, and folktales.[8] She had a reputation as a beautiful and intelligent divination expert who knew how to use jadeite *magatama* in religious rituals. A culture hero and deity in Izumo named Ōkuninushi heard about the lovely shaman in Itoigawa and traveled there in pursuit. Ōkuninushi has his own body of legendary tales and a reputation as a connoisseur of women. The stories make it clear that he engaged in "night crawling" (*yobai*). This is the term given to a rural practice of secret-not-secret nighttime visits to a young woman's room with her consent and the disguised awareness of her family. After a first night of unconsummated courtship, Nunakawa and Ōkuninushi spent another night together, and thereafter she became one of his wives. Their mutual courtship was accomplished through an exchange of somewhat erotic poems, which are embedded in the *Kojiki.* Nunakawa's poem makes it clear that she was a willing participant in Ōkuninushi's night crawling. Nunakawa became the deity of jadeite and is often depicted holding or wearing *magatama.* She is a resident deity in several shrines in the Itoigawa region, most notably at Nunakawa Jinja, Amatsu Jinja, and Hakusen Jinja. While fascinating, the story of the shaman Nunakawa-hime is relatively unknown in other parts of Japan. She is overshadowed when contrasted with another legendary shaman who is also tied to the teardrop-shaped jewel through centuries of well-known imagery. This is the shaman queen known as Himiko.

Himiko, described in prior chapters, is the first Japanese person whose name appears in writing. The Chinese history *Wei zhi* says that after Himiko's death a male ruler was briefly installed but quickly booted out. He was followed by a thirteen-year-old female relative of Himiko named Iyo. Iyo sent tribute to the Chinese court that included five thousand white beads and "two large blue perforated comma-shaped beads" (Kidder 2007, 18). The *magatama* was so cherished it was a suitable gift to present to the emperor of China! Representations of Himiko wearing *magatama* are found in numerous contexts as a symbol of local identity and historical authenticity and as a heroine in today's divination industry (L. Miller 2018). This use of the legendary figure of Himiko takes us to the explosion of *magatama* imagery used for a variety of secular purposes, discussed in the next section.

Magatama Commodification and Promotion

Magatama are unique and beautiful artifacts that often function as a regional symbol of ancient life. Museums, towns, and cultural centers use the bead for workshops, as an insignia, or as a fun activity. Cities in Izumo and Itoigawa use *magatama* imagery or create mascots that incorporate *magatama*. *Magatama* goods are sold as cheap souvenirs and by bead sellers as an elite prestige item. *Magatama* not only transport people today back to the past but redeem the bead itself to its original status. In the same way that the DeBeers diamond company successfully elevated an unexceptional stone, the common diamond, to one of the most sought-after gems through savvy slogans and marketing, *magatama* entrepreneurs have been adding value to the jadeite, agate, and other mineral beads through presentation, text, naming, and slogans that link them to Japan's ancient past.

Nunakawa, the deity of jadeite mentioned above, has been commodified in order to buttress regional tourism and identity. There is a statue of Nunakawa, now nicknamed the "Niigata Daughter" by city promoters, holding a large jade *magatama* at the Itoigawa train station. She is also a cute mascot for Itoigawa Geopark named Nuna. She wears a robe decorated with tiny white *magatama* icons and holds a rounded green *magatama* (figure 37).

Figure 37. Itoigawa Geopark mascot Nuna

Sōma, the man who helped activate the search for jadeite in Itoigawa, is commemorated on a 1995 postage stamp that depicts him next to a large *magatama*.

The third-century shaman ruler Himiko is similarly promoted in stores that sell powerstones and *magatama*. A tiny shop on the edge of the Hashihaka Tomb in Sakurai is named Jade Garden, or Himiko's Garden. It specializes in *magatama* made from Itoigawa jadeite. Masako, the shopkeeper I met on a visit there, gushed about the beads and told me that jadeite *magatama* carry spiritual qualities. The business card she gave me has two drawings, one of a regular *magatama* and one of the piggyback *komochi magatama* (child-bearing curved bead).[9]

The global living history movement, in which educators urge institutions and groups to perform or offer recreations of historical lifestyles or activities, was especially well received in Japan. It is therefore not surprising that *magatama* are often used as a gimmick to pull in participants to museums, cultural centers, and historical parks. All over Japan these institutions offer one-day workshops on making *magatama*. The Sōka City History Folk Museum in Saitama offers workshops targeted to children. The museum curators believe that making the curved beads will enable "the mysterious power from ancient times" to take root. A poster for one such workshop depicts an adorable male character wearing Kofun-era clothing and hairstyling, holding aloft a chubby green *magatama*. The method uses cheap talc or soapstone, which is easy to carve by hand. First, a *magatama* is drawn on it, then it is scraped against a larger stone to achieve the desired shape. It takes more than thirty minutes before a rough *magatama* emerges from the small block. The bead is then polished with water and carbon paper. One may also buy small *magatama*-making kits in shops and online. One kit is sold through an educational supply store. On their subsidiary craft-making website named Tanoden (2018), they provide ideas for using the materials they sell. These *magatama*-making kits include background text claiming that making the beads entices children to connect with the values of people from the past: children will "be able to perceive the sensibilities and aesthetics of ancient people." Tangible encounters with *magatama* are intended not only to connect members of communities with their local history but also to transport Japanese back to imagined ethnic roots.

Nara Prefecture is the site of Japan's most ancient culture, and the earliest of the large keyhole-shaped earthen tombs are located there. It is not surprising that local tourism goods exploit the *magatama* icon to highlight this history. The famous temple of Tōdaiji is always thronged with tourists. On a visit I followed the proscribed path behind the Buddha statue to

Figure 38. Secular *magatama*

arrive at an area where one may obtain both sacred items and secular merchandise. At one kiosk a woman was selling plastic *magatama.* There were deer charms dangling from the tail of the *magatama,* and they were available in five colors corresponding to feng shui. Another type had a tiny buddha charm and bell attached to the *magatama.* The juxtaposition of the *magatama* and the other charms did not reflect any religious logic. Two Japanese women looked at them: "Oh, they are kawaii [cute]!" said one, and "Let's get them!" said the other. They each bought several, obviously intending them to serve as souvenirs for friends. Of course, aesthetic judgments are subjective. However, it should be noted that the word kawaii has multiple meanings in interaction: unusual, small, or perhaps humorously appealing (Miller and Stevens 2021). In a similar vein, after showing a photo of cell phone straps from a Kyoto tourist kiosk to a Japanese friend, this person said they were kawaii (figure 38). The metal *magatama* have an image of a cat, a pagoda, and writing that says "Kyoto meow." When I protested that description, the friend said, "Okay, then they are *guro kawaii!*" (grotesque cute). *Magatama* charms, no matter their design or style, are appealing to many people.

Magatama Amulets and Other Spiritual Goods

In his discourse on *magatama* and other customs of "relic-worship," the Meiji-era bureaucrat and scholar Kanda Takahira (1884, 7) stated that "it is a well-known feature among all semi-civilized peoples to regard the remains of ancient times with superstitious awe and reverence, and from this error the Japanese people have not been free." Despite Kanda's condemnation and attempt to make fandom of *magatama* equivalent to primitive nonmodernity, Japanese continue to love the jelly bean–shaped beads. Although *magatama* have been disparaged by intellectuals, they are beloved by participants in Shinto practice, entrepreneurs, divination experts, and history buffs. The supernatural traits ascribed to the bent stone are highly regarded.

Magatama have made a conspicuous appearance on Shinto shrine amulets since the early 2000s. In view of the mythology in the *Kojiki* and elsewhere connecting the deity Amaterasu with *magatama,* I assumed that the places where she is enshrined might have *magatama* amulets. Out of curiosity I visited the Ise Jingū shrine complex where she is honored. I was surprised that the *magatama* amulet was not offered at the Naikū or Inner Shrine at Ise that is the abode of Amaterasu. However, an amulet I received from the Geikū or Outer Shrine at Ise Jingū is in the shape of a *magatama.* It is made of brocade material, with a purple background with pale flowers, a gold flower in the center, and a tiny gold bell attached. The Geikū enshrines Toyouke Ōmikami, the deity who oversees the three human lifestyle essentials of housing, food, and clothing.

Other shrines that offer *magatama* items include Hibita Jinja in Kanagawa, which also hosts a *magatama* festival. It is not so much a celebration of the ancient bead stone but rather a general festival with performances, *magatama*-making, a flea market, an old-style lottery, and various exhibitions. Shirasaki Hachimangū in Yamagata offers several types of unusual *magatama* amulets. One type, more Goth than Shinto, has a metal dragon wrapped around the bead. Another type fills in the *magatama* hole with a diamond and includes an earphone jack to attach the amulet to a cell phone.[10] Beginning around 2000, many shrines that did not have folktales, jadeite, or other specific reasons to hype connections to *magatama* began to add them to their menu of good luck charms and souvenir offerings anyway. In 2015 when I visited Kasuga Taisha, one of the oldest shrines in Nara, I noticed that the kiosk was displaying cell phone straps with *magatama.* Four deities are enshrined there: two are deities of the Nakatomi clan (later to become the Fujiwara), one is a deer-riding deity, and a fourth is a warrior deity. There is no obvious link between them and *magatama.* I asked the *miko* shrine attendant at the *juyosho* (shrine office) about them. She told me the shrine had only been providing *magatama* amulets for five years. Some of these new amulet offerings are tasteful, such as the Kasuga Taisha's simple strap of six small round beads with a green *magatama* at the end. Some are of inferior quality, such as the one at

Kanda Myōjin in Tokyo, which is a pink plastic bracelet with a pink *magatama* strung on it. Others, I found baffling. A souvenir kiosk in Kyoto sold a clear resin *magatama* encasing a purple blob with a gold image of the temple on it. Beyond the normal type of hybridity one expects, we have an example of a temple artifact that does not appear to be pointing to the ancient past, or to the power of female shamans, or to any of the usual meanings linked to the bead. The addition of a *magatama* is simply showing awareness of a trendy design element.

Outside museum exhibits and shrines, *magatama* have found a welcome home in the occult domain. Within this context is a sensual and tactile understanding of *magatama*. They are seen as having material sanctity, so one should "treat it like a living being with a soul," as one divination provider told me. They are a natural extension of interest in powerstones. *Magatama* enable vicarious shamanism. They are handheld mojo. Magatama no Wa is a specialized spiritual bead shop in Osaka. They sell *magatama*, crystals, bead bracelets, earrings, glass globes, and powerstones. The shop has a massive collection, more than a hundred types of *magatama* in assorted colors and minerals. Some miniature *magatama* are sold for ¥1,000, while a black Itoigawa jadeite bead sold for ¥127,440. The range of types includes the archaic clove-head *magatama*, crystal *magatama* engraved with butterflies, and Dalmatian *magatama* (variegated white with black spots). Magatama no Wa (2012) provides many suggestions for the care and use of a bead, advising that it be handled as a living thing with power. The bead should periodically be washed and given sunlight. It should not be placed near TVs, speakers, phones, and laptops. When not in use, it should be wrapped in paper or cloth and placed in a box. Because the *magatama* are viewed as sacred objects, the guidelines for their care are similar to those for tarot cards. In both cases they are accorded respect and special attention.

Tamamoto Yōko is an author who claims to have studied folklore and Shinto history at Kokugakuin University. This is a private university in Tokyo dedicated to fields such as Shinto and Japanese history. It was founded in 1882 and today is considered one of the popular powerspots. There is no evidence that Tamamoto graduated from this university, although it is possible that she took a few classes there. Her name, Tamamoto, was most likely selected as a pen name because it contains the *tama* (spirit, soul) morpheme. She holds workshops on divination, spirituality, and powerstones. Her book *Spirit Beckoning and the Laws of Good Fortune: Japanese Spiritual Magic* (Tamamoto 2012) combines ideas about conducting a special ritual called *tamafuri* (spirit beckoning) with *magatama*. She writes that use of the "ancient powerstone of Japan" will help the country overcome problems such as the birthrate decline and the economic slump. She provides methods for using *magatama* to enhance or perform the *tamafuri* ritual. It is intended to rouse the spirit, *tama* being the animating spirit that gives life to the physical body (Ebersole 1999). The idea is to liven up the soul and recharge its energy through ritual shaking or through "beckoning spirit" into the body. One method for doing that is by waving the *magatama* in front of the sluggish person. The power within the bead activates the *tama* of the person doing the ritual or for whom the ritual is performed.

Efforts to indicate the occult through *magatama* imagery are plentiful in women's magazines, books, and blogs. An article in a divination magazine provides elaborate instructions for using *magatama* for various aspects of life such as finances, home life, or romance (Noguchi 2009). Readers are told which color and type of bead to use, the procedure for the magical ritual, and in some instances the spells to recite.[11] With its association with ancient divination and ritual, finding *magatama* resurrected for modern religious purposes is to be expected. Yet *magatama* travel beyond this domain. The iconic beads pop up in games, manga, culinary creations, and in the beauty industry as well.

Magatama in Secular Settings

Magatama allude to great antiquity. Perhaps not many Japanese associate the polished teardrop with the Jōmon era, but it is almost always mentioned in sections of textbooks that describe the Kofun era and also, occasionally, the Yayoi era.[12] They are straightforwardly classified as part of the ancient period more generally. In a history manga, the first *magatama* to appear are worn by Himiko (Ohishi and Himekawa 2012, 66–67). Later, Emperor Kinmei (509–571) wears two *magatama* necklaces, one very heavy looking with around fourteen *magatama* strung on it (Ohishi and Himekawa 2012, 100). The idea was to emphasize the status of the ruler.

Magatama make a unique appearance in one of the hundreds of postwar monster films released in Japan. The genre is known as *kaijū eiga* (strange beast film) and was inaugurated with the classic 1954 film *Godzilla* (Honda 1954). One series of *kaijū eiga* stars Gamera, a giant turtle monster.[13] A strange type of *magatama* appears in the film *Gamera: Giant Monster Mid-Air Battle* (Kaneko 1995). In the film's story, a group of researchers investigate a floating atoll and discover artifacts on its surface. Littering the ground are *magatama* made of orichalcum, a precious metal mentioned by Plato in his description of Atlantis. It turns out that the atoll is home to Gamera. The odd *magatama* are taken back to Japan, where the daughter of one of the team members, Asagi, holds one of the beads. It becomes warm with glowing energy. She is given permission to keep one, which she strings and wears as a necklace. For a Japanese audience, it is clear that Asagi becomes a type of shaman priestess similar to Himiko. She is able to communicate with Gamera through the medium of the *magatama*.

A unique use of *magatama* is found in the game *Counterattack Fantastic* (Silicon Studios 2012), released as *Fantasica* in English. It is a free-to-play cell phone role-playing game and card-collecting game. Although disliked by some game fans, others appreciate its beautiful graphics and card designs by the video game artist Minabe Hideo. In the game, *magatama* is the name given to squirmy, worm-type digestible entities that confer power. After eating them the host gains certain skills. Normal, nonanimate bead *magatama* are also used to illustrate cards for different characters, including Himiko, Nunakawa Hime, and others. In the card for Himiko, for example, she is depicted as a young woman using both hands to levitate or bounce a huge magenta *magatama* in the air.

Traditional Japanese confections are sometimes made in the shape of *magatama*. Saiundo Wagashi in Matsue, open since 1874, sells a set of *magatama*-shaped sweets in different flavors, such as tea and strawberry. They are called *monaka* and have a center of sweet red-bean paste encased in a crisp sticky-rice wafer. *Magatama*-shaped cookies are easy to make and are sold at locations with a connection to ancient history.[14] A food blogger who posts on cake-making and other baking projects described how she made *magatama* cookies. She was pleased with the result: "Cute! A gust of archaeological wind! My children are super happy and I'm glad too" (Moron 2015).

Magatama are so powerful that they have been imagined as a useful device for more than spiritual endeavors. The common linguistic process called semantic extension or semantic broadening, in which word meanings are increased or extended into more contexts, allows cosmetic and beauty work providers to draw on existing meanings in novel ways. Tamatsukuri Onsen's putative skin-beautifying water also affords some new interpretations. An example is the product named Kirakira Mist Beauty Spa Water, made by a company named Tamatsukuri Onsen Bihada Kenkyūjo Hime Lab. They produce a line of soaps, face packs, lotions, and cleansing gels. According to their promotional material, the special water from the hot springs will enhance the skin's appearance: "The effects of sulfate ions and chloride ions give the skin firmness and luster." Following the path of semantic extension even further, we find that the connection between *magatama* and beauty is sufficient for unusual beauty industry concepts. A beauty expert named Momoki Yūko developed a facial technique she calls the "face bone reset" (*gankotsu resetto*). It uses a borrowed Chinese folk remedy imported into Japanese beauty culture. Named *kassa,* it is a massage treatment using a plate that is rubbed on the skin to detox stagnant blood flow. Momoki (2015) came up with the idea of using a *magatama* in place of the plate, and the bead is therefore rubbed all over the face. Supposedly, this will stimulate blood flow that will improve the appearance of the skin.

Given the freedom in how people use imagery and themes that are mashed up, distorted, or extended in often unexpected ways, it is notable that the *magatama* is most often used to represent itself, an object from ancient tombs and archaeological sites. It does not usually allude to any specific historic event, although stories of its appearance in various myths may be linked to it. It may lend nuances and symbolism and semiotically denote the ancient and the supernatural, but its core form is not usually altered. An exception is when designers attempt to incorporate *magatama* into imagery for regional mascots. In those cases the *magatama* may be anthropomorphized or cradled or worn by mascots. An example is the adorable, chubby *magatama* held by a character in the Sōka City History Folk Museum poster, which almost comes to life as a character itself. Another less successful example is the mascot created for the town of Tamatsukuri Onsen, discussed below.

I do not have good answers to questions about when *magatama* were resurrected to serve modern tasks. Like fashion trends, it is impossible to pinpoint the exact year or place that people began to renew interest in *magatama,* repurposing them for new functions such as jewelry-making or as objects used in divination or to symbolize female magical power. As mentioned at the start, I first noticed them as actual objects available for purchase in craft stores. However, unlike the fashion industry, where subsidiary businesses are invested in tracking the latest trends from coolhunters to fashion photographers, *magatama* meanings and uses are diffuse and linked to both sacred and secular contexts. They are not a simple use of symbols to sell things, a "gimmick" in the sense that Ngai (2020) describes. Her thesis is that if too much work goes into a concept or product, it will disappoint us due to a mismatch between its price or attraction and its actual economic value. Although some *magatama* merchandise and objects are overwrought or corny, they are not quite commodities like Coke or Nike sneakers. They have an existing history and mythology that are not fabricated by marketers. After reading about the historic location for *magatama* bead-making in the Izumo region, I decided to visit and see why they are attractive destinations for occult hunters.

Tamatsukuri Onsen

Tamatsukuri Onsen is touted in tourism literature as the place "where the gods of hot springs and *magatama* are enshrined." The place that is now Tamatsukuri Onsen is mentioned in an eighth-century text titled *Chronicle of the Land of Izumo Province,* where it was lauded as a place of beauty and relaxation (Aoki 1997, 88). People in Tamatsukuri Onsen embrace both the secular and sacred meanings of *magatama,* but the hot spring is mainly visited by those seeking relaxation and spiritual rejuvenation. The hot spring is promoted in guidebooks and women's magazines as a powerspot, a place to recharge energy and gather spiritual vitality. It was mostly women, traveling with friends or solo, who were wandering around the town and visiting the shrine. At a mom-and-pop pub, I saw a solitary woman, fresh from a hot spring soak and wearing her hotel's cotton yukata, enjoying drinks and appetizers. My friend Rebecca went with me on the journey, and as soon as we exited the small train station, we were greeted with evidence of *magatama* used for civic boosterism. There was a large rabbit statue holding a *magatama* and posters featuring the town's mascot Tamahime-chan, a princess with a *magatama* for a head who also wears a small *magatama* necklace. She holds the things people would carry with them to a public bath or hot spring. Like most regional mascots, she has a biography: Tamahime-chan is a matchmaker eager to help people find a partner and also works as the Tamatsukuri Onsen beauty advisor. Among her favorite goods is a skin lotion named Kirakira Mist Beauty Spa Water (mentioned above). When we arrived at the train station, our hotel had a van waiting to pick us up. On the ride Rebecca casually told the driver about my interest in *magatama.* He lit up! He offered to escort us to the Tamatsukuriyu Jinja and to introduce us to the resident priest. He also drove us to the Izumo Magatama no Sato Denshōkan, a combination *magatama* museum, workshop, restaurant, and retail space. This complex was founded in Tamatsukuri Onsen in 1901 as Menōya Shingū.[15]

Walking the narrow streets along the Tamayu River that runs through the town, we encountered many *magatama* decorations. A bridge over the river featured four enormous, green-painted cement *magatama,* each perhaps six feet wide and four feet high (figure 39). In spots one could see *magatama* patterns traced with rocks on the shallow riverbed. A few streets had manhole covers with *magatama* on them. Like many other resort towns, Tamatsukuri Onsen refurbished its identity and added some new invented traditions along the way. There has been extensive landscaping and ground work along the riverbank and elsewhere, as well as the addition of a few fictional riverside attractions, such as the cheesy Himekami Square

Figure 39. Tamatsukuri Onsen

Footbath and statue of the "goddess" Himekami.[16] At a point along the river is a public water basin decorated with a large green *magatama.* Although this fountain is not an authentic Shinto ablution pavilion for ritual cleansing, it is designed to resemble one. Named Yakushi Hiroba Taraiyu, visitors are encouraged to help themselves to the esteemed hot spring water that flows into the basin. Visitors may use their own bottles or buy one self-service from a little wood cabinet made to resemble a miniature Shinto shrine for the home. The water from Tamatsukuri Onsen is touted in women's magazines and beauty blogs as beautifying for the skin. We skipped the water and availed ourselves of the offerings found at the small bars and eateries instead.

The Izumo Magatama no Sato Denshōkan is two miles north of the resort town's center on the shore of Lake Shinji. The *magatama* workshop employs four resident bead artisans; three are male and one is female. The museum section includes exhibits that illustrate the progression in *magatama*-making, from raw stones to finished beads. When Senge Takatoshi, descendent of one of the Izumo priestly lineages, became the chief priest of Izumo Taisha in 1947, he presented a distinctive *magatama* necklace that was crafted at the Denshōkan to the imperial family. The style, called *mihogidama,* is composed of alternating Izumo agate beads of three colors: tubular red ones, round white ones, and *magatama* green ones.

The colors are said to denote the following: white bead, longevity; red, health; and green, rejuvenation and life source. Images of this necklace are found everywhere, and reproductions may be purchased in shops and online. The Denshōkan now displays a high-quality replica. One area of the museum displayed text and images about the TV minidrama series titled *Shōtoku Taishi* (Satō 2001). It told a version of the story about the semimythological politician who served as the regent for the Female Emperor Suiko (554–628). Notable was that the actors wore accurate period attire and also prominent *magatama* necklaces, including the famous but anachronistic Izumo red, green, and white *mihogidama* necklace.

The shop had products ranging from tasteful jewelry to cute or gimmicky goods. There were *magatama*-themed herbal bath salts, pouches, pickles, and incense burners. Matcha powdered green tea–flavored cashews were sold in green packages adorned with bunnies. The packages said, "The image of a blue agate *magatama* is made by wrapping flavorful cashew nuts in matcha." The cashews remind us of the crescent bead, and the bunnies are a nod to a famous tale found in the *Kojiki* and other texts known as Inaba no Shirousagi (the White Hare of Inaba). In the story the Izumo deity Ōnamuchi (a.k.a. Ōkuninushi) shows compassion and saves a white rabbit who had been abused. The white rabbit and *magatama* were often paired in decorative motifs, as seen in the train station statue and elsewhere.

One of the bead craftsmen, Murata, spent more than an hour talking to me about the history and production of *magatama*. An important lesson I gained from him is that *magatama* are more than touristic baubles. Murata was deeply attached to his craft and said he felt part of his spirit went into the bead as he was creating it. This ensoulment took three or more hours of work. Murata provided me with copies of materials he wanted me to read, and he also gave me a handwritten sheet of paper with information in English about *magatama*, along with points he wanted to emphasize. One thing he had written for me included the following: "The shape represents the sun and the moon, symbolizes energy which comes from them, and shows admiration for the whole universe. The hole symbolizes the relationship between ancestors and descendants. And the green color represents a vivid life, just like green leaves in the Spring."

Murata felt a deep connection to *magatama* and exhibited enormous pride in his work and its history. About the Three Sacred Treasures, he told me, "It was said the *magatama* of the kami [deity] was made here in Shimane prefecture."[17]

In addition to this *magatama* workshop, the other key location tied to *magatama* was the local shrine. Tamatsukuriyu Jinja is mentioned in a Fudoki list, so it dates to at least 733 (Aoki 1997). The three primary deities enshrined there are Kushiakarutama, Ōnamochi, and Sukunabikona. Kushiakarutama (another name for Tamanoya) is named as the creator of the Yasakani no Magatama, one of the Three Sacred Treasures. This deity is also considered the progenitor of the Tamatsukuri-be beadworking guild. Ōnamochi is a central cultural hero and deity of Izumo (Ōkuninushi is called Ōnamochi in the Izumo). He is the deity of abundance, medicine, luck, and happy marriages. Sukunabikona is the deity of *onsen* (hot springs), agriculture, healing, magic, sake brewing, and knowledge.

The shrine was nestled on a forested hillside with flowering camellia, tall evergreens, and moss-covered stone Inari fox statues. Our van driver walked with us to the home of the head priest named Endō in order to introduce us. He was dressed casually and asked us to return in twenty minutes. When we did, he had changed into traditional vestments and escorted us into the interior of the shrine sanctuary, where he had us sit on a cedar bench. We were purified with prayers and the *gohei* staff used to sanctify participants. Endō gave us a thirty-minute lecture on the shrine's resident deities, explaining the story of Kushiakarutama (Tamanoya), as found in the *Kojiki*. He wanted us to hear about this guardian of lapidaries. I was struck by his deep sincerity and seriousness and the concern he expressed that we learn about the shrine's place in Shinto mythology. He was willing to take the time to talk to unexpected foreign visitors and to perform priestly duties when he could have been lounging in a tracksuit. As Smyers (1999, 44) reported for other Shinto priests at Inari shines, they "pride themselves on carrying out their tasks with formality and solemnity." Endō did his best to impart the meaning and sacredness of the *magatama* to us.

The shrine storehouse at Tamasukuriyu Jinja (closed to the public) is smaller than the one I visited at Tamatsukuri Inari Jinja in Osaka, but it contains ancient and rare *magatama* tools, such as rectangular granite grinding stones with parallel grooves and flat stones used for polishing *magatama*. Endō's father was passionate about preserving the beadworker's tools: "Momoye Endo, priest of the Shinto Shrine of Tamatsukuri-yu-no-Jinsha, was especially enthusiastic in the collection of these remains, and he was the first man who noticed and took care of the grindstones used for beads" (Hamada, Shimada, and Umehara 1927, 1).[18] People in the Shimane region are proud of their *magatama* tradition and say theirs are a distinctive, rounder shape than those found in other parts of Japan. Talking to a *magatama* artisan and a priest deeply related to *magatama* were critical correctives to my cavalier attitude prior to the visit to Tamatsukuri Onsen. They experienced forms of intimacy with *magatama* that I had not considered. I had believed that *magatama* had made a transition from sacred object in the ancient period to exploited symbol and secular commercialized motif in the current moment. I learned from them and others that for many people *magatama* continue to have genuine spiritual resonance.

Magatama reveal enormous diversity in meaning and representation. A focus on one small artifact that surfaces in historical accounts, mythological vignettes, ethnographic observations, and modern media convinces us that material culture and visual culture, apart from the usual grand narratives of great battles and famous people, are essential aspects of the historical and cultural record. In a land where transformation is normal, the *magatama* are not often changed significantly. Even the once sacred Buddhist symbol called *manji* (a backward swastika) has transformed into a popular word and symbol among schoolgirls. It is used as an exclamation when taking photos (like saying "cheese!") or as an emoji added to text messages. Returning to the theories about the origins of *magatama*—that they represent fetuses, fish, animal teeth, kidneys, and so on—we might expect to see uses or alterations in their form that draw on those primordial associations. Yet I have not seen or learned about fang-like *magatama* necklaces sold at zoos. Are there kidney-looking *magatama* used in medical settings, such as posters for kidney disease in doctors' offices? Recalling my friend's words "It looks like a fetus!," I am surprised to have never seen *magatama*-fetal mascots used in pregnancy manuals or fertility posters.

Even in cases in which the *magatama* is anthropomorphized, this is only done through the addition of human attributes to the unaltered shape of the bead. Unlike some types of religious objects that require the device of a narrative or text to anchor it, the *magatama* stands alone. It needs no cushioning explanation. The Christian cross began as a symbol of a specific event, the Crucifixion scene. But *magatama* can reference various mythological episodes, personages, or just the notion of *kodai*, the ancient period in general. Children learn about the beads from an early age, including their history in the ancient eras and their significance as part of the Three Sacred Treasures of the imperial line.[19]

Although the *magatama* is rather stable in its iconography, people have found many new ways to reanimate the bead, to let it speak to us. The precise origin of *magatama* remains unknown. We find them in ancient sites inhabited by the earliest people in the Japanese Islands, the Jōmōn. In later centuries massive immigration of Yayoi people from the Korean peninsula introduced a slightly differently shaped *magatama*. This extremely long history attests to its influence on the human imagination, making *magatama* resistant to change in shape or meaning. Even though the obtainability and treatment of the bead has changed dramatically, the *magatama* continues to resist erasure and exert its magical impression.

CHAPTER 8

Powerspots

"My worries were not entirely resolved, but my mood was refreshed." This was the response one woman gave to the question of whether or not a visit to a powerspot had any beneficial outcome (Yanada 2010, 123). Asked what their objective was in visiting powerspots, women in the survey said things such as "To reset!," "To get power from nature," "To increase my own energy," "To enhance my love life," "To seek better health," and "It was an inauspicious year [*tenchūsatsu*]."[1] The editors noted that more than specific benefits, most people were seeking an infusion of positive energy, or *pawā chāji* (power charge). The media and many scholars have proposed that it is mainly young women intent on attracting a boyfriend or husband who are driving the powerspot boom. However, similar to the editors who conducted the survey above, I found a broad range of reasons people of all ages give for their interest in powerspots, and certainly searching for short-term refreshment from hectic everyday life stands out as a key motivation.

In this chapter I want to look at some of the ideas and attitudes circulating about powerspots. Numerous Anglophone scholars have explored powerspot and spirituality trends in Japan (Carter 2018; Gaitanidis 2022; Horie 2017; Okamoto 2019; Roth 2019; Rots 2019). Although plentiful background and analysis on powerspots are available, I believe a somewhat altered perspective will nevertheless provide further insights. My goal is to delve deeper into some powerspot literature, seeking aspects of these spiritual expressions that have been overlooked. It might be that elements of humor, irony, and self-reflective awareness are missing from prior studies. The interest in powerspot hunting was driven by female seekers of the occult, who also desire to engage in supernatural play. Thus, powerspots should be considered related to other activities (divination, interest in *magatama,* desire for pilgrim stamps, etc.) that are studied in this book. Although media does play a role in promoting this and other female interests and activities, unlike other scholars and critics I neither believe that it was primarily the media that created or drove the trend nor see women as unwitting tools of its efforts. The first section below begins with a brief history of the powerspot concept, from its inception outside Japan to its entrenched status within Japan. The following section examines the qualities that people look for in powerspots. How do sites become objectified as having spiritual energy? What do people expect when they visit a powerspot? A few polls on powerspot visiting invite us to challenge some media and scholarly claims about visitor motivations. I am also interested in how powerspots are advertised and promoted and how they appear in popular culture. The last section looks at a few prominent individuals who have promoted powerspot awareness and tourism.

In my quest I was interested in viewing visits to locations named as powerspots as an individual spiritual practice. In this regard I follow the classic thinking of Luckmann (1967), who sketched the concept of "privatized religion." This refers to religious behavior that occurs outside established religious ritual settings and with little contact with religious intermediaries such as priests. I looked for insights into powerspots through a variety of media, especially books and magazines, and through on-site observations. I was not particularly concerned about individual beliefs about the efficacy of their visits but rather about how powerspots are understood, experienced, promoted, and marketed. I began collecting data and thinking about powerspots in 2013 and visited many in the Tokyo area that year.[2] In the following years, I also visited designated powerspots in the Kansai area, in Shimane Prefecture, and Ise in Mie Prefecture.

A powerspot (*pawā supotto*) has a number of meanings and attributes, but at its core it describes a place where people can acquire positive luck or spiritual energy. Powerspots serve as places of mental refuge. Powerspot hunters have given impetus to publishing and tourism industries devoted to traveling to powerspots around the world, but the primary focus is Japan. Although both sacred and natural spaces might be objectified and branded as part of powerspot tourism, many of them are Shinto shrines. Powerspot visits are framed as special spiritual endeavors, yet much of the activity surrounding them, such as buying *omamori* amulets, praying at the shrine or temple, stopping in at a local eatery, and purchasing unique souvenirs, are not very different from traditional pilgrimages or visits to such places.

The Hybrid Powerspot Concept

The hybridity of the powerspot concept combines Japanese ideas about sacred places with imported New Age notions of power vortexes. Starting with a 1960s trend in travel to exotic places for spiritual development, New Age adherents in North America began to suggest that there are power centers, or "vortexes," that emanate intense spiritual energy. A psychic counselor named Page Bryant produced an audiotape and books promoting the idea of the powerspot or vortex. It was most likely her book *The Earth Changes Survival Handbook,* that spread the powerspot and vortex notions to a wide audience. She stated that "the Native Americans knew Geomancy quite well, though they didn't use that particular term. They knew of power spots on the Earth, but didn't call them vortices" (Bryant 1983, 158). Her writing led to the idea that a network of power lines span the globe and express intense energy in certain locations. The concept of the powerspot took one very public form in 1987 as an event called the Harmonic Convergence. The organizers proposed that 144,000 people gather at world vortexes and take part in synchronized meditation for global peace. Divine energy was believed to be especially strong in convergence sites such as Stonehenge, Machu Picchu, Sedona, and elsewhere. People in Japan similarly seek out landscapes and locations considered to hold concentrations of vital energy, sometimes called *ki* in Japanese. Hatanaka (2003, 134–143) claims that some powerspots in Japan, such as Ise Jingū, are located in high-energy places called "zero magnetic fields" (*zero jiba*).

As the idea spread to Japan, it was popularized by writers, psychics, and occult providers as the *pawā supotto,* or powerspot. These powerspots offer a quiet haven and the promise of personal transformation. They give people relief from the regimentation of everyday existence. They are where tired women can go to get "powered up" and receive spiritual cleansing. The powerspot concept has been domesticated and fully incorporated into the Japanese lexicon. Thus, one finds claims by history buffs writing about the Edo period (ca. 1603–1868) that "Asakusa was the powerspot of the common people!" (Futabasha 2012, 28). The concept of the powerspot is so well known that an American living in Japan recalls going to the breathtaking Takachiho Gorge and the Amano Iwato Jinja in Miyazaki Prefecture. Later, as she talked about these locations with Japanese associates, they said, "Oh yes, those are powerspots." She had not encountered the term "powerspot" before and thereafter used it as a way to organize other trips.[3]

Powerspot hunters in Japan are predominantly female, and much of the mass media reporting on the trend have expressed denigrating and disparaging attitudes. Assessing popular powerspot writers, a journalist named Hughes (2010) says, "It's unclear exactly what spiritual philosophy people like Shuhei and Wakatsuki Yuu are spouting, but that reflects the fuzzy logic of the movement itself." Her article presents powerspot interest as an irrational "craze." Another example is found in a *Japan Times* interview with a male professor of the sociology of religion. He warned people about the dangers of believing in "dubious things" and went on to say that "we must bear in mind our experience with Aum—that the will to seek healing and spirituality, once taken the wrong way, can lead to major and ferocious errors" (Wijers-Hasegawa 2007). He equates individual powerspot seekers with Aum Shinrikyō, an aberrant and murderous cult responsible for the 1995 killing of Tokyo subway riders with sarin gas.

Pilgrimage has a very long and entrenched history in Japan, and some of the associated meanings that scholars have noted for famous pilgrimages are also seen in powerspot visiting. In his study of the Shikoku Henro Pilgrimage, Reader (2006) found that pilgrims have a variety of reasons for going on the pilgrimage, from spiritual atonement to the memorialization of dead relatives. But he also discovered that pilgrims value the pilgrimage as a chance to escape everyday reality. Pilgrims and powerspot enthusiasts, therefore, similarly see their activities as a time-out for the soul, an excuse to have a trip away from family and, in many cases, a chance to discover their dreams of an authentic, old Japan. The powerspot pilgrimage (*pawā meguri*) also emulates the Shichifukujin Meguri, a circuit visit to seven temples and shrines dedicated to the Seven Lucky Deities. These various pilgrimage types confer economic benefits for locals through hotels, cafés, souvenir shops, goods, and amulets, as well as some newer marketing and business endeavors, which I discuss in the next section.

Identifying Powerspots

What qualifies as a powerspot from a Japanese perspective? Any place can theoretically be named a powerspot depending on the criteria one uses. Once someone designates a place as a powerspot, it takes on a status that allows multiple uses and meanings to be generated. The powerspot is a type of "religious objectification." Various locations are named as powerspots and then objectified once they are thus nominated. Included are natural locations and expected sacred compounds, such as Buddhist temples and Shinto shrines. Some places are designated as powerspots for a variety of idiosyncratic reasons.

It is important to survey some of the ways that powerspots are understood, presented, and advertised in media. I will provide a few details about the content found in popular powerspot guides and articles. One of my goals is to offer a corrective to the mostly condescending or cursory reports about powerspots written by news media and other writers. These reports describe female hunters of powerspots in voices rich with disdain.

They are the same voices that denigrated other feminized occupations, cultural activities, and industries, not because of anything inherent about the activities and jobs but because it is primarily women doing them.[4]

Powerspot literature is quite diverse, representing different attitudes and stances (figure 40). Hardly any of this writing presents dogma or a narrow theology. Almost always, these places are methodically promoted as sanctuaries from daily life and worries and as an opportunity to reevaluate one's life situation. Neither the writers nor the readers approach the concept of powerspots with doe-eyed credulity. Even if readers want to access site chakras or some type of prana space, they ask for hard details. They want to know where their money will be spent. Most writers accommodate this demand with information about the history and special features of the powerspot, as well as directions for getting there and information about eating and shopping in the vicinity. Guides, websites, and cell phone apps provide all the information one needs to plan a visit to a powerspot. A few writers also offer suggestions for how to prepare for the visit, such as clearing one's mind or dressing in simple white clothing, as traditional pilgrims do (Rinoie 2012). It is interesting that several

Figure 40. Powerspot guides

guides provide basic etiquette for going to a shrine or temple, such as how many times to clap your hands prior to offering prayers and how to use the water ablution pavilion (*chōzuya* or *temizuya;* Ikkojin Henshūbu 2010, 57–71; Katsuki 2010; Shimada 2010b). Manners when gathering samples of sacred water are also common. Morimura (2007, 42) cautions that taking massive amounts of water is "NG" (no good).

Natural waterfalls, mountains, hot springs, and locations with enormous ancient trees are often designated as powerspots. For example, a giant ginkgo tree growing in the grounds of the Kamo Jinja in Kinokawa City, Wakayama Prefecture, became a famous powerspot. Mostly, however, it is shrines that are specified as indigenous powerspots. Shinto shrines have a history of association with supernatural power, so this makes sense. Buddhist temples are less frequently named as powerspots, perhaps because of their association with death rituals. The sacred spaces identified as powerspots are not necessarily those that people expect. Locations claimed to be shamanistic portals and sites, such as Mount Ōmine, are not often included. Although Shinto shrines dominate most lists, many other diverse places are also designated as powerspots. A special issue of the weekly news magazine *CREA* (a mook, or magazine-book) includes Ishibutai Tomb in Asuka (ca. 592–645 CE), Shuri Castle in Okinawa (palace of the Ryūkyū Kingdom between 1429 and 1879[5]), and Iwaidaki waterfall in Okayama (Kurabayashi 2010). The guide also devotes six pages to the multiplex Buddhist Kōya-san temple settlement in Wakayama Prefecture. Natural powerspots are highlighted, too, including ten waterfalls, ten giant trees, ten mountains, and ten hot springs.

When contemplating powerspots, some promoters call up ideas such as electromagnetic energy grids or the flow of *ki* energy from or between mountains, valleys, and bodies of water, recasting planetary kundalini into the idioms of Taoist thought. Yamamichi (2010), a feng shui specialist, innovatively taps into Google Earth technology to link topographic features based on the Five Element/Phases. His guide uses diagrams next to aerial shots in order to indicate a power vortex. It should be noted that Yamamichi includes more Buddhist temples and natural spots, such as mountains, gardens, and hot springs, than Shinto shrines. He graduated from Tōyō University (with a focus on Indian philosophy) and also studied in Taiwan and South Korea, at National Taiwan Normal University and Sogang University. He has done fieldwork on Taoism and other topics.

Some powerspot sites were already sacralized centuries or decades ago as attractive religious destinations, such as the Ise Jingū (Teeuwen and Breen 2017). But new guides often include unexpected locations. In a guide to powerspots in the Tokyo vicinity are a few unanticipated sites

(M. Itō 2010). The guide highlights nine shrines, three temples, three nature spots such as gardens and mountains but also unusual spots such as the Tokyo Skytree in Sumida (a broadcasting and observation tower), and Kokugakuin Daigaku, a prominent academic center for philosophical and Shinto studies. All the illustrations in the guide are endearingly hand-painted, and each location includes information on types of *ema* votive plaques, souvenirs, and local eating spots. For example, for one's visit to Kameido Tenmangū, Itō recommends a stop at the Kameido potsticker shop. A useful appendix provides detailed maps for each location and directions for getting to each site. Even if the impetus for creating this charming guide was merely crass economic gain, it nevertheless is a useful and pretty guide that anyone might appreciate.

A special issue on powerspots in one magazine included some of the usual material as well as amusing sidebars (*Koiunreiki* 2010). One ploy is to designate putative "Three Sacred Treasures" that are associated with selected sites. The Three Sacred Treasures (Sanshu no Jingi) are the mirror, sword, and *magatama* that were given to Ninigi by the sun goddess Amaterasu when he descended from heaven, later forming the set of regalia denoting authority for the imperial line. Writers have often played with this notion in a humorous manner, such as calling the three desired postwar commodities—the television, the refrigerator, and the washing machine—the Three Sacred Treasures. There have been many other satirical "Treasures" since then; therefore, using this trope is not seen as offensive. For Izumo Taisha the powerspot treasures are Izumo-style soba, Tamatsukuri Onsen, and *magatama.* For the Mount Fuji mountain girl (*yama-gāru*) they are a water bottle, socks, and a compass. Articles that combine information and humor are common in this literature.

Powerspots are marketed as locations to visit when seeking good fortune, often in ways no different from how shrines and temples have presented themselves for centuries. Reader and Tanabe (1998) extensively discuss the guidebooks that provide information for those seeking "practical benefits" (*genze riyaku*). They illustrate how this publishing niche combines information on temples and shrines with basic travel tips. An example of this genre is Oka's (2007) *Complete Guide to Kyoto Blessings and Benefits.* In his entry for Higashimuki Kannonji, he provides a history and details about what sort of benefits visitors may receive (Oka 2007, 209–211). It is a Buddhist temple on the grounds of Kitano Tenmangū, the Shinto shrine dedicated to Tenjin, the deity of scholarship. The guide names Kannonji as dedicated to good fortune, protection from evil, protection for pregnant women, protection for raising children, and recovery from illness. A photo is included of an unusual amulet in the shape of a

Native American dream catcher.[6] Within the precincts is a mausoleum and pillar dedicated to Sugawara no Michizane's mother, Tomo-uij. This and Oka's other entries are not that different from powerspot guide entries. Interest in powerspots interacts with other occult and spiritual pursuits. An example is the Feng Shui Talisman Deck created by Namatame (2010) as a supplement insert (*fuzoku*) in a magazine. There are ten cards divided into three categories: five for different aspects of life (love, marriage, work, money, health), three for areas (water, mountain, holy ground), and two for concepts (purity and guardian). Readers are advised to take whatever cards they like, depending on their objective, when they visit a powerspot. They can use them for inspiration or for engaging in divination at the site.

It is clear from research and observation that activities at temples and shrines are frequently embedded in touristic sightseeing. The extensive literature on pilgrimage in Japan also documents the blurred lines between religious activity and touristic pleasures. Powerspot visits are similar to traditional pilgrimages to religious sites in a number of ways. As Hoshino (2007, 68) noted, few pilgrimages are purely for religious reasons and are often for "refreshing life" and "challenging the spirit." Both pilgrimage and powerspot guides list not only the locations but also the type of local foods to eat, the best souvenirs to get, and, if staying overnight, the nicest inns and hotels.

I am not convinced by the argument that the media played a dominant role in creating interest in powerspots. In her overview Roth (2019, 99) asks us to attend to the "important role in the propagation of the powerspot trend, starting off with targeting women's magazines." In addition, she offers a comparison between celebrities who promote powerspots and "joker-like figures" (Roth 2019, 99). Tsukada and Ōmi (2011) also allude to the power of media, especially television and magazines, as the main drivers of interest in powerspots. Are we really at the point where we believe that putatively clueless hordes of women are swarming powerspots simply because some magazines and celebrities talk about them? We know that editors and writers of women's magazines work closely with their readerships. They normally seek out reader comments, feedback, and questions that are the basis for the development of features in their publications. In her study of *shōjo manga* (girls' comics) magazines, Prough (2011) has provided evidence of the extremely close relationship between readers, artists, and editors that is unlike anything outside Japan. This close relationship between magazine editors or writers and their readers is one of the distinguishing traits of Japanese print media. Magazines are quick to notice trends among readers and to feature those in their issues. Although these feature articles might help to buttress a trend, in a type of dialectic between readership wishes and representation they are rarely the primary driver of fads.

In addition, as seen in the history of pilgrimage in Japan, especially to Ise during the Edo period, visits to shrines and temples have often been combined with, and perhaps serve as justification for, other hedonistic pleasures (Ambros 2006; Reader 2006; Teeuwen and Breen 2017). Powerspot scholars and critics often position women as dense suckers taken in by the media spin and present spiritual hustlers as having low opinions about female agency and intelligence. Consider this: What if all the stressed women simply say they need time out and will decamp to somewhere relaxing with interesting food and good baths? They might be accused of the ultimate sin for women, that of selfishness or self-centeredness (*wagamama*). Thinking about themselves and not being other-directed violates Japanese gender norms, especially gender ideology about female self-sacrifice for family and others. One way around the prohibition against hedonistic pursuits and "wasteful" economic activity is to tie it to religious seeking. If the quest for relief shifts to admirable spiritual development, it becomes a valid activity. It takes effort to imagine women as meekly driven by celebrity endorsements and media attention when they go on "religious" travel away from work and home. They stay in luxurious inns, steam away muscle aches in hot spring baths, and dine on local specialties. Questions about powerspots I have heard women ask over the years include some such as, "Okay, there is energy around there, but where is the open-air hot springs bath?" One wonders who the real dupes are in this situation. Furthermore, imagining women as the clueless victims of swindles negates the subversive potential of transforming traditionally male-dominated spaces into female-oriented destination spots. For example, stones found at the Ise Jingū became minipowerspots for female visitors, to the utter bewilderment of the male Shinto priests. "Priests were initially puzzled by the crowds of worshipers who gathered around these stones, stretching their hands to soak up energy" (Teeuwen and Breen 2017, 6). Supernatural energy attributed to nondescript stones was an idea generated outside the control of Shinto functionaries.

One form of powerspot behavior that some say is not appreciated by religious gatekeepers occurs when the visitor spends time, with eyes closed, touching rocks or trees that are thought to contain energy. I saw evidence of this type of powerspot hunter during my visit to Ise Jingū. For example, two women spent ten or more minutes with their arms straight out touching tall trees, eyes closed, as they drew in energy. The shrine is set in a forested area with many stately imposing conifers. Although not as old as people might think, these majestic trees attest to the enduring power of nature so are attractive to occult hunters as sources of energy. They may appear to be a "forest of trees that seem as old as humanity itself" (Smith 2021), but most of the trees around the Ise complex are less than eighty years old.[7] I overhead a woman saying to her friend as she walked away from the complex, "I got the power" (*pawā o itadkimashita*). It is ironic that women were once excluded from pilgrimage to certain sacred sites such as the temple complex on Mount Kōya yet today are the target of belittling characterizations for powerspot pilgrimaging. Perhaps priests and journalists have been puzzled, but those who go forth on powerspot visits have reasons for doing so, and numerus polls, briefly discussed in the next section, attest to the spectrum of motivations involved.

Powerspot Surveys

There are thousands of polls about powerspot visiting. Some focus on unique aspects of the cultural activity; others are not as useful.[8] Most highlight a few star attractions such as major shrines, temples, and places of natural beauty. A survey on marriage, fortune, and powerspots for the year 2018 is given in table 7. Women nationwide between the ages of twenty and forty-nine (one thousand total: five hundred unmarried women, five hundred married women) were asked which powerspot they most wanted to visit (Medikea Seimei Hoken 2018). The poll was conducted via the internet over a two-day period. The top pick was Izumo Taisha. In 2017 and 2016, the number one choice was Ise Jingū, which fell to the number two spot in 2018. Number three was the lush subtropical island of Yakushima.

The next question for the respondents who indicated they wanted to visit a powerspot was "Why do you want to visit a powerspot this year?" The top reason among all the answers was "to refresh" (this is a different survey than the one mentioned at the beginning of the chapter). Apparently,

Table 7. Powerspots women wanted to visit in 2018

18.5%	Izumo Taisha
16.3%	Ise Jingū
14%	Yakushima
12.6%	Itsukushima
11.8%	Sensōji

Source: Medikea Seimei Hoken 2018.

Table 8. Reasons women visited a powerspot

37.7%	Want to refresh
32.3%	Seek economic good fortune
30.4%	For sightseeing
26.1%	To ward off bad luck
26.1 %	To increase good fortune
25.8%	Want to be healed
19.3%	To recharge energy
18.1 %	To become positive
17.1%	To improve career
15.7%	To get well
14.2%	Want to relax
13.0%	Desire for a partner
5.3%	Want to marry current partner
4.9%	Escape reality
11.2%	Other reasons or no particular reason

Source: Medikea Seimei Hoken 2018.

many women want to visit powerspots to renew their spirits and regain their energy rather than wish for human relationships. Around one in three women sought good luck in money, and one in four wished for other things, such as exorcising bad luck, healing, and recharging energy (table 8).

For the majority of women, a hunt for supernatural help in finding lovers or marriage partners is not what is propelling them to powerspots. Even when the survey creators refined the data to focus only on the answers from unmarried women, the top three reasons given for visiting powerspots were "To refresh myself," "For sightseeing," and "Because I want a partner." A different poll of fewer women is interesting because it draws from the subculture of spiritual enthusiasts (table 9). The title for the discussion of the poll includes the shortened slang term for "spiritual," *supi.* The poll included only 101 women with an average age in the midthirties.

Table 9. If you went to powerspot where was it?

Tokyo Daijingū
Meiji Jingū
Izumo Taisha
Suzumushi-dera in Kyoto
Taiwan Alishan Mountain
Kirisuto no haka (Tomb of Christ) in Shingo
Mauna Kea Mountain in Hawai'i

Source: Yanada 2010, 123.

The poll reveals that most respondents had knowingly visited a powerspot that may not be well known to the general public. For example, when I mentioned powerspots to a few friends, they usually said something like "Oh, you mean Kiyomasa's Well?" They were thinking of the spot at Meiji Jingū that received intense media attention in 2009, discussed below. We notice, too, that in another poll asking people what powerspot they want to visit, there are some novel destinations in addition to the top three renowned spots (table 10). For example, Suzumushi-dera is off the beaten track for most visitors to Kyoto. It is where caged bell crickets provide background chirps in a meditation space. The Kirisuto no haka (Tomb of Christ) in Shingō, discussed below, is visited as a powerspot without any sense of Christian devotion involved. Their answers to the questions reveal some insider knowledge, such as knowing that Yakushima is a hot spot among natural powerspots and that Sedona, Arizona, is a destination within the New Age milieu.

In some cases powerspots are blended into other notions, such as heritage sites that have power by virtue of their special status. A special issue of the women's magazine *AnAn* included an article that

Table 10. What powerspots do you want to visit?

1	Izumo Taisha (tied)
1	Ise Jingū (tied)
2	Yakushima
3	Sedona, Arizona

Source: Yanada 2010, 123.

asked eight different people, including a photographer, a designer, a musician, and a celebrity, to name their top three powerspot-heritage sites (Sakimi 2006). Of the twenty-four sites, five were in Japan, while the others were in diverse countries and included the Statue of Liberty and the Grand Canyon in the United States, Luang Prabang village in Laos, the Palace of Versailles in France, and the Basilica of the Sagrada Familia in Spain.

Promoting Powerspots

Powerspot imagery and themes pervade many forms of popular culture. The business of marketing sacred locations has proven to be necessary for survival for many regional areas and their temples and shrines. Sakai (2016) traced the positive economic impact from fans of popular culture products. Temples and shrines have experienced more tourism because they are mentioned in fan media, and whether they like it or not, most are doing their best to appeal to this new demographic. Travel agencies have joined the action, and there are powerspot bus adventures and hotel deals for powerspot tours. The Tokyo Metro subway system participated in this strategy in 2010 when it launched the "Love Realization Fortune Powerspot Circuit Pilgrimage Ticket" campaign. It ran from January 8 to July 7, when only five thousand one-day tickets, packaged with a cute photo album of the sites, were made available for ¥710.[9]

In some cases, writers jump on the powerspot bandwagon to promote other initiatives. Kondo (2014), the globally prominent expert on minimalist living spaces, dipped into these waters when she included a short section on making one's own personal powerspot in one's home. She talked about a client who collected numerous amulets. She proposed that they make a personal powerspot on a high bookshelf. "One theme underlying my method of tidying is transforming the home into a sacred space, a power spot, filled with pure energy" (Kondo 2014, 161). Evidently, turning one's own home into a powerspot was a hot idea: an entire book riffing on it was published by the spiritualist Ehara (2015). A prolific writer on powerstones, tarot cards, astrology, and aromatherapy named Morimura (2007) insists that not every powerspot is useful for everyone and that we must find one that suits us individually. One's own powerspot (*mai pawā supotto*) might be determined by asking questions that explore an affinity for certain types of places. She also suggests that powerspots may be correlated with each person's Western astrological sign. For example, Cancer might like water resorts, while Capricorn will appreciate ancient cultural locations such as the Egyptian pyramids.

Powerspot marketing ideas and efficacy claims may be openly imaginative. *Speedy! Hearing Powerspot and Beauty Diet* (Igarashi 2010), which is really acupressure of the ear for relaxation, appropriates the trend in a novel manner. More prosaic are things such as powerspot calendars. One annual wall calendar contains scenes of mountain vistas created by the feng shui celebrity Rinoie (2012). She claims to be a descendent of a Joseon dynasty aristocratic clan in Korea. In 2002 she was a guest on a reality TV program, during which she gave advice to shops that were in danger of closing. All the shops made a quick comeback, doubling their sales within a month and pushing Rinoie into the mediascape. She went on to publish more than one hundred books on feng shui.

The DVD *Let's Take a Virtual Trip to Powerspots* is a relaxing mix of music and exquisite scenes (Pony Canyon Media Lab 2011). The hour-long program highlights four powerspots: Izumo Taisha in Matsue Prefecture, Yakushima Island in Kagoshima Prefecture, Mount Kōya in Wakayama Prefecture, and the three Grand Shrines of Kumano in Mie Prefecture. The scenes range from lush panoramas of dense mossy forests to ornamental Shingon altars while ambient music provides the score. A similar musical appropriation is the female group named Power Spot (2011–2015). The six members, between sixteen and twenty-one years old, were an artificially constructed "idol" group selected because of their appearance rather than outstanding talent. A generous review of Power Spot (video embedded) said that "they seem like a group that has a really nice energy. Nothing about them is really revolutionary or stands out, but the girls themselves really seem like they're having fun. They're a happy bunch, and their PVs are very pleasant. Not necessarily the most interesting, mind you, but they're cute and fun" (Serenyty 2013). The powerspot DVD and the idol group are illustrations of popular culture's appropriation of trends in the spiritual domain. The appropriation of religion is common in the US, where it surfaces in games and toys (Bado-Fralick and Norris 2010). Other examples are the faith-based theme parks in the US, such as the Ark Encounter in Kentucky or the Holy Land Experience in Florida. However, powerspot appropriations in Japan are not linked to religious texts or interpretations, and many illustrate a cheeky irreverence.

Some manga artists and writers also find the concept of the powerspot irresistible. The creator of a popular girl's horror manga series, Nagakubo (2012), turned his skills to the description of powerspots (figure 41). He wrote that while doing prior work he met many mediums, divination

Figure 41. Powerspot manga

providers, and Okinawan shamans with unusual powers. His interest led him to investigations of powerspots, and he wanted to illustrate the spiritual benefits of such locations. His powerspot manga features the same twin sisters from his horror manga series, Shōko and Miako. There are four main characters: himself as the curious artist, a divination provider named Hoshino-san (who contributes seven pedantic sidebar columns), and the manga sisters Shōko and Miako. They visit each powerspot and learn about the enshrined deities and local customs. The manga has some unusual bits of esoteric lore. For example, if you are at the water basin for ritual cleaning and the water tastes off, then the power at that location is not suited to you (Nagakubo 2012, 150).

One of the more unusual books in the powerspot genre contains a collection of manga episodes about adventures and is written by ten artists who have large female fandoms (Amamiya et al. 2017). Each of the artists contributes a short essay or comic about a powerspot destination, few of them locations most occult hunters visit. The choices range from ancient tombs to an enormous cedar tree. Among the rarities they picked was the Sudō Jinja in Kyoto, built to pacify the vengeance ghost of Prince Sawara.

History is a major theme in the guide, as seen in another rare section, the Miyataki archaeological site next to the Yoshinogawa River, thought to have been an eighth-century palace. There is also a section that asks readers to determine their "type" in order to choose the best powerspot to visit. A chart cross-tabulating birth year and month produces a number that leads one to five types named after the Taoist Five Elements/Phases. Famous writers and manga artists who have been pulled into the powerspot domain are joined by other celebrities, including comedians and religious specialists. Three of these notable people are discussed in the next section.

Prominent Powerspot Promoters

The reputation of some powerspots may get a boost because of their connection to famous celebrities, although in most cases interest in religious travel predated such attention. Anyone who has read women's magazines since the 1990s would know that powerspot awareness had long been circulating in female culture before the wider mainstream media paid any attention. In addition, it is useful to evaluate the manner in which the media and some scholars have characterized celebrity involvement in powerspot consciousness.

One well-known powerspot star is Shimada Shūhei, a comedian who morphed into a charisma divination specialist with a focus on palm reading. During a 2009 TV interview, he reported that a photo he took of a well at Meiji Jingū brought him excellent fortune. The unimpressive well, a small round bubbling hole in the ground of a garden outside the shrine, is named Kiyomasa's Well (Kiyomasa no Ido). Shimada used the well photo as the wallpaper for his cell phone and computer and subsequently had a surge of good luck. Not long after his cell phone story aired on TV, Kiyomasa's Well became a popular powerspot deluged with visitors. During my underwhelming visit in 2013, I paid admission to the Inner Garden and waited in a long line that slowly shuffled past the well. There was a security guard present who urged us to move along. Visitors are not allowed to take water from the well.

Shimada's powerspot experience at Kiyomasa's Well launched him into this new domain, and he went on to publish a powerspot guide and DVD (Shimada 2010a, 2010b). The book is packed with information and is written in an irreverent style. For example, when talking about Imado Jinja in Tokyo, he reports that his mother, who accompanied him on his visit, said, "This isn't really a powerspot." The book contains sections on powerspots for specific life issues, such as love and marriage, working life and careers, gambling, health, and dealing with disease. An example of one suggested location is Izumo Taisha, famous for *enmusubi,* the creation of good interpersonal ties and relationships. For people seeking romance and marriage, this is one of the most famous shrines. He notes that every October deities from all over Japan are said to convene at the shrine, making it especially powerful. One section of Shimada's guide focuses on powerspots for "pinpoint worries." The "Pin Points" highlight queries from readers about specific problems (another example of the close connection between writers, publishers, and the readership). Shimada recommends a powerspot for their issue, which is then featured in the section together with his advice. For example, someone wrote that they were just beginning to learn how to play the piano and were already scheduled to give a performance (Shimada 2010b, 118). Shimada recommended that the novice player visit a subshrine located within the grounds of the Kurumazaki Jinja in Kyoto. The smaller shrine, named Geinō Jinja, is dedicated to Ame no Uzume, the goddess who lured the sun goddess Amaterasu out of her cave by performing a suggestive dance. The shrine has long been popular among entertainers and artists. I visited Kurumazaki Jinja on a rainy day and was impressed by the number of entertainers and writers who had visited the subshrine Geinō Jinja. On the red slats of the fence around the shrine, called *tamagaki,* celebrities who have visited the shrine and made donations have their names inscribed in black ink. A few I noticed were for a former member of the Super Girls idol group Ishibashi Hotaru, comedian Sugiyama Eiji (known as Sugi-chan), and CLAMP, the all-female Japanese manga artist group.[10]

Other segments in Shimada's book are devoted to palm reading, feng shui, and the types of unique *omamori* amulets one may get at some of the powerspots. Included in his recommendations are pet *omamori* (in the shape of dog and cat paws) from the Ōmiya Hachimangū in Hyōgo and a *magatama* bead necklace from Sumiyoshi Taisha in Osaka (Shimada 2010b, 30–33). In the guidebook he retells the story about Kiyomasa's Well but some years later mentioned a second powerspot also located at Meiji Shrine, one that he much preferred. During a lecture he gave at Ōtsuma Women's University, he said that power emanates from a stone named Kameishi (Turtle Stone), also located at the site (Rika Riko Twins 2017). Reminding us that any place considered to hold supernatural energy may become a powerspot, Shimada includes not only Shinto shrines and Buddhist temples in his guide but also Kirisuto no haka (Tomb of Christ). Also called Toraizuka, it is located in the hamlet of Shingō in Aomori Prefecture. A myth began circulating in the village during the 1930s, followed by the discovery of the tomb. According to the legend, Jesus studied in Japan before returning to Palestine for his ministry. When the time came for his crucifixion, however, one of his brothers named Isukiri took his place, and Jesus returned to Japan to live out a long life. Most villagers are aware that the tomb is a sham, but it is still revered as a spot connected to the ancestors who created it: "Even something so obviously counterfeit can become a holy place because of the subjective interpretations of the people associated with it" (Okamoto 2019, 105).[11] Someone who visited the site for the hamlet's Jesus Festival tweeted about the attitude of the residents (Yoda 2022). She mentioned that the local Shinto priest resides over a ceremony, that a convenience store in front of the grave bears a sign with a related linguistic gag on it, and that because Aomori is known for garlic farming, they created garlic ice cream with the name "Dracula" to celebrate the Jesus legend.

Attitudes toward Shimada are benign or slightly dismissive, but the same cannot be said about another celebrity connected to powerspots. Ehara Hiroyuki is one of the most frequently mentioned media personalities in both news and scholarly articles about the powerspot boom. In particular, if the tone of the writing is to present powerspots as spiritual sales scams or something like "gate crashing religion" (Roth 2019, 99), Ehara is inevitably mentioned (see Brasor and Tsubuku 2011; Horie 2017). Ehara is a spiritualist and psychic researcher who uses the term "spiritual counselor" to describe his work as a medium and past-life reader. Writers like to add the term "self-proclaimed" to his occupational description as a snide move to discredit him. He was born in Tokyo in 1964 and endured a difficult childhood with the loss of his parents (his father died when he was four; his mother, when he was fifteen). He studied fine arts at Wako University and later attended Kokugakuin University, receiving training as a Shinto priest. He spent a few years as a Shinto clergy intern at Kitazawa Hachiman in Setagaya before traveling to London, where he studied European-style spiritualism. After returning to Japan in 1989, he began writing columns for women's magazines and eventually hosted two popular TV programs from 2004 to 2009, which launched him into celebrity status. The media dubs him a "pop fortune teller" or "TV psychic." He has published hundreds of books and also performs as an opera singer (baritone). He is a complex person often tied to various scandals. Regardless of one's evaluation of Ehara, his promotion of powerspots attracts much criticism. Yet, compared to other books in the genre, it is hard to see his guides as anything unusual or bizarre. Perhaps the only deviation is that Ehara coins his own method for talking about powerspots, often referring to them using borrowed English as "spiritual sanctuaries" (*supirichuaru sankuchuari*). He has produced numerous guides under the Spiritual Sanctuary series name, each covering a different region of Japan. He wants readers to view these places as repositories of *reiteki enerugii* (spirit energy).

One book in the series is his guide to Shikoku, Izumo, and Hiroshima (Ehara 2005). Excluding the full-page maps, 14 percent of the content is devoted to food, baths, and shopping. For example, in the section on Izumo Taisha are a few pages on the shrine, followed by several on local inns, restaurants, and smaller shrines. There is also a section on the nearby resort town of Tamatsukuri Onsen. Featured are three hotels or inns, including the Tamatsukuri Grand Hotel. Because of my interest in *magatama* beads, I visited Tamatsukuri Onsen, and one reason I selected the Tamatsukuri Grand Hotel for lodging is because of Ehara's description of its "power stone bath." I found the Megumi no Yu (Goddess Bath) to be just as he depicted it: plated with thousands of red, green, and white agates. The agate bath was so named because it was inspired by mythology surrounding Amaterasu and is related to the cave legend and her emergence into light when lured outside. This bath certainly qualifies as a site of supernatural play and enjoyment even if the mythical associations are not taken seriously.

Many scholars insist that Ehara is only interested in promoting Shinto shrines as powerspots, yet in reading his guides, I did not find this to be completely true or see his selections as reflecting an intentionally nationalist bias, as insinuated. The Sanctuary Series volume on Kyoto begins with Daigōji, to which he dedicates six pages (Ehara 2006). In the rest of the guide, Shintō shrines on average are given two pages each. He also devotes several pages, including hotels and eating places, to a visit to the Buddhist multiplex at Hiezan. Perhaps as someone trained in Shinto theology he feels more comfortable talking about shrines, but he does not exhibit aversion to Buddhist temples, and to characterize him as doing so is incorrect. In the Kyoto volume, he calls the *omamori* amulets one buys at shrines "spiritual supplements" (*sapurimento,* sometimes clipped to *sapuri*) similar to vitamins (Ehara 2006, 68).

The last powerspot personage I want to highlight is Ichino Tomoe, a professional illustrator as well as the head priest (*gūji*) at Imado Jinja in Asakusa. Imado Jinja is featured in most powerspot guides, primarily because of Ichino's unstinting efforts. One of the few female Shinto priests, she is the force behind the refurbishing of a formerly neglected shrine. Unlike some of the national shrines that maneuver centuries of built-in fame, Imado Jinja is located in what was once a stigmatized part of the city just north of Sensōji, one of the more popular tourist destinations in Asakusa. The way this shrine rose to prominence illustrates how women, both the priests and the hunters of sacred spaces, have played a central role in the creation and popularity of powerspots. Ichino masterfully manipulated media to bring economic benefits to her shrine and community.

Imado Jinja currently enshrines multiple deities, a common enough occurrence. The heavenly couple Izanami and Izanagi, the progenitors of all the other deities, are worshipped there as appropriate divinities to pray to for fertility and marriage. Also inducted is the Taoist figure of Fukurokuju, one of the Shichifukujin (Seven Lucky Deities). The spirit of Emperor Ōjin, fifteenth emperor of Japan, is also deified there.[12] The shrine was destroyed during the Great Kantō Earthquake of 1923, rebuilt again, and then demolished by wartime fire bombing in 1945. The current main hall was built in 1971. A well-known pottery site was once located in Imado, where clay from the Sumida River was used to manufacture unglazed earthenware roof tiles. In 1722 the Tokugawa government insisted that all buildings have tile or earthen roofs to prevent fires, so the Imado kilns date from around that time. On the grounds of the Imado shrine are two guardian dog statues inscribed with the name of Imado pottery-makers and a date of 1752. Pottery-makers used the same clay to make small cat, fox, and human figurines, as well as other items such as dishes and braziers. These *imado-yaki* (Imado-ware) items were one of the famous souvenirs of Edo. A woodblock illustration from a series by Utagawa Hiroshige titled "Flourishing Business in Balladtown" (Jōruri-machi hanka no zu, 1852) shows a busy scene of various forms of commerce, along with people buying snacks at food stalls, divination providers, hair groomers, storytellers, and used clothing dealers. In one print an Imado-yaki pottery-maker is selling beckoning cats, or *maneki-neko.*

Analogous to today's powerspot guides were Edo-period guides to the famous sites, the shops, and the best souvenirs. These guides were read not only by those visiting Edo from other places but also by Edo residents as well. An example is *Guide to Famous Spots in Edo,* compiled by Saitō Chōshū (ca. 1737–1799) and painted by Hasegawa Settan from 1834 to 1836. It features a drawing and text about *Imado-yaki* (Saitō and Suzuki 2000). The billowing smoke from the fires that fed the Imado kilns are also depicted in numerous woodblock prints. One notable print is a scene of men working at the kilns at Imado by Utagawa Kuniyoshi (1798–1861). It was one of ten prints published around 1834 as part of the collection called *Famous Views of the Eastern Capital* (*Tōto meisho*). Other prints of the Imado kiln site would depict the place from afar, marked by swirls of smoke. In this one Kuniyoshi gets up close and illustrates two men shoveling into huge burning kilns. Next to the men looms the huge stack of pine needles used to fuel the kilns. Visitors on their way to the Yoshiwara licensed pleasure district passed Imado by boat on the Sumida River. As Screech (2006, 275) alludes to, perhaps the "dry, all-swathing smoke" from the Imado kilns along the river symbolized the divide between the metaphoric realms of heaven and hell.

At one time Imado and its neighboring San'ya district were also home to tanneries and slaughterhouses, marking them as hamlets for outcasts, or Burakumin (Heine 2012, 152). Burakumin is a name for a social group historically stigmatized based on occupation, including meat processing and leather production. The Imado slaughterhouses and leather factories were relocated elsewhere in 1892 because of an ordinance, but traces of the leather industry remain in the form of shoe stores still found on streets around the shrine. Another well-known shoe district is located in Hanakawado just south of Imado. In an effort to combat the severe discrimination faced by Burakumin, many of the hamlets are periodically renamed or reorganized with other neighborhoods under new names. Currently, Imado Jinja serves parishioners in five neighborhoods historically identified as outcast hamlets: Imado 1-Chōme, Imado 2-Chōme, Nihonzutsumi, Higashi Asakusa, and Senzoku. Senzoku is the current name for the area where the Yoshiwara was located. Today it is a sketchy place with hundreds of modern sex-service industries.[13]

Shinto priests, male and female, are allowed to marry and have children. Imado Jinja is one of the thousands of small family shrines that generally follow a custom that allows children or grandchildren to inherit the position as chief priest. The current head priest, Ichino Tomoe, was born in 1976, and from the age of twelve she served as a *miko* (shrine attendant) at her family shrine.[14] After graduating from Tokyo Kasei Gakuin Junior College, a private women's college, she worked as a designer of stuffed toys at a toy company. She subsequently passed the qualifications to serve as a priest from Kokugakuin University in 2002 and eventually assumed the role of head priest at Imado Shrine.

During the Meiji era, female Shinto priests were outlawed, but the ban was lifted following the Pacific War. By the end of 2012, there were only 667 women *gūji* (head priests), fewer than 10 percent of all head priests (Nishide 2014). Similar to Ichino, most female priests work at small family shrines rather than national shrines or large regional shrines. Often these are family succession shrines where daughters or wives may be the designated inheritors of the priest role, once they have been certified. Almost all priests are required to pass certification exams administered by the Association of Shinto Shrines (Jinja Honchō).[15] In an interview Ichino talked about some of the challenges she has faced as one of the few female priests. She often thought that parishioners would have preferred her grandfather to officiate at rituals: "In general, people think being a Shinto priest is a man's profession. If you're a woman, they think you're a shrine maiden, or a supplementary priestess. People don't know women Shinto priests exist, so they think we can't perform rituals. Once, after I finished performing *jiichinsai* (ground-breaking ceremony), I was asked, 'So, when is the priest coming?'" (Hanai 2017).

Outgoing and charismatic, Ichino talks freely with visitors and actively promotes shrine affairs and offerings. She has been especially proactive in tying the shrine to local events. One method has been to link it to one of the many circuit pilgrimages that entice pilgrims to visit a series of shrines and temples in adjacent neighborhoods. Imado Jinja participates in two circuit pilgrimages. One is the well-known Asakusa Shichifukujin Meguri (Asakusa Seven Lucky Deities Circuit Pilgrimage), which directs people to seven different shrines where seven of the Lucky Deities are housed. Imado Jinja lays claim to the Taoist deity Fukurokuju. The shrine also participates in Shitamachi Hachi Fukujin Meguri (Downtown Eight Lucky Deities Circuit Pilgrimage). This is a relatively new pilgrimage linked to a tour bus company.

The beckoning cat (*maneki-neko*) mentioned above is now ubiquitous in Asian shops and restaurants outside Japan. Ivakhiv (2003, 128) notes that often pilgrimage sites might be places where stories are edited or staged. This is certainly the case for some powerspot sites, as revealed in the beckoning cat origin stories claimed by both Imado Jinja and Gōtokuji, a Buddhist temple in northeast Tokyo. Although Imado boasts variant versions of the tale, the main story goes something like this: A destitute woman who lived in Hanakawado (adjacent to Imado) had a beloved cat. Eventually, she was forced to leave her house and give her cat up due to poverty. One night the cat appeared to her in a dream and said, "If you make a figurine of me and deify it, you will become happy and prosperous." She followed this suggestion, and her luck changed enough for her to return to her house. Afterward she began making Imado clay cat figurines, which she sold at the large torii gate of Asakusa Jinja. These cat figurines proved to be extremely popular and she became wealthy.

In contrast, the Gōtokuji story makes a brutal warrior the centerpiece of the tale: A feudal lord from Ōmi Province was beckoned into Gōtokuji by a white cat, a detour that saved him from a bad fate (either being struck by lightning or slayed by enemies). In gratitude he donated to the temple, which then became prosperous. Because *maneki-neko* figurines made of Imado-ware are attested to in a number of Edo-period writings, are preserved in artifacts, and are represented in woodblock prints naming the cat as *imado-yaki,* the origin of the beckoning cat at Imado appears to be the most credible. Imado Jinja capitalized on female interest in cats and cuteness by reformulating the two enshrined deities Izanami and Izanagi as a beckoning cat couple. The adorable couple illustrate the shrine's *ema* in a unique form—they are round. Numerous statues of the deity pair can be found around the grounds and in the main shrine hall (figure 42). The word for round, *en,* is also a homonym for "fate." The shrine's *omikuji* lottery fortunes and pilgrim stamps also include *maneki-neko* imagery. Cat statues and watering cans are found around the shine precincts, and there is a separate, nonsacred *maneki neko* shrine housed in converted living quarters on the side of the main shrine.

Ichino Tomoe was commissioned to work on a mook (magazine-book) about powerspots by Futabasha, and this publication enhanced her reputation and brought attention to Imado Jinja (Ichino 2010). The shrine began to host matchmaking events in 2008. Ichino wrote in her blog that the first few meetings were failures because she had not carefully planned how to facilitate them. Even so, with the upsurge in powerspot visitors the shrine has been able to upgrade the appearance of the grounds and add signs in the vicinity to help people navigate their way there. Ichino is often photographed or interviewed for TV programs in front of the shrine, wearing a pink priest's robe. In looking into her profile, I noticed that she

Figure 42. Deity pair as beckoning cats, Imado Jinja

often wore pink ritual garments. The traditional clothing worn by Shinto priests, called *shōzoku,* are based on Heian-era (794–1185) court costume. The ritual outfits may be of three basic types: formal, ritual, or casual/everyday. In most cases the colors worn will denote the rank of the priest. I noticed that higher-ranking priests wore white or purple robes, while junior priests wore aqua. Ichino talked about the time she was still a junior priest at the shrine in an interview: "At first, I wore my grandfather's light green garment because I thought it's better to look like a man. But after a while I decided to be proud of the fact that I am a female priest and I began wearing a pink robe, like today. I thought I can be more confident if I stop thinking too much [about my gender]" (Hanai 2017). Ichino reflects on the "power of pink" in *Imado Shrine's Beautiful Shinto Priest Teaches Ten Daily Behaviors for Inducing Happiness* (Ichino 2014). Discussing her selection of hue, she wrote, "If you harvest your expertise in use of color, you will better express yourself" (Ichino 2014, 124–125). She suggests that women should not be afraid to wear the color pink, especially when looking for a partner: the color pink will lead men to think you are a happy person, which will attract them.

In a blog published while the book was in press, Ichino (2013) wrote that the publisher selected the title of the book, and she apologized for the use of the word *bijin* (beautiful woman). The book is a collection of short essays about how to live a brighter and happier life and at times serves as a general conduct guide to proper manners. A section on speech cautions the reader to be mindful and to speak kindly and politely. Other essays promote similar general self-development themes: the present time is the best time; cherish nature and love trees and plants; become a person with a smiling face who easily laughs; visit shrines to receive power; the most important things in life are those that cannot be seen. She reminds the reader that the beckoning cat is an *engimono* (good luck object) that if treated with respect will bring you good fortune. She also mentions the Imado-ware makers (Ichino 2014, 202). Ichino wrote a personal blog from 2005 to 2016. Her blog tracked some of her ritual duties, such as officiating at festivals and purification rituals and meeting visitors to the shrine.[16] Much of her blogging focused on her artistic and creative activities, the breadth of which is impressive. She makes her own New Year's *kumade* (ornamental good luck rakes). In order to "rake in good luck," they are usually made of bamboo and decorated with small auspicious objects and talismans. Ichino recycles the small, narrow wood boards found under fish cakes (*kamaboko*), paints these with cute images of cats and the Seven Lucky Deities, then adds them to her *kumade.* She also makes various types of dolls, including stuffed buddha and Jesus dolls. She produces many paintings and illustrations for different civic groups and charity events. She designed an *ema* votive plaque for the Hato Bus Asakusa Shichifukujin Meguri, on which she used an image of a white pigeon (*hato*). She produced an enormous painting of the Shichifukujin Treasure Ship for a 2016 display at a Sōgo department store at Omiya, in which the deities are depicted as cats.

I believe it is important to notice Ichino's activities because in her case the promotion of her shrine through cat imagery is not simply a marketing device but an extension of her creative drive. It is women like her and her fans who have been able to create a powerspot in a location once considered polluted. Imado Jinja is a remarkable tale of the spatial and perceptual transformation of a place once famous for atrocious odors and smoke but now associated with cute cats and romantic relationships.

In the 1980s I was taken to a US pilgrimage site named the National Shrine of Lady of the Snows in Illinois. It was the winter holiday season, and crowds of people walked through its two hundred acres to admire the small illuminated grottoes and other snowy religious scenes. I wondered if the people around me were there because of religious devotion or simply to see the massive lights? The site includes a gift shop, restaurant, and hotel, so it has successfully combined tourism and religion. Not surprisingly, there are many other religious pilgrimage sites in the US, ranging from the formal to the peculiar. The Shrine of Saint John Neumann in Philadelphia displays his skeleton with a mask over his face. In Utah one may visit the Gilgal Sculpture Garden to see a Joseph Smith sphinx, a sculpture of a dismembered giant, and numerous other stone monuments accompanied by cryptic Mormon writings. These pilgrimage sites in the US remind us that any site may be turned into a religiously ascribed location that attracts visitors. Turning to the powerspot trend in Japan, by comparison, I do not think that seeking energy or a mind cure is bizarre or silly and thus find media and scholarly representations to generally be flawed and biased.

In the case of Shinto shrines regarded as powerspots by female visitors, the general lack of devotional interest in the specific deities housed at the sites is not appreciated by everyone. Some official bodies such as the main administrative organization, the Jinja Honchō (Carter 2018), are not particularly pleased by massive numbers of young women visiting their sacrosanct shrines for their own personal reasons. Yet every site has multiple audiences and understandings, a point most beautifully unpacked by Rots (2019) in his description of the Okinawan Sēta Utaki sacred place. He found many different narratives and contentious claims to the site, most operating completely outside a firm understanding of its actual history. Female shamans, community members, tourist companies, and tourists claim the site as their own and carry their own understandings with them. This means that regardless of the opinions and attitudes of shrine functionaries and regardless of media hype, visitors will always have a range of motivations for undertaking powerspot visits and will continue to journey to the spots that appeal to them. Depending on the person and their individual interests, some places will perhaps be experienced as more intensely charged with supernatural power than others. I met someone named Mayumi when I visited Izanagi Jinja, a small shrine not far from the Yanagimoto station in Nara Prefecture. We talked a little about powerspots. She said that during a visit to Izumo Taisha in Shimane Prefecture, often on the list of the top three powerspot destinations, she did not "connect" with the space. Instead, even though Izanagi Jinja is not nearly as beautiful or old, she felt more sympatico toward it. Perhaps, she added, she felt energy from the nearby tumulus of one of the early Yamato rulers (referring to Andonyama Kofun, allegedly the burial place of Emperor Sujin). Mayumi had read many powerspot guides and had visited several recommended ones, but she said the guides were only suggestions and that of course she had her own preferences.

Kracauer wrote about travel as a "liberation from earthly woes," going on to say that "through their travels (and for the time being it doesn't matter where they are headed) the shackles are burst, and they imagine that infinity itself is spreading out before them. In trains they are already on the other side, and the world in which they land is a new world for them" (Kracauer and Levin 1995, 72). This description also fits the way many occult hunters talk about powerspot tourism. Japanese powerspots are also close to what Ivakhiv (2003) found in his study of New Age pilgrimage. He studied the pilgrimages made to "power places" in Sedona, Arizona and stated, "It is possible to experience religion without belonging to a particular religious organization" (Ivakhiv 2003, 21). The powerspot trend is reinvigorating existing shrines, temples, and other locations with new meanings. Visiting a powerspot is a spiritual experience anyone can participate in without actually endorsing any particular religion. Sacred and natural spaces are objectified as destinations for women in search of a balm for life's disappointments and as short-term refreshment from their hectic, everyday existence. One way to contain women's sense of contribution to wider society is to ascribe the trends they create or engender to something beyond them, usually the media.[17] It is important to keep in mind the emancipatory possibilities of powerspots and other forms of occult hunting and supernatural play.

Conclusion

Ten women and girls of varying ages, each carrying a miniature basket, were crammed into a tiny shop named Strawberry Nice. They were intently combing through containers full of beads, Swarovski crystals, and loose semiprecious stones. In 2008 I joined them on this quest in a wholesale jewelry-making store in Asakusabashi in Tokyo, where there were more than forty other shops just like it within a six-block radius of the Bead Town neighborhood. It was nearly a female-only place where women and girls roamed in pairs, groups, or alone, spending hours visiting store after store stroking the ropes of hanging beads and digging through containers full of colorful feng shui bracelets. Asakusabashi is best known as a wholesale business district where small-shop owners buy seasonal decorations, boxes, paper bags, and stationery goods. The area is also famous for its doll and craft stores. Bead shops such as Strawberry Nice were added to the mix, and the stores targeted female customers.[1] Buying things for do-it-yourself crafts is not unusual behavior in Japan. What was notable, however, was that many of the items and displays in Bead Town had occult themes. There were charms from Western, Chinese, and Hindu astrology; beads sorted by their associated feng shui color; and baskets of loose curved *magatama* beads that denote ancient female power. Objects with occult themes appearing in numerous craft stores indicates that the domain has broad appeal and vibrancy even if it occurs below mainstream interest or business school faculty considerations about appropriate research. This same interest extends to the various areas investigated in *Occult Hunting*. A *reifu* paper charm is more than a small slip of paper, visiting powerspots serves numerous functions, and a comma-shaped bead tells many stories.

Many other forms of material religion and occult pastimes have not been covered in *Occult Hunting*. An example gaining attention are paper petals called *sange*. They originated from a Buddhist ritual involving the scattering of lotus petals as part of memorial services. Eventually, the lotus petals were substituted with papers cut in the shape of petals, and some visitors took them home as amulets or mementoes. Temples commissioned artists to create original art to print on them, and now they are a folk art form. Occult hunters seek them out, too, and many powerspot guides include a page or section describing them. The small paper petals are decorated with everything from dreamy scenes of flying celestial beings to manga-like images of bodhisattvas. Similar to *goshuin* pilgrim stamps, the temples periodically change their designs. *Sange* may be handed out as a gift by the temple when obtaining pilgrim stamps or other objects. Some are offered in sets of three or five but require a monetary offering. An example is a set of three large woodblock-printed paper petals I obtained at Tanzan Jinja in Sakurai (although today it is a Shinto shrine, Tanzan was originally a Buddhist temple). One print by Miyata Nagisa is of the thirteen-story pagoda with van Gogh–like swilling clouds above it and flower blooms in the foreground (figure 43). I saw many other beautiful *sange* elsewhere and read about them in numerous magazines and books targeting the occult hunter. For example, Nishimura (2018, 50) mentions the beautiful *sange* that are found along a pilgrim stamp pilgrimage circuit in Nara called the "Lotus Road."

Figure 43. Sange paper petal, Tanzan Jinja

I am curious about how these artifacts are used and displayed by collectors and look forward to seeing more research on *sange* trends and fandoms in the future.

When people care about the cultural spheres explored in *Occult Hunting,* when they themselves define them as important and worthy, pronouncements about their nonscientific nature, triviality, and wastefulness by other groups of people (older men, sneering journalists, snarky academics, and so on) are irrelevant. A paraphrase of the sociological maxim known as the Thomas theorem states that "if people define situations as real, they are real in their consequences" (based on Thomas and Thomas 1928, 572). For each of the aspects of the supernatural and the occult that I looked into, multiple spin-offs and innovations generated widespread interest, extensive cultural production, and great profit, whether or not the tarot, *reifu,* powerspot visiting, or other objects and activities were "real" or not. *Occult Hunting* illustrates how objects and media from the occult domain acquire a variety of meanings as they move from production to acquisition. This is not unlike the complex interplay between the desire for healing services and the way healing has been marketed in the publishing industry, the music industry, toy-making, and tourism (Matsui 2013).[2] Women have had a core role in driving the production and marketing of occult goods and media. The case is similar to the "merchants of cool" (Goodman 2001) who used market data, surveys, observation, and focus groups to track teen trends in the US. Marketing agencies made use of coolhunters to pinpoint the latest fads. Japan's "merchants of the occult" do the same to track the desires of the female demographic. It is not simply the case that businesses, media producers, shrines, and temples are creating the market: they also respond to and embody the interests and aesthetics of female occult hunters. Thus, the occult domain reflects an interplay between commerce and a sincere search for transcendental meaning.

Women have held core roles in religious movements globally, often in ways that have challenged established religious organizations. Tøllefsen and Giudice's (2017) edited volume explores Hindu groups, African churches, pagan groups, Christian groups, and other movements. Japan in particular has a history of female founders of religious groups (especially the New Religious Movements) and female religious reformers. As noted by Ambros (2015, 172): "Rather than serving as marginal actors, Japanese women have taken leading roles." Globally, however, women have long resisted oppressive dominant religious organizations without forming new religious movements, although their efforts have not always been recognized. For example, female members of a Chinese vegetarian

Buddhist group were successful in resisting pressure to marry from the late nineteenth century until around 1935 (Sankar 1985). The occult hunting activities tracked in this book do not support the notion that Japanese women are on the verge of revolutionizing religion in Japan in any institutional manner. On the contrary, they are often full participants in a spectrum of traditional religious activities and rituals, from visiting established shrines and temples to serving in official roles such as head priest. Instead, we see an extension of religious behavior to include newly created realms from tarot cards to *magatama*. Women are also galvanizing new attitudes toward religion by experiencing the supernatural and the occult in ways that include enjoyment, creativity, and the search for individual meaning. We also see the impact of female interests and aesthetics (especially kawaii cuteness) in almost every religious domain, from established temples and shrines to the powerspot.

Most religious institutions in Japan addressed the COVID-19 pandemic in some manner. McLaughlin (2020) details a few of the rituals held to expel the virus, as well as the media efforts to reassure people: photographs were taken of priests and pastors from different religious groups lined up in solidarity in front of the enormous Tōdaiji in Nara, and the largest Shinto shrine organization created specific prayers aimed at eradicating the virus. Lowe (2020) looked at a few responses from Buddhist temples in Nara, finding, for example, that Yakushiji advocated for parishioners to copy sutras at home to petition for an end to the pandemic. A notable event was held in 2020 at Kitano Tenmangū in Kyoto (*Kyodo News* 2020). A ritual called Goryō-e, meant to appease an angry spirit, was revived as a joint Buddhist-Shinto effort to exorcize the pandemic. Buddhist priests from the Enryakuji in Otsu joined the resident Shinto priests for an event that had not been held for 550 years. Powerspot hunting tapered off, and shrines and temples shifted to different or enhanced strategies to keep occult hunters connected. They stepped up their menu of online amulets and pilgrim stamp ordering on their web pages. Seimei Jinja in Kyoto offered a thin vinyl pilgrim stamp book with a *goshuin* insert that it mailed to those who ordered them online. New items for protection against the COVID-19 virus were added to the existing offerings, or older ones were repurposed and resanctified for the new cause. One interesting effort to help those isolating at home to feel connected was created by Kaneko Reiko, a priest at Wakeoe Jinja. She came up with the idea of using a webcam to allow people to worship from their homes during the pandemic. She also suggested that potential visitors check the webcam to see if the shrine was too crowded prior to visiting.

The ritual purification basin at Tsuno Jinja was filled with roses and sweet peas instead of water, and the long-handled bamboo scoops were removed. The revamped purification basins at different shrines attracted the attention of journalists, and articles about the phenomenon became common. *Miyazaki nichinichi shinbun* (2021) ran an article about the many visitors to the Tsuno Jinja who were posting photos of its flower-stuffed basin on social media.[3] Guests at other shrines also posted bittersweet photos of the altered ablution pavilions all through the first years of the pandemic. An inability to ritually purify with flowing water was distressing, but people appreciated the presence of fresh hydrangeas, sweet peas, and daisies, which helped mitigate the discomfort. It signified that the shrine was concerned about public health and was trying to lift up everyone's spirits. The idea became so popular that a new term was coined for the substitute flower basin, *hana chōzu*. Flowers were donated to shrines by flower shops, local farmers, and merchants. Shrine staff used the *hana chōzu* as yet another avenue for artistic expression, with colors and themes to match the seasons. In October some of the flower basins became flower arrangements, with sprigs of brown wheatgrass and maple leaves mixed in with yellow chrysanthemums and orange marigolds. A shrine attendant at Hebikubo Jinja in Tokyo tweeted an artistic video of bright-pink flowers and floating crystal balls in the purification basin, noting that they heralded the upcoming Valentine's Day colors (Miko Hebi 2022).

The pandemic also generated an unusual development, the revival of an obscure folklore sea creature named Amabie.[4] She dates to 1846 when a government official went to Kumamoto Prefecture to look into stories about a shimmering form that emerged from the sea at night (E. Nagano 2005). She rose from the water, introduced herself to the official, and predicted six years of abundant harvest that would occur along with an epidemic. She recommended that the bureaucrat draw her likeness and show it to other people as protection. A special type of woodblock-printed sheet called a *surimono* was produced from this drawing and disseminated as a news event. In the print Amabie has long hair, a beak in an otherwise human face, three legs, and scales from the neck down. When the pandemic arrived in Japan, Amabie experienced a rebirth (Alt 2020; K. Tanaka 2022). In the first week of March 2020, people were ironically tweeting images of her, which prompted the Japanese Ministry of Health, Labor and Welfare to use her in a public awareness poster aimed at young people. Soon, Amabie was everywhere. There were Amabie drawing contests and cosplay as the odd mermaid. Some people dressed up their cats with tiny wigs made of yarn and colorful scale-print cloth bibs to look like the chimera. Personal items such as face masks, face mask charms, and name stamps with her corona-fighting image were produced. Amabie appeared in food products and packaging, and she adorned new labels put on sake and beer bottles. Character lunch boxes featured her, and cookies and delicate rice-dough confectionary were made in her shape. Amabie cookie cutters were sold on Amazon. A friend found an Amabie amulet for cleaning one's cell phone screen sold at 7-Eleven.[5]

Many shrines and temples began to offer Amabie-themed good luck amulets and other items. The woman who designed the globally famous Pikachu characters, Nishida Atsuko, drew two characters to adorn an upbeat *ema* votive plaque meant to ask for protection against COVID-19. Nishida wanted to do something for people during the pandemic, so she created and dedicated the votive plaque at Kasuga Taisha (Okada 2020). The *ema* depicts a cute white deer wearing a red ribbon bow, named Haku-chan, along with a white-haired Amabie with red eyes given the name Haru-chan (figure 44). Nishida said she drew the images in the hopes that the viewer would feel soothed and relaxed.[6] Some shrines began offering pilgrim stamps with an image of the mermaid-like figure. An example is the Muraya shrine in Nara, with its Amabie-sama's Yukata Cosplay Goshuin. Amabie is dressed up in a festive magenta and aqua

Figure 44. Amabie votive plaque, Kasuga Taisha

yukata with a yellow obi (Murayanimasumifutsuhime Jinja 2022).[7] Amabie reflects the polysemic nature of occult hunting. She may be playfully used for beer-bottle labels or kitty cosplaying, yet she is also depicted on small slips of paper tucked into wallets and purses for added reassurance and protection.

The 1958 American film *The Barbarian and the Geisha* is alleged to be based on the historic figure of Townsend Harris, a merchant from New York tasked by President Franklin Pierce to serve as the first US consul to Japan in 1856 (Huston 1958). The starring role of Harris was played by John Wayne, and in the film's trailer, he introduces its exoticized background (Biggest Trailer DataBase 2020). It includes a scene of *miko* shrine attendants performing a sacred dance at a Shinto shrine. In his voiceover narration about this common ritual, Wayne intones, "Weird ceremonies and superstitions barred from the view for centuries." Both "weird ceremonies" and "superstitions" are ethnocentric judgments of non-Christian religious behavior. This type of denigration runs through the trailer and at that time was most likely accepted as a reasonable description by the majority of the intended American audience. There is always the danger of outsiders being unable to make sense of what they are seeing, and even when making an effort at cultural relativism, I still experience episodes of cultural ignorance. An industrial designer from California wrote a widely circulated blog post about his visit to Ise Jingū (Rose 2019). While I appreciated his intention to praise the long-term thinking of the shrine builders, there were many errors and cringe-inducing moments in his essay. One unfortunate description referred to the shrine office that offers *omamori* amulets as "a place that sells commemorative gifts." He later referred to it as a "gift shop" and *ema* votive plaques as "hand-screened prints on wood." While writing this book, I worried that the material might feed into the hard-wired ethnocentrism that never seems to dissipate. I fretted about how to write my views on religious and occult subjects without falling into the "weird Japan" trap.

There is a rich scholarship on the problem of orientalism in media and perceptions of Japan. Wagenaar (2016) suggests that another bias has joined traditional orientalisms (Zen aesthetics, geisha, samurai) and techno-orientalism (cyborgs, robots). The new type of orientalism is seen in well-known media like WTF Japan YouTube videos: a fascination with woodblock prints featuring tentacle sex, Yoyogi Park rockabilly dancers, Christmas spent eating Kentucky Fried Chicken, and putative "rent-a-family" businesses.[8] Wagenaar calls this trope "wacky Japan." Spaeth (2020) mentions the general problem with journalistic Anglophone treatments of Japan that incline toward the weird: "In the Western imagination, Japan is rife with shut-ins, celibates, suicides, loners, and obsessive geeks. It is the place where the men fall in love with busty Power Rangers, and the women vanish like ghosts into the gloomy mist of the suicide forest." The entrenchment of interpretations that assume "weird Japan" came up in a Facebook post. A friend posted a photo of cookies shaped as human-like *haniwa* (Kofun-period clay figurines). One of their friends guessed it might be "some part of the penis festival," most likely imagining the Kanamara Matsuri. The festival originated in 1969 and features genitalia-themed foods and imagery that tourists and foreign media love to photograph. To me the cookies looked like a nice variation of a gingerbread man. An adage in anthropology is that the researcher's goal should be that of "making the familiar strange, and the strange familiar" (Spiro 1990, 49). In an effort to avoid contributing to the weird Japan discourse, my discussion of *reifu* paper charms, *magatama* bead veneration, and other occult pursuits were embedded within their respective cultural and historical contexts. The aim was to enable understanding of occult hunting as meaningful for people with their own concepts and cosmologies. By locating material religion and supernatural pursuits within a world of graspable meanings, *Occult Hunting* has presented logical adaptations based on female interests and aesthetics, linking them to larger systems of meaning.

Notes

Introduction

1. In Japan studies the term "Five Elements" is often used for this concept based in the syncretic and native *onmyōdō* (the way of yin and yang). It should not be confused with the Buddhist term *godai,* which includes earth, water, fire, wind, and the void.

2. Other scholars of religion in Japan have also made this point (i.e., Shields 2010).

3. "Occult" was used by the American astronomer Percival Lowell (1894) in his traveler's account of esoteric mountain rituals in Japan. Mixed with his observations are ethnocentric speculations about the cognitive and emotional endowment of the Japanese. In his case, use of the term "occult" denotes illogical and primitive thinking.

4. Within many academic disciplines, a common term used for supernatural power is "mana," which was adopted from Melanesian and Polynesian settings.

5. For a cogent overview of recent studies on Shinto, see Thomas (2017). Bender (2016) discusses the hegemony of Buddhist perspectives in the study of early Japanese religions, especially in regard to a reluctance to name the early indigenous religion as Shinto.

6. Weber's essay was originally a speech, "Wissenschaft als Beruf," given at Munich University in 1918.

Chapter 1: Divination

1. Perhaps it is more accurate to call it the "refeminization" of divination because some of the earliest forms of divination are tied to ancient female shamans (see Kidder 2007).

2. A detailed description of their preparation and ritual process is found in Blacker (1981).

3. Examples of *futomani* mentioned in the Man'yōshū are in Naumann (1993).

4. At least two shrines conduct bone divination. Musashi Mitake Jinja in Ome City holds a *futomani matsuri* (animal bone divination festival) each year to determine crop success. It is not open to the public. It seems that the ritual is not very ancient at this shrine, with verification only going as far back as around 1830. At the Ichinomiya Nukisaki Jinja in Tomioka City, a priest performs *rokuboku* (deer scapula divination) during a ritual named *shikaura shinji.* It is to determine whether or not fires will occur in the area.

5. Divination by sorting (sortilege) itself has a precedent in *I Ching* divination, which is much older.

6. Aston (1908) appears to describe the book in his article on divination.

7. At Meiji Jingū, the *omikuji* have twenty *waka* composed by Emperor Meiji (1852–1912) and Empress Shōken (1849–1914).

8. A novel method is to use an Android application for daily *omikuji* on your cell phone. You may also get virtual ones online. After clicking on the link, you are taken to a screen

with a hexagonal *omikuji* cylinder between two shrine attendants. Soon a fortune appears! (Kaiun Omikuji, n.d.)

9. However, one shrine that provided Mandarin-language *omikuji* eventually stopped the practice. Yatsushirogū in Kumamoto Prefecture decided to end efforts to accommodate Chinese cruise ship tourists because they were too disruptive. The shrine closes on the days the ship docks (*Asahi shinbun* 2019).

10. An extensive compilation of *omikuji* information and types found at different shrines and temples is also found online at Omikuji Gaido (2019).

11. A different ancient type of divination had the same name, *mizuura* (water divination). A future prediction was based on a rope sent drifting down a river, where whether it floated or sank would indicate things such as when one would meet a lover.

12. The shrine's nickname is Tama no Koshi Jinja. It arose from an expression that means "to ride in a beautiful palanquin" but is clipped to suggest "marry a wealthy man." It derives from the story of a woman named Otama, who was a subsidiary wife of a Tokugawa leader. She contributed funds to the shrine.

13. Some shrines have tapped into the interest in *yōkai* (ghosts or goblins). Fudaten Jinja in Tokyo has *omikuji* illustrated with *yōkai* figures from the manga series *GeGeGe no Kitarō* by Mizuki Shigeru, and Takaosan Yakuōin Yūkiji has one decorated with cute *tengū*, a supernatural being with a long nose.

14. There is a long-standing dispute among Californian foodies about the origin of the fortune cookie. Jennifer Lee (2009) has shown that they are most likely based on the Japanese *tsujiura sembei* (divination crackers) once sold in Kyoto.

15. A YouTube of the Omikuji robot is at Amago Kiichi Channel (2015).

16. All the names used for those I interviewed or spoke to are pseudonyms.

17. Another animal system uses typical zoo creatures: gorilla, panda, elephant, penguin, giraffe, alligator, cheetah, polar bear, zebra, hippo, and owl (Primavera 2008). The seekers find their zoo type by consulting a chart that lists types by birth year and date.

18. However, in terms of worldwide distributions Japan is not unique in this regard. Among Latvians, Hungarian Rom, Egyptians, Persians, and other populations, the blood type frequencies are similar to those found in Japan.

19. There also is Endearing Divination, or *moe uranai*, which includes female icons such as Osaka Dialect Girl, Goddess, Literature Girl, Miss Maid, Magic Girl, and Shrine Attendant (Moe Uranai Seisaku Iinkai 2005).

Chapter 2: Occult Business

1. Osaka had an indoor theme park named Dōtonbori Gokuraku Shōtengai (now closed) that featured Taishō-era (1912–1926) recreations of stylized cafés and restaurants. On the fifth floor were several retro-style divination booths.

2. There was an interesting non-Japanese divination provider named M. Amin Kohi who dubbed himself the Shibuya no Papa (the Dad of Shibuya). His business card claimed he was a specialist in Silk Road divination, Persian astrology, palmistry, physiognomy, and tarot cards. His prices were extremely high.

3. Another author with a similar combo set is Taguchi (2002), who wrote *Abe no Seimei Cosmography Divination*.

Chapter 3: Tarot Cards

1. A video YouTuber who presents a persona as an anime maid provides a tarot layout and explains each card's meaning (Angelina Maid Channel 2019).

Chapter 4: Pilgrim Stamps

1. Unlike *goshuin*, some types of Buddhist inscriptions are mainly treated as objects of worship themselves, and as Dobbins (2020, 192) notes, "Historians point out that their popularization in Japan was not based on aesthetic qualities."

2. A collector of pilgrim stamps has a blog that includes images of stamps from the Edo period (Murakami 2022). The sutra receipt from Higashi Betsuin's collection in Fukui, dated 1795, looks very much like one of today's *goshuin* stamps.

3. In the late 1970s, I studied calligraphy with Abe-sensei when I lived in Nishinomiya. I did not pursue further training afterward but retained a lifelong interest in it as a scholar and learner-practitioner.

4. I appreciated the feedback from Marc L. Moskowitz.

5. The mascot designed for Wakeoe Jinja named Bekki-chan has a theme song. A video from the shrine's YouTube channel includes the song and imagery of the mascot (Wakeoe Jinja 2019).

6. In 2017 the town created Yukimaru Skywalker, a mechanical drone puppy that soars over the landscape (Kazuki Tanaka 2021).

7. Thanks to Kathryn Ugoretz for bringing this version to my attention.

8. There are hundreds of polls on *goshuin* rankings on the internet, published by magazines and specialized groups. They are mostly idiosyncratic or focused on the Tokyo area. For example, it is not surprising that some of the shrine organizations list Meiji Jingū as the number one stamp.

9. Thanks to Kathryn Ugoretz for alerting me to this (Momiji Hachimangū 2022).

10. An unexpected appropriation of the pilgrim stamp concept is the train station lunch box pilgrim stamp (*ekiben goshuin*). Niigata Prefecture began the promotion at the end of 2021: The collector visits seven stations to get a stamp in a special commemorative booklet (Mochizuki 2021). The lunch box pilgrims visit seven shops that sell the local train station lunch and either stamp their own books or ask a clerk to do it. The beautifully designed retro stamps for the box lunch in Minamiuonuma feature a cow representing the local Sakurai Japanese cattle breed.

11. Another riff on the idea of the pilgrim stamp targets visitors to the ancient earthen tombs called *kofun*. This type of stamp is called *gofuin*.

12. Ushi-Tenjin Kitano Shrine in Tokyo stopped offering single-sheet pilgrim stamps because of online resales (they continue to do regular in-person calligraphy and stamps).

Chapter 5: Taoist Paper Talismans

1. Yamashita (2012, 87) links these Taoist strands with esoteric Buddhist Mikkyō (Shingon and Tendai).

2. Kim (2022) asserts that Chintaku reifu were borrowed directly from China prior to the *onmyōdō* tradition in Japan.

3. A nicely produced promotional video, including an "image song," was created for Hoshida Myōken-Gū by New Age musical artist Kamimura Shigezo (2015).

4. *Ofuda* may have their origin in the talismans that had the word *monoimi* (abstinence or confinement) written on them and which were hung on gates of residences during the Heian era (Iwai 2007).

5. Onmyōji Miko appears to have shut down her business. Matsu Rika-sensei is in the online menu of specialists at Sutā Supirichuaru (n.d.).

6. *Bonji* is found on some *omamori* amulets at Buddhist temples such as Nankokuji and Sensōji in Tokyo.

7. Perhaps the dramatic pose of characters holding the *reifu* is an extension of the way characters in other popular culture media hold swords, weapons, or other objects thrust forward. Thanks to Steve Covell for this observation.

8. Fans of the Inuyasha manga series might notice similarities with the paper slips adorned with messy pseudo-writing that the monk Miroku uses to stop demons. Miroku is introduced in Takahsahi (2010).

Chapter 6: Votive Tablets and Amulets

1. I appreciated that fellow anthropologists James Roberson and Gordon Mathews accompanied me on this outing.

2. A photo taken at Kigandō of an *ema* for petitioning for abundant lactation was used in L. Miller (2006, 98).

3. The owners closed the Yūshima shop and reopened in Yanaka with the new name Emadō.

4. *O-ema* means "big *ema*" and is not the same as the honorific marker *o-*.

5. Perhaps there is one type of enthusiast who is not very welcome at shrines and temples—the bring-your-own *ema* traveler. Bureaucrats at Kiyomizu-dera in Kyoto were unhappy when counterfeit *ema* turned up on their *ema* stands (*Kyoto shinbun* 2015). These "BYO *ema*" had Chinese writing on them and were apparently being brought to the site by Chinese tourists.

6. Other shrines offer similarly interactive *ema*. A complete-your-own *ema* type is found at Tsuyu no Tenjinsha in Osaka. The shrine is linked to a tale about a sex worker named Ohatsu and an apprentice trader named Tokubei who committed a double suicide at the shrine in 1703. On the *ema* visitors draw in the eyebrows, lips, noses, freckles, glasses, and other traits. In defiance of the sad tale, most of the completed drawing are humorous or intentionally homely.

7. The film was about an Italian girl searching for her missing fiancé near Poltava, Ukraine (De Sica 1970).

8. I once saw what was inside an *omamori* in an appalling manner. I was at a conference at the University of Nebraska not long after the September 11, 2001, attack by terrorists. I was returning home on the same plane as a friend from Japan. At the Transportation Security Agency checkpoint, the officer searched inside her purse and found an *omamori*. He ripped it open and pulled out the contents. We stood there in shock at this malicious act of desecration. Did he expect to find explosives inside the dainty brocade pouch that measured less than two and a half inches long?

9. On other *omamori*, Hello Kitty is represented by a folk dancer (Hirota Jinja in Aomori) or shown holding a fish (Nishiki Tenmangū in Kyoto).

10. The blog site does not provide any information about the author, but it is clearly a native speaker of English outside Japan. The author said they needed to use Wikipedia to describe *omamori*.

11. Secular *omamori* packaging is common. The candy brand KitKat created an *omamori*-like pack that includes a pouch for a personal message.

12. Perhaps a double meaning was intended? *Chōzetsu* also means transcendental, thus "transcendental cuteness" for a transgender person.

13. An example is a romance manga written for a female audience titled *The Devilish Boy Next Door* (Moto 2009). A female character named Ai obtains an *omamori* in the hopes that it will attract a boyfriend.

14. The *omamori* theme is also found in men's soft pornography manga (Ōishi 2012).

Chapter 7: Precious Curved Beads

1. Kidder (2007, 261) wonders if a few of the Nara bead-makers were recruited from Izumo.

2. There are many versions of *The Pillow Book*, and the two main lineages are the Nōinbon and the Sankanbon (Ivanova 2018, 21). The reference to the three *onsen* is only found in the Nōinbon version in section 117 (Matsuo and Kazuko 2008, 486). Thanks to Edward Kamens and Gergana Ivanova for helping me track down this information.

3. Smyers (1999, 24) reports that Suzuki's father visited Korea to learn more about shared *magatama* culture.

4. The name is also found in an American glossary of pottery terms published in 1898: "Magatama tsubo. Very ancient vases, found in Japanese tombs" (Jewelers Circular Publication Company 1898).

5. Today the deity Tamanoya is also in charge of glasses and cameras.

6. The Chinese bronze mirrors found at Kofun-era sites are notable because of the ability to date them. It is thought that the disbursement of mirrors from the Miwa court to peripheral chieftains was a crucial strategy for creating political alliances in the early Kofun period (Kidder 2007).

7. In the *Nihon shoki*, Emperor Tenmu (ca. 631–686) asked to have the sword moved out of the Imperial Palace to Atsuta Jinja because its great supernatural power was causing harm. According to a later account in the *Heike Monogatari*, a collection of oral stories assembled sometime before 1330, it disappeared beneath the waves of the sea during a historic battle. Despite this version of the sword's fate, its presence at Atsuta Shrine is commonly accepted.

8. The official webpage of Itoigawa City (n.d.) lists numerous legends about Nunakawa from local gazettes and other sources.

9. Masako's *magatama* were somewhat expensive but not exorbitant, unlike an online shop named Kamakura Hijiriishi Sacred Stones (n.d.). It sells a special line of twenty-five *magatama*, including one designated as "Himiko." Each is presented in a beautiful cypress box, similar to the way high-end art objects are packaged. The more expensive ones are around ¥270,000. The less expensive model is a light-green *magatama* strung from a brown macramé cord together with a white bead. The contextualizing text states that this item has strong "yang energy" and that it reflects the "heart and soul of the Japanese from that which is handcrafted by Japanese."

10. To protect themselves against a type of aquatic doppelgänger goblin, Ama shellfish divers in Shima would use the two symbols associated with two Heian-period wizards, Abe no Seimei and the Ashiya Dōman, usually shortened to Seiman Dōman. Now it is popular on tourist goods such as towels and charm straps. Some shops sell a charm that is a red carnelian *magatama* strap with the Seiman Dōman inscribed on it in gold. The Seiman Dōman symbol works well on towels and other textiles but lacks pizazz on cell phone straps, so the addition of the *magatama* gives it a needed boost.

11. *Magatama* also appear in a divination card deck named Kamisama Cards (Ōno 2008). Ōno's oracle cards are used for divination and represent deities from the *Kojiki*. The deity of *magatama*, Tamanoya, has his own card.

12. The shop Magatama no Wa (2012), for example, dates *magatama* from the Yayoi period only.

13. The monster's name is derived from the word for "turtle" (*kame*) together with the *-ra* suffix, a morpheme found in other monster names such as Gojira (Godzilla), Mosura (Mothra), and Gidora (Ghidorah).

14. The Mon Reve bakery in Moriyama, Shiga Prefecture, churns out *magatama* cookies during the summer in conjunction with a local campaign honoring Himiko (L. Miller 2018).

15. The Menōya Shingū company later opened stores in numerous locations around Japan, many with the name Anahita Stones (2023). Anahita is the name for a Persian goddess. It also has links to the Denshōkan.

16. Most resort towns have made similar efforts. There are numerous studies of tourism in Japan and how it shapes the way traditional inns (*ryōkan*) are structured and operated. McMorran's (2022) ethnographic research was especially sensitive and insightful.

17. Some months later, Murata mailed me some beautiful green jasper *magatama* that he had made to commemorate our visit.

18. Occult hunters who visit this shrine are also interested in a different stone. This is the large round Negai Ishi (Granting Stone) found in the precincts. Prior to asking for their wish at the Negai Ishi, the visitor obtains an envelope from the shrine office that will contain a small "wishing" stone, a small amulet pouch, and two prayer sheets.

19. Denoting "ancient Japan" as well as imperial patriarchy, a blue *magatama* adorns the cover of a modern translation of the *Kojiki* by a nationalistic writer and defender of male-only imperial succession (Takeda 2011).

Chapter 8: Powerspots

1. *Tenchūsatsu* is an unlucky time in four pillar divination (*shichūsuimei*). It is slightly different from the better-known *yakudoshi* (inauspicious year) based on the Chinese zodiac.

2. I presented an early version of this chapter at the American Anthropological Association Annual Meeting, Chicago, in 2013.

3. Personal communication from Genevieve Sawicz.

4. An example is the elevator girl occupation (L. Miller 2013).

5. In 2019, a fire destroyed nine structures at the Shuri Castle site. Ongoing reconstruction has been in progress since 2022.

6. However, this amulet was not available when I visited in 2019.

7. The forested area around Ise Jingū was replanted and rejuvenated in the 1950s because visitors had raided the trees for firewood (Omura 2002, 181).

8. Tsukada and Ōmi (2011) share other polls on powerspots but only for responses given to the question "Do you believe in powerspots?"

9. The powerspot circuit pilgrimage sites were Tokyo Daijingū, Meiji Jingū, Imado Jinja, the Tokyo branch of the Izumo Taisha, and Hie Jinja.

10. There are other subshrines in the Kurumazaki Jinja precincts in addition to the Geinō Jinjia (Tatusumi Inari Jinja, Benten Jinja, Ōkuninushi Jinja, and more).

11. It should be noted that unlike Kakure Kirishitan, the underground Christians still found in or near Nagasaki, no Christians lived in Shingō at any point in the village's history (Okamoto 2019, 107).

12. Imado Jinja also has a weak association with the cultural hero Okita Sōji (ca. 1842–1868), a member of the famed Shinsengumi police force. At the shrine is a stele commemorating his death. He died while staying with an associate who lived in a temporary residence in the shrine grounds.

13. The old district of San'ya was split up and renamed Higashi Asakusa, Nihonzutsumi, and Kiyokawa. Descriptions of the day laborers who once lived in San'ya are found in Fowler (1996).

14. For more history and descriptions of female religious, see Ambros (2015).

15. A discussion of the reasons there are so few female Shinto priests is found in Hardacre (2016, 523), who notes that because of demographic changes it is estimated that the number of female Shinto priests will gradually increase in the coming years.

16. Including Ehara Hideyoshi, who visited Imado Shrine on February 24, 2009.

17. The same is true for linguistic changes in standard language, which are often inspired by innovative forms created in female youth dialects but later attributed to male copywriters (L. Miller 2004).

Conclusion

1. As of 2021, Strawberry Nice was still in business, as were around nine other shops.

2. See also Gaitanidis (2022).

3. The *Miyazaki nichinichi shinbun* (2021) provides the reading for the Chinese characters as *hana temizu*, but most often it is read as *hana chōzu*.

4. In addition to Amabie, the pandemic also renewed interest in the figure of Tsuno Daishi, an avatar of the tenth-century Buddhist priest Ryōgen. Paper amulets bearing the image of Tsuno Daishi are posted outside one's home to prevent disease.

5. Thanks to Cody Poulton for sharing information about the Amabie cell phone cleaner.

6. Isahaya Jinja (2020) began offering an online downloadable papercraft figure of Amabie for free in order to address "anxiety about what you can't see."

7. The Amabie pilgrim stamps are ranked in popularity (Goshuin/Jinja Memo 2020).

8. It was later revealed that the *New Yorker* was duped into reporting on a nonexistent "rent-a-family" industry in Japan (Spaeth 2020).

References

Afro Fukuoka. 2016. "JR Kyūshū-san ni kiku! #02 Kanizaki eki" (Let's ask Mr. JR Kyūshū! Number 2: Kanizaki Station). April 28. Accessed July 21, 2021. https://afro fukuoka .net/archives/trivia/vol2/2.

Akatsuki Reika and Aya Takano. 2010. *Supirichuaru tarotto nyūmon: Ketteiban* (A spiritual tarot primer: The definitive edition). Tokyo: Shufu no tomosha.

Alexy, Allison, and Emma E. Cook, eds. 2019. *Intimate Japan: Ethnographies of Closeness and Conflict.* Honolulu: University of Hawai'i Press.

Allison, Anne. 2013. *Precarious Japan.* Durham, NC: Duke University Press.

Alt, Matt. 2020. "From Japan, a Mascot for the Pandemic." *New Yorker,* April 9. Accessed January 26, 2022. https://www.newyorker.com/culture/cultural-comment/from -japan-a-mascot-for-the-pandemic.

Amago Kiichi Channel. 2015. "Paper Fortune Robot: Kurosaki-eki omikuji robatto" (The Kurosaki station paper fortune robot). YouTube video, 1.37. September 20. Accessed July 21, 2021. https://www.youtube.com/watch?v=IBFP72UYtgw.

Amamiya Miko, Mimika Itō, Kaya Uesugi, Tamago Uno, Nanami Kamon, Taimu Zenigata, Reiko Terao, Nami Himuro, Kyōko Mafune, and Sarukoro Mizutan. 2017. *Pawā supotto no arukikata: Kyōto Nara hen* (How to walk the powerspots: Kyoto and Nara areas). Tokyo: Asahi Shinbun shuppan.

Ambros, Barbara. 2006. "Geography, Environment, Pilgrimages." In *Nanzan Guide to Japanese Religions,* edited by Paul Swanson and Clark Chilson, 289–308. Honolulu: University of Hawai'i Press.

———. 2015. *Women in Japanese Religions.* New York: New York University Press.

Anahita Stones. 2023. Website for agate and semiprecious stone products. Accessed May 22, 2023. https://www.anahitastones.com.

Anderson, Richard W. 2002. "Jingū Kōgō 'Ema' in Southwestern Japan: Reflections and Anticipations of the 'Seikanron' Debate in the Late Tokugawa and Early Meiji Period." *Asian Folklore Studies* 61 (2): 247–270.

Andō Kenji. 2019. "Asuka Jinja ga 'Sanja Matsuri' no tokubutsu goshuin o hanpu chūshi ni" (Asakusa Shrine discontinues the distribution of special pilgrim stamps for the "Sanja Festival"). *HuffPost Japan,* May 13. Accessed January 26, 2022. https://www.huffingtonpost.jp/entry/goshuin_jp_5cd8df80e4b054da4e8bab80.

Angelina Maid Channel. 2019. "Tarotto uranai" (Tarot divination). YouTube video, 9.25. December 31. Accessed March 13, 2022. https://www.youtube.com/watch?v =tHX6hwYgp2o.

Aoki, Michiko. 1997. *Records of Wind and Earth: A Translation of Fudoki, with Introduction and Commentaries.* Monographs and Occasional Paper Series 53. Ann Arbor, MI: Association of Asian Studies.

Aoyama, Tomoko. 2018. "Ame no Uzume Crosses Boundaries." In *Diva Nation: Female Icons from Japanese Cultural History*, edited by Laura Miller and Rebecca Copeland, 34–50. Berkeley: University of California Press.

Arichi, Meri. 2006. "Seven Stars of Heaven and Seven Shrines on Earth: The Big Dipper and the Hie Shrine in the Medieval Period." *Culture and Cosmos* 10 (1): 195–216.

Asahi shinbun. 2019. "Bad Behavior Forces Facilities to Reject Foreign Group Tourists." March 5. Accessed June 14, 2019. http://www.asahi.com/ajw/articles/AJ2019030 50001.html.

Asami Hohoko. 2007. *Uranai o doko made shinjite imasu ka?* (How far will you take your belief in divination?). Tokyo: Gentōsha.

Ashikaga, Ensho. 1954. "Votive Pictures: A Japanese Superstition." *Western Folklore* 13 (1): 29–33.

ASNetworks. 2007. Fujimori Midori no Let's tarotto (Fujimori Midori's *Let's Tarot*). Nintendo DS game. Saitama: ASNetworks.

Aston, William G. 1908. "A Japanese Book of Divination." *Man* 8:116–120.

BAB Japan, ed. 2011. "Tarotto no kai ga watashitachi ni tsutaeru" (What the tarot community can convey to us). In *Kokoro to karada o iyasu: Serapii ōru gaido* (Healing the heart and the body: Complete therapy guide), 15–19. Tokyo: BAB Japan.

Bado-Fralick, Nikki, and Rebecca Sachs Norris. 2010. *Toying with God: The World of Religious Games and Dolls*. Waco: Baylor University Press.

Ban Nobutomo. 1903. *Seibokukō* (Lecture on divination). Vol. 1. First published in 1858. Kyoto: Hayashi Yoshibē. National Diet Library Digital Collection. Accessed June 4, 2023. https://dl.ndl.go.jp/pid/760504/1/59.

Barnes, Gina. 2001. "Ritualized Beadstone in Kofun-Period Society." Paper presented at "Man, Nature, and Art," British Museum, September 6–8.

Barnhart, Richard. 1972. "Chinese Calligraphy: The Inner World of the Brush." *Metropolitan Museum of Art Bulletin*, n.s., 30 (5): 230–241.

Becker, Howard S. 1998. *Tricks of the Trade: How to Think about Your Research While You're Doing It*. Chicago: University of Chicago Press.

Bender, Ross. 2016. "Shinto in Nara Japan, 749–770: Deities, Priests, Offerings, Prayers, and Edicts in Shoku Nihongi." PMLS Papers: Premodern Japanese Studies, November. Accessed June 15. http://www.meijigakuin.ac.jp/~pmjs/papers/.

Bi Anjeri and Saki Umezawa. 2004. *Anjeri no yasashii tarotto nyūmon* (Anjeri's simple tarot manual). Tokyo: Interwork.

Biggest Trailer DataBase. 2020. "The Barbarian and The Geisha (1958) Theatrical Trailer." YouTube video, 2:53. December 18. https://www.youtube.com/watch?v =-myaBC1ux0A.

Blacker, Carmen. 1975. *The Catalpa Bow: A Study of Shamanistic Practices in Japan*. London: George Allen & Unwin.

———. 1981. "Japan." In *Divination and Oracles*, edited by Michael Loewe and Carmen Blacker, 63–86. Boston: George Allen & Unwin.

Bornoff, Nicholas, and Michael Freeman. 2014. *Things Japanese: Everyday Objects of Exceptional Beauty and Significance*. Clarendon, VT: Tuttle.

Brasor, Phillip. 2006. "Weekly Magazines Joust over Trillion-Yen Fortune Telling Trade." *Japan Times*, March 12.

Brasor, Philip, and Masako Tsubuku. 2011. "Heal Me: Spirituality Business Redefining Religion." *Japan Times*, September 15. Accessed July 23, 2019. https://www

.japantimes.co.jp/news/2011/09/15/business/heal-me-spirituality-businesses-redefining-religion/#.XVg7DkdOmAY.

Brinkley, Frank. 1902. *Japan, Its History, Arts and Literature,* Vol. 7. Boston: J. B. Millet.

Bryant, Page. 1983. *The Earth Changes Survival Handbook.* Correlated by Eva Prang. Albuquerque: Sun Books.

Bunkasha Komikkusu, ed. 2006. *Uranai no karisuma! Shinjuku no haha no sōzetsu jinsei dorama* (Divination charisma! The heroic life of the Shinjuku Mother). Multiauthor comic anthology. Tokyo: Bunkasha.

Burarinko. 2020. "Daikakuji no omamori & goshuin" (The amulets and pilgrim stamps at Daikakuji). *Kyōto Burari Sanpo & Gurume Techō* (blog). (Strolling around Kyoto & gourmet notebook). July 26. Accessed September 24, 2021. https://www.kyotowalk-gourmet.com/entry/daikakuji_omamori.

Carter, Caleb. 2018. "Power Spots and the Charged Landscape of Shinto." *Japanese Journal of Religious Studies* 45(1): 45–73.

Cavanaugh, Jillian R., and Shalini Shankar, eds. 2017. *Language and Materiality: Ethnographic and Theoretical Explorations.* Cambridge: Cambridge University Press.

Collins, Kevin. 1997. "Seizing Spirits: The Chinkon Ritual and Early Japanese Literature." PhD diss., Department of East Asian Literatures and Cultures, Columbia University.

Darumaji. 2022. *Yukimaru no goshuin* (Yukimaru pilgrim stamp). Shrine website. Accessed February 21, 2022. https://www.darumaji.jp/infoDetail.html?id=21.

Dein, Simon. 2016. "The Category of the Supernatural: A Valid Anthropological Term?" *Religion Compass* 10 (2): 35–44.

De Sica, Vittorio. 1970. *I Girasoli* (Sunflower). Feature film. Rome: Compagnia Cinematografica Champion.

DeSmet, Peter A. G. M., and Ian Reader. 2017. *Health-Related Votive Tablets from Japan: Ema for Healing and Well-Being.* Leiden: Leiden University Press.

Dobbins, James C. 2020. *Behold the Buddha: Religious Meanings of Japanese Buddhist Icons.* Honolulu: University of Hawai'i Press.

Dorman, Benjamin. 2007. "Representing Ancestor Worship as 'Non-religious': Hosoki Kazuko's Divination in the Post-Aum Era." *Nova Religio: The Journal of Alternative and Emergent Religions* 10 (3): 32–47.

———. 2016. "Spiritual Tourists and Local Healers at a Hawaiian Power Spot." *Bulletin of the Nanzan Institute for Religion and Culture* 40:90–103.

Drexler, Monika. 1994. *Daoistische Schriftmagie: Interpretationen zu den Schriftamuletten Fu im Daozang* (Daoist writing magic: Interpretations of the Fu amulets in the Daozang). Stuttgart: Steiner.

Drixler, Fabian. 2013. *Mabiki: Infanticide and Population Growth in Eastern Japan, 1660–1950.* Berkeley: University of California Press.

Ebersole, Gary L. 1999. "Tama Belief and Practice in Ancient Japan." In *Religions of Japan in Practice,* edited by George J. Tanabe, 141–152. Princeton, NJ: Princeton University Press.

egg. 2007a. "Animaru tōku" (Animal talk), 124:102.

———. "Model 11," 124:31.

Ehara Hiroyuki. 2005. *Kami kikō 2: Shikoku, Izumo, Hiroshima* (Deity travelogue 2: Shikoku, Izumo, Hiroshima). Supirichuaru sankuchuari shirīzu (Spiritual sanctuary series). Tokyo: Magajin hausu.

———. 2006. *Kami kikō 2: Kyōto* (Deity travelogue 3: Kyoto). Supirichuaru sankuchuari shirīzu (Spiritual sanctuary series). Tokyo: Magajin hausu.

———. 2015. *Jibun no ie o pawā supotto ni kaeru saikyō no rūru 46* (46 ultimate rules to change your own home into a powerspot). Tokyo: Shōgakukan.

Eller, Jack David. 2007. *Introducing Anthropology of Religion.* London: Routledge.

Eno, Brian, and Peter Schwalm. 2002. *Music for Onmyōji.* Music CD. Yokohama: JVC Victor.

En Tenshoku. 2017. *Jinja ya otera omamori no kikaku eigyō* (Shrine or temple amulet project planning business). Accessed July 28, 2021. https://employment.en-japan.com/desc_811244/?aroute=6&arearoute=1&PK=E39604.

Eubanks, Charlotte. 2013. "Reading by Heart: Translated Buddhism and the Pictorial Heart Sutras of Early Modern Japan." *International Journal of the Sociology of Language* 220:7–25.

Figal, Gerald. 1999. *Civilization and Monsters: Spirits of Modernity in Meiji Japan.* Durham, NC: Duke University Press.

Fleming, Benjamin, and Richard Mann, eds. 2014. *Material Culture and Asian Religions: Text, Image, Object.* New York: Routledge.

Fowler, Edward. 1996. *San'ya Blues: Laboring Life in Contemporary Japan.* Ithaca, NY: Cornell University Press.

Fujimori Midori. 2008. *Hajimete no hito no tame no rakuraku tarotto nyūmon* (Easy introduction to tarot for first-time users). Tokyo: Setsuwasha.

Fuji TV. 2006. "Shinjuku no haha monogatari" (The tale of Shinjuku Mother). *Kin'yōbi puresutēji* (Friday prestige). TV Drama. Aired December 22, 9:00 p.m. to 10:52 p.m.

Fujiwara, Satoko. 2019. "Practicing Belonging? Non-religiousness in Twenty-First Century Japan." *Journal of Religion in Japan* 8 (1–3): 123–150.

Futabasha, ed. 2012. *Yomigaeru edo* (Reanimated Edo). Tokyo: Futabasha.

Gaitanidis, Ioannis. 2022. *Spirituality and Alternativity in Contemporary Japan: Beyond Religion?* London: Bloomsbury Academic.

Gakushū Kenkyūsha Plus. 2019. *Hajimete no gojōin gaido* (The first castle stamp book guide). Tokyo: Gakushū kenkyūsha.

Gandamu Uranai Chō Seisaku Iinkai. 2001. *Chō! Gandamu uranai* (Super! Gundam divination). Tokyo: Wani Books.

Goodman, Barak, dir. 2001. *The Merchants of Cool.* Documentary. Arlington, VA: Public Broadcasting Service.

Goo Research. 2010. "Tekichūritsu ga takai to omou uranai ranking" (Rankings for divination we think has the highest predictive value). Accessed December 11, 2011. http://ranking.goo.ne.jp/ranking/010/fortune_cometrue_2010/.

———. 2011. "Yatte mitai netto urani ranking" (Ranking of divination I'd like to try). Accessed December 11, 2011. http://ranking.goo.ne.jp/ranking/010/net_uranai/.

Goshirakawa Anju. 2019. *Kamakura goshuin gāru* (Kamakura pilgrim stamp girl). Tokyo: Shūeisha.

Goshuin/Jinja Memo. 2020. "Amabie no goshuin ranking" (Ranking of Amabie pilgrim stamps). Minna no ranking (Everyone's ranking). October 29. Accessed May 10, 2023. https://ranking.net/rankings/maker-3114ca/f5bacd76.

Gyappu Japan. 2010. *Fortune guide book: Nayamera otona joshi no kaiun ōru gaido* (Complete good luck guide for worried adult women). Tokyo: Gyappu Japan.

Hall, Jenny. 2020. *Japan Beyond the Kimono: Innovation and Tradition in the Kyoto Textile Industry.* London: Bloomsbury.

Hamada Kōsaku, Sadahiko Shimada, and Sueji Umehara. 1927. "Izumo ni okeru jōdai tamatsukuri no iseki to ibutsu no kenkyū" (Studies on the sites and remains of the ancient bead-workers in Izumo). With ten-page English summary. *Kyōtō Teikoku Daigaku Bungakubu kōkogaku kenkyū hōkoku* 10:1–78.

Hanai, Toru. 2017. "Tomoe Ichino." *Women at Work around the World.* Reuters the Wider Image, March 8. Accessed July 10, 2019. https://widerimage.reuters.com/story/women-at-work-around-the-world.

Hara Chieko. 2018. "Mihiraki 3-men, dohakuryoku no goshuin" (Three-page spread, impactful pilgrim stamps). *Asahi shinbun digital,* May 21. Accessed January 16, 2022. https://www.asahi.com/articles/ASL586F66L58OIPE036.html.

Harada Minoru. 2008. *Zusetsu jindai moji nyūmon: Yomeru kakeru tsukaeru* (Introduction to illustrated script of the age of the deities: Readable, writable, and usable). Tokyo: Biingu netto puresu.

Hardacre, Helen. 2016. *Shinto: A History.* Oxford: Oxford University Press.

Hashimoto Kyōmei. 2016. *Onmyō senjutsu* (Yin-yang divination). Tokyo: Taibundō.

Hatanaka Mioko. 2003. *Tōkyō goriyaku sanpo shichifukujin meguri* (Seven Lucky Deities Pilgrimage, walking for spiritual benefit in Tokyo). Tokyo: Heibonsha.

Hayami Yoku and Junji Koyanagi. 2003. *Gōsuto basutā Abe no Seimei* (Ghost buster Abe no Seimei). Tokyo: Gakushū kenkyūsha.

Hayashi, Toshiyuki. 2015. "Animal Bone May Have Told Fortunes in Third-Century Japan." *Archaeology,* February 9. Accessed March 21, 2022. https://www.archaeology.org/news/2970-150209-japan-fortune-telling.

Heine, Steven. 2012. *Sacred High City, Sacred Low City: A Tale of Religious Sites in Two Tokyo Neighborhoods.* Oxford: Oxford University Press.

Hieda On Mayura. 1994. *Nikui otoko, iya na jōshi no noroi-kata oshiemasu* (I'll teach you the way of cursing a difficult guy or obnoxious boss). Tokyo: Tokuma shoten.

———. 2012. "Kōshiki kontentsu 'genzai ni yomigaerishi Himiko Hieda On Mayura'" (Official Content: "Hieda On Mayura, Himiko resurrected in our time"). *Uranai-shi Hieda On Mayura Jimusho renraku-ban* (blog). February 28. Accessed May 10, 2023. http://ommayurahieda.cocolog-nifty.com/blog/cat23363438/index.html.

Himiko Rōzu. 2013. *Za mira tarotto* (The mirror tarot). Tokyo: Jitsugyo no Nihonsha.

Himuro Nami. 2010. *Tarotto uōzu 1* (Tarot wars 1). Tokyo: Hōmusha.

Hirata Jinja. 2022. Accessed May 10, 2023. http://hirata-jinja.org/.

Hiroshima keizai shinbun. 2021. Hiroshima, Miyajima ni kiri-e 'goshuin' Daishōin ga sūryō gentei de (In Hiroshima, Miyajima papercut 'pilgrim stamp': Limited edition at Daishōin). July 20. Accessed February 6, 2022. https://hiroshima.keizai.biz/headline/3561/.

Hirota Chieko. 2008. *Shitte iru to ureshī Nihon no engimono* (I'm happy I got to know Japan's lucky charms). Tokyo: Tokuma shoten.

Hirota, Ryūhe. 2021. "Traversing the Natural, Supernatural, and Paranormal Yōkai in Postwar Japan." *Japanese Journal of Religious Studies* 48 (2): 321–339.

Holtom, Daniel Clarence. 1928. *The Japanese Enthronement Ceremonies with an Account of the Imperial Regalia.* Tokyo: Kyo Bun Kwan.

———. 1938. "Japanese Votive Pictures (The Ikoma Ema)." *Monumenta Nipponica* 1 (1): 154–164.

Honda Ishirō, dir. 1954. *Gojira* (Godzilla). Tokyo: Tōhō.

Hori, Ichiro. 1968. *Folk Religion in Japan: Continuity and Change.* Chicago: University of Chicago Press.

Horie, Norichika. 2017. "The Making of Power Spots: From New Age Spirituality to Shinto Spirituality." In *Eastspirit: Transnational Spirituality and Religious Circulation,* edited by Jorn Borup and Marianne Qvortrup Fibiger, 192–217. Leiden: Brill.

———. 2018. "Dentō kaiki? Soretomo chihō shōmetsu?" (Regressing to tradition? Or perhaps the vanishing rural?). In *Gendai Nihon no shūkyō jijō* (The status of religion in contemporary Japan), edited by Horie Norichika, 25–34. Tokyo: Iwanami shoten.

Horiuchi Katsuhiko. 2012. "Hajimete no goshuin" (Our first pilgrim stamps). *Kaiunchō,* June, 32–38.

Hoshi Saori and Yūichirō Satō. 2013. *Aisare gāru no gaikotsu tarotto: Happī ōra o te ni ireru* (The Loveable Girl's Skeleton Tarot: A happy aura in your hands). Tokyo: Tōhō shuppan.

Hoshida Yoshiko, dir. 2006. *Shinjuku no haha monogatari* (The tale of Shinjuku Mother). *Kin'yōbi Puresutēji* (Friday prestige). TV Drama. Aired December 22, 9:00 p.m. to 10:52 p.m. Fuji TV.

Hoshino, Eiki. 2007. "Current Increase in Walking Pilgrims." In *Pilgrimages and Spiritual Quests in Japan,* edited by Maria Rodríguez del Alisal, Peter Ackerman, and Dolores P. Martinez, 65–83. New York: Routledge.

Hughes, Felicity. 2010. "Power Spots: Japan's Latest Spiritual Craze." *Japan Times,* September 2. Accessed December 10, 2018. https://www.japantimes.co.jp/news/2010/09/02/national/media-national/power-spots-japans-latest-spiritual-craze/#XVk6IuNKiAY.

Hultkrantz, Ake. 1983. "The Concept of the Supernatural in Primal Religion." *History of Religions* 22 (3):231–53.

Huston, John, dir. 1958. *The Barbarian and the Geisha.* Feature film. Los Angeles: 20th Century Fox Studios. Movie trailer. Accessed March 2, 2002. https://www.youtube.com/watch?v=-myaBC1ux0A.

Ibaraki shinbun dōga nyūzu. 2020. *Ibaraki goshuin meguri, Omitama Soga Jinja* (Ibaraki pilgrim stamp tour, Omitama Soga Shrine). YouTube video, 1.41. July 3. Accessed December 16, 2021. https://www.youtube.com/watch?v=Y-9yAL2XYuE.

Ichino Tomoe. 2010. *Imado Jinja shinshoku Ichino Tomoe ga susumeru shiawase o yobu pawā supotto* (The priest of Imada Shine Tomoe Ichino recommends powerspots that will bring you happiness). Tokyo: Futabasha.

———. 2013. "Oshirase" (Notification). *Ichino Tomoe Burogu* (Ichino Tomoe blog). December 11. Accessed December 15, 2020. http://imado.blog40.fc2.com/blog-date-201312.html.

———. 2014. *Imado jinja no bijin kannushi ga oshieru shiawase o jūbai yobikomu mainichi no shosa* (Imado shrine's beautiful Shinto priest teaches ten daily behaviors for inducing happiness). Tokyo: Gakken.

Idol Formerly Known as Ladybaby. 2016. *Sampai! Goshuin girl* (Worship! Pilgrim stamp girl). Music CD. Tokyo: King Records.

Igarashi Yasuhiko. 2010. *Sokkō mimi pawā supotto to bi daietto* (Speedy! Hearing powerspot and beauty diet). Tokyo: Seihōdō.

Ikkojin Henshūbu, ed. 2010. *Kaiun nihon no pawā supotto annai* (Information on Japan's good fortune powerspots). Tokyo: Besuto Serāzu.

Imahashi, Rurika. 2023. "Japan Logs 3.8m Visitors for 2022, 15 Times More than 2021." *Nikkei Asia,* January 18. Accessed May 10, 2023. https://asia.nikkei.com/Business/Travel-Leisure/Japan-logs-3.8m-visitors-for-2022-15-times-more-than-2021.

Inomata, Ryūichi. 2010. *Shodō gāruzu: Watashitachi no Kōshien* (Calligraphy girls: Our Kōshien). Feature film. Tokyo: Nippon TV.

Isahaya Jinja. 2020. "Nihon ichi no 'Amabie-sama' mokuzō, hōnō" (Japan's No. 1 "Amabie-sama" wooden statue, dedication). *Isahaya Jinja* [blog]. Accessed March 26, 2022. https://isahaya-jinja.jp/amabie-mokuzou-no1-hounou/.

Isaki Jurei. 2008. *Kojiki tarotto kiso kaisetsu* (Basic commentary on Kojiki tarot). Tajimi: Murasakidō.

Ishida Chihiro. 2008. "Shiawase o maneku onmyō-jutsu" (Invite happiness with yin-yang techniques). Tokyo: Magajin hausu.

Isshūkan Henshūbuhen, ed. 2007. *Shin Yamanotesen uranai* (The new Yamanote Line divination). Tokyo: Kōdansha.

Itateyama Misuzu. 2012. *Wa tarotto* (Japan tarot). Fukuoka: Azusa shoin.

Itō Miki. 2010. *Tōkyō burari pawā supotto sanpo* (Casual walks to Tokyo powerspots). Tokyo: Kōdansha.

Itō Yumi. 2007. *Kei kā fūsui* (Easy Chinese feng shui for your car). Tokyo: Taiyō shuppan.

Itoigawa City. n.d. "Nunagawa hime no densetsu" (Legends of Nunekawa Hime). Accessed May 10, 2023. https://www.city.itoigawa.lg.jp/3790.htm.

Ivakhiv, Adrian. 2003. "Nature and Self in New Age Pilgrimage." *Culture and Religion* 4:1, 93–118.

Ivanova, Gergana. 2018. *Unbinding the Pillow Book: The Many Lives of a Japanese Classic.* New York: Columbia University Press.

Iwabuchi, Koichi, ed. 2004. *Feeling Asian Modernities: Transnational Consumption of Japanese TV Dramas.* Hong Kong: Hong Kong University Press.

Iwai Hiromi. 2007. *Ema ni negai o* (Making requests with votive plaques). Tokyo: Nigensha.

Iwai, Hiroshi. 2007. "Monoimi." *Encyclopedia of Shintō.* Tokyo: Kokugakuin University. Accessed March 21, 2022. http://eos.kokugakuin.ac.jp/modules/xwords/entry.php?entryID=1458.

Iwatsutsukowake Jinja. 2020. Facebook, December 7. Accessed December 14, 2020. https://www.facebook.com/permalink.php?story_fbid=3961103057252083&id=306534876042271.

Izumi Ryūichi. 2004. *Tarotto taizen: The complete book of Tarot: Rekishi kara zuzō made* (Encyclopedia of tarot: The complete book of tarot: From history to iconography). Tokyo: Kinokuniya shoten.

Izumi Ryūichi and Ken Kumagai. 2009. "Pātikuru tarotto" (Particle tarot). Magazine insert supplement. *Koiunreki,* no. 96, May.

Jewelers Circular Publication Company. 1898. "Japanese Terms as Applied to Pottery." *Jewelers' Circular and Horological Review* 36:77–78. New York: Jewelers Circular.

Jiji News. 2019. "Goshuin from Shrine, Temple, Church Becoming Boom." December 22. Accessed May 10, 2023. https://sp.m.jiji.com/english/show/1970.

Jitsugyō no Nihonsha, ed. 2012. *My Birthday: Otona ni natta shōjotachi e: Ichigō kagiri no fukkan* (My birthday: For all the girls who became adults. One-time limited-edition reissue). Tokyo: Jitsugyō no Nihonsha.

Joshidō-sha. n.d. *Joshidō-sha to wa?* (What is the Women's Road Company?). Accessed July 21, 2021. https://omikuji-joshidosya.hatenadiary.jp/joshidosya1.

Kaburagi Maya. 2017. *Nippon no omikuji: Nihon zenkoku nihyaku-sanjū-ni shu no omikuji o hiku* (Japanese lottery fortunes: Take one of the 232 from all over Japan). Tokyo: Gurafikkusha.

Kagami Ryūji. 2000. *Shinsei rūn tarotto senjutsu* (Sacred runes tarot divination). Illustrated by Kazumi Akutsu. Tokyo: Gakushū kenkyūsha.

———. 2007. *Kirakira koi no tarotto uranai* (Sparkling love tarot divination). Tokyo: Futami shobō.

———. 2009. *Harō kitei no tarotto uranai* (Hello Kitty tarot divination). Tokyo: Takeda Random House Japan.

Kagami Ryūji and Akiko Ikeda. 2005. *Dayan no tarotto kādo* (Dayan tarot cards.) Tokyo: Hakusensha.

Kahoku shinpō. 2016. "Eto dai ema kigō" (Commissioned painting of zodiac huge *ema.* November 29. Accessed July 28, 2021. https://kahoku.news/articles/20161129kho000000027000c.html.

Kaiunchō. 2012. "Mon gai bu shutsu no chintaku reifu" (Household *reifu* that you will treasure and never take out of the building). June, 1:80–81.

Kaiun Omikuji (Good fortune *omikuji*). n.d. Accessed July 21, 2021. http://www.omikuji.co3.jp/pc/.

Kamakura Hijiriishi Sacred Stones. n.d. "Chitose magatama" (Millennium *magatama*). Accessed September 15, 2021. http://sacredstone.jp/shopbrand/ct14/.

Kamimura Shigezo. 2015. "Hoshi no tomodachi" (Star friends). YouTube video, 6:13. Accessed October 2, 2021. https://www.youtube.com/watch?v=P81Thw_yAxI.

Kamoshida Takumi. 2022. "Himawari no ema ni 'hayaku sensō owatte'" (A votive plaque with sunflowers says 'Quickly end the war'") *Sankei News,* April 20. Accessed February 15, 2023. https://www.sankei.com/article/20220420-RYNSRNFMEFN5ZH256XIY5KTOPY/.

Kanazawa shinbun. 2020. "Goshuin manā akka de kujū no ketsudan" (A tough decision due to deteriorating pilgrim stamp manners). January 19. Accessed February 15, 2022. https://www.kanaloco.jp/news/social/entry-246609.html.

Kanda Myōjin Kanshō, ed. 2008. *Miko-san nyūmon: Shokyūhen* (Primer for shrine attendants: Beginning level). Tokyo: Asahi Shinbun shuppan.

Kanda Takahira. 1884. *Notes on Ancient Stone Implements, &c., of Japan.* Translated by N. Kanda. Tokyo: Kokubunsha.

Kaneko Shūsuke, dir. 1995. *Gamera: Daikaijū Kūchū Kessen* (Gamera: Giant monster mid-air battle). Tokyo: Tōhō.

Ka-Pya! Sisters. 2014. "Omamori Charm Workshop: Video Tutorial." YouTube video, 11:02. July 28. https://www.youtube.com/watch?v=L4kfgTnFvnU.

Kasai Ayumi and Moon Princess Himiko. 2002. *Ai to shinbi no tarotto uranai: Kasai Ayumi orijinaru kādo 78 mai* (Love and mystery tarot divination: 78 original cards by Kasai Ayumi). Tokyo: Seibidō shuppan.

Kashiwagi Tamai. 2013. *Uranai ni itte kimashita: Kaiun mania no "ataru uranaishi" taikenki* (I went to a divination provider! A journal of "popular providers" in divination mania). Illustrated by Aki Tsuruha and Nihon Manga Juku. Tokyo: Ōizumi shoten.

Kasulis, Thomas. 2004. *Shinto: The Way Home.* Honolulu: University of Hawai'i Press.

Katsuki Miho. 2010. "Shintō to Bukkyō kihon no ki" (The fundamental "heart" of Shinto and Buddhism). In *Crea Due Trip Todōfuken no pawā supotto* (Crea Due Trip powerspots of the 47 prefectures), 67–74. Tokyo: Bungei shunjū.

Kawahashi, Noriko. 2000. "Seven Hindrances of Women? A Popular Discourse on Okinawan Women and Religion." *Japanese Journal of Religious Studies* 27 (1): 85–98.

Kawano, Satsuki. 1995. "Gender, Liminality and Ritual in Japan: Divination among Single Tokyo Women." *Journal of Ritual Studies* 9 (2): 65–91.

Keesing, Roger M. 2012. "On Not Understanding Symbols: Toward an Anthropology of Incomprehension." Transcribed and edited by Jordan Haug. *HAU: Journal of Ethnographic Theory* 2 (2). Accessed July 28, 2021. https://www.journals.uchicago.edu/doi/10.14318/hau2.2.023.

Kendall, Laurel. 2021. *Mediums and Magical Things: Statues, Paintings, and Masks in Asian Places.* Oakland: University of California Press.

Kidder, Edward J. 2007. *Himiko and Japan's Elusive Chiefdom of Yamatai: Archaeology, History, and Mythology.* Honolulu: University of Hawai'i Press.

Kim, Sujung. 2022. "A Star God Is Born: Chintaku Reifujin Talismans in Japanese Religions." *Religions* 13 (5): 431.

Kisha Ichi-go. 2018. "Wakamono ni mo ninki 'mai goshuin-chō' te nani?" (What are "my pilgrim stamp books" that are so popular with young people?). *Tsukuru madoguchi,* April 4. Accessed February 20, 2022. https://tsukumado.com/column/664/.

Kobayashi Yoshinori. 2010. *Gōmanizumu sengen special: Shin tennō-ron* (A special arrogant manifesto: The new emperorism). Tokyo: Shōgakkan.

Kogure Masao and Toshihide Kunimatsu. 2006. *Noroi no tarotto kādo* (The cursed tarot cards). *Heisei uwasa no kaidan* 19 (Rumored ghost stories of the era no. 19). Tokyo: Iwasaki shoten.

Koiunreki. 2008. "Supiricharu no oshigoto" (Doing spiritual work). *Koiunreki* 90 (November): 156–157.

———. 2010. "Pawā supotto gaido" (Powerspot guide). *Koiunreiki* 114 (November): 12–16.

Koizumi Norihiro. 2016. *Chihayafuru: Kami no Ku* (Chihayafuru: Part I). Tokyo: Nippon TV.

Kondo, Mariko. 2014. *The Life-Changing Magic of Tidying Up: The Japanese Art of Decluttering and Organizing.* New York: Ten Speed Press.

Kory, Stephan N. 2015. "From Deer Bones to Turtle Shells: The State Ritualization of Pyro-Plastromancy during the Nara-Heian Transition." *Japanese Journal of Religious Studies* 42 (2): 339–380.

Kracauer, Siegfried, and Thomas Levin. 1995. *The Mass Ornament: Weimar Essays.* Translated, edited, and with an introduction by Thoman Leven. Cambridge, MA: Harvard University Press.

Kubo Kiriko. 1999. *Dōbutsu uranai* (Animal divination). Tokyo: Shōgakkan.

Kunisawa Yū. 2016. *Tarotto uranaishi miyu no rashingi* (The tarot fortune-teller's pearl dream compass). Tokyo: Kosumikku shuppan.

Kurabayashi Satomi, ed. 2010. *Crea Due Trip Todōfuken no pawā supotto* (Crea Due trip powerspots of the forty-seven prefectures). Tokyo: Bungei shunjū.

Kusaba Kazuhisa and Toshihiko Yayama. 2010. *Shiawase o yobu kannon no e* (Kannon pictures to summon happiness). Tokyo: Makino shuppan.

Kuse Tsukiko. 2015. *Kamigatari: Onna onmyōji to bōsō no ao oni.* Vol. 1. (Deity narration: The female wizard and the blue ogre of Bōsō). Bonita Comics. Tokyo: Akita shoten.

Kuyōgi Shūkei. 2001. *Abe no Seimei hiden onmyōji: "Shikigami" uranai* (The secret wizard Abe no Seimei: "Spirit helper" divination). Tokyo: Futami shobō.

———. 2002. *Abe no Seimei higi: Onmyōdō jusengu shihō shinsho* (Abe no Seimei's secret tricks: Writings on the Four Treasures and tools of the Way of the Wizard for spells and incantations). Tokyo: Futami shobō.

———. 2003. *Onmyōdō, katatagae, yakuyoke, jusen: Abe no Seimei gokui* (The Abe no Seimei codes: The wizard's craft, circumvention of directional taboos, charms for the prevention of bad luck, and spells). Tokyo: Futami shobō.

Kyodo News. 2019a. "New Emperor Naruhito Vows to Stand with People." *Kyodo News,* May 1. Accessed June 15, 2021. https://english.kyodonews.net/news/2019/05/2a76518b06aa-hold-emperor-naruhito-ascends-throne-reiwa-era-begins.html.

———. 2019b. "Turtle-Shell Divination Conducted at Imperial Palace in Tokyo Ahead of Key Succession Rite." *Kyodo News,* May 13. Accessed July 21, 2021. https://english.kyodonews.net/news/2019/05/3b93f5f50f46-turtle-divination-conducted-ahead-of-key-imperial-succession-rite.html.

———. 2020. "Kyoto Shrine Revives Shinto-Buddhist Rite after 550-Year Hiatus." *Kyodo News,* September 4. Accessed July 21, 2021. https://english.kyodonews.net/news/2020/09/87a15ab06213-kyoto-shrine-revives-shinto-buddhist-rite-after-550-year-hiatus.html.

Kyōto Iju Keikaku. 2016. "Inori tokyō ni aru mono o tsukuru" (Making things with prayers). Community Newsletter, March 23. Accessed September 22, 2021. https://kyoto-iju.com/works/omamori.

Kyoto shinbun. 2015. "Mochi-komi ema ni kuryo" (Concerns about bring-your-own votive plaques at Kiyomizu-dera). December 26.

Latour, Bruno. 2010. *On the Modern Cult of the Factish Gods.* Durham, NC: Duke University Press.

Lee Byung-Hoon, dir. 2003. *Dae Jang Geum* (The Great Dae Jang). TV series. Seoul: Munhwa Broadcasting.

Lee, Jennifer. 2009. *The Fortune Cookie Chronicles: Adventures in the World of Chinese Food.* New York: Hachette/Twelve.

Lewis, William F. 1993. *Soul Rebels: The Rastafari.* Prospect Heights, IL: Waveland Press.

Long, Susan Orpett. 2005. *Final Days: Japanese Culture and Choice at the End of Life.* Honolulu: University of Hawai'i Press

Lowe, Bryan D. 2017. *Ritualized Writing: Buddhist Practice and Scriptural Cultures in Ancient Japan.* Honolulu: University of Hawai'i Press.

———. 2020. "Protection without Punishment: Turning to Buddhist Gods during Covid-19." *Immanent Frame,* June 25. Accessed March 15, 2022. https://tif.ssrc.org/2020/06/25/protection-without-punishment/.

Lowell, Percival. 1894. *Occult Japan; or, The Way of the Gods: An Esoteric Study of Japanese Personality and Possession.* Boston: Houghton-Mifflin.

Luckmann, Thomas. 1967. *The Invisible Religion: The Problem of Modern Society.* New York: Macmillan.

Magatama no Wa. 2012. "Magatama no pawā" (The power of magatama). Accessed September 15, 2021. https://magatamanowa.co.jp/original2.html.

Maruyama Nobuhiro. 2019. *Jindai moji nazorigaki* (Tracing the characters from the Age of the Deities). Tokyo: Nagaoka shoten.

Matsui Takeshi. 2013. *Kotoba to māketingu: "Iyashi" būmu no shōhi shakaishi* (Language and marketing: A social history of the "healing boom" in Japan). Tokyo: Sekigakusha and Chuokeizaisha.

Matsukawa Atsushi and Naoki Ogawa. 2011. "After Aum 1: Occult Subculture Makes a Comeback." *Asahi shinbun,* December 7. Accessed December 15, 2020. http://ajw.asahi.com/article/behind_news/social_affairs/AJ201112070063a.

Matsuo Satoshi and Nagai Kazuko, trans. 2008. *Makura no sōshi: Nōinbon* (*The Pillow Book:* Nōin text). Tokyo: Kasama shoin.

McLaughlin, Levi. 2020. "Japanese Religious Responses to COVID-19: A Preliminary Report." *Asia-Pacific Journal: Japan Focus* 18 (9): 1–22.

McMorran, Chris. 2022. *Ryokan: Mobilizing Hospitality in Rural Japan.* Honolulu: University of Hawai'i Press.

Medikea Seimei Hoken. 2018. "Enmusubi, kin'un jōshō to pawā supotto ni kansuru chōsa 2018" (2018 survey about marriage and romance, better economic fortune, and powerspots). *Minna no risāchi. Chōsa ripōto* (Research on everyone. Survey reports). February 7. Accessed December 19, 2019. https://www.medicarelife.com/research/022/.

Midori Mayu. 2007. *Panda uranai* (Panda divination). Tokyo: Orange Page Books.

Miko Hebi (@http_hebimiko). 2022. "Ohayōgozaimasu. Samui desu ne" (Good morning, It's really cold). Twitter, February 7. Accessed March 6, 2022. https://twitter.com/http_hebimiko/status/1490837674848305152?cxt=HHwWgIDSse29wrApAAAA.

Miller, Laura. 1997a. "People Types: Personality Classification in Japanese Women's Magazines." *Journal of Popular Culture* 31 (2): 133–150.

———. 1997b. "Wasei eigo: English 'Loanwords' Coined in Japan." In *The Life of Language: Papers in Linguistics in Honor of William Bright,* edited by Jane Hill, P. J. Mistry, and Lyle Campbell, 123–139. The Hague: Mouton/De Gruyter.

———. 2004. "Those Naughty Teenage Girls: Japanese Kogals, Slang, and Media Assessments." *Journal of Linguistic Anthropology* 14 (2): 225–247.

———. 2005. "Bad Girl Photography." In *Bad Girls of Japan,* edited by Laura Miller and Jan Bardsley, 127–141. New York: Palgrave Macmillan.

———. 2006. *Beauty Up: Exploring Contemporary Japanese Body Aesthetics.* Berkeley: University of California Press.

———. 2008a. "Extreme Makeover for a Heian-Era Wizard." *Mechademia: An Annual Forum for Anime, Manga and the Fan Arts,* no. 3: Limits of the Human, 30–45.

———. 2008b. "Korean TV Dramas and the Japan-Style Korean Wave." *PostScript: Essays in Film and the Humanities* 27 (3): 17–24.

———. 2010. "Japan's Zoomorphic Urge." *ASIA Network Exchange* 17 (2): 69–82.

———. 2011a. "Subversive Script and Novel Graphs in Japanese Girls' Culture." *Language and Communication* 31 (1): 16–26.

———. 2011b. "Tantalizing Tarot and Cute Cartomancy in Japan." *Japanese Studies* 31 (1): 73–91.

———. 2013. "Elevator Girls Moving in and out of the Box." In *Modern Girls on the Go: Gender, Mobility, and Labor in Japan,* edited by Alisa Freedman, Laura Miller, and Christine Yano, 41–65. Stanford, CA: Stanford University Press.

———. 2014. "The Divination Arts in Girl Culture." In *Capturing Contemporary Japan: Differentiation and Uncertainty,* edited by Satsuki Kawano, Glenda S. Roberts, and Susan Long, 334–358. Honolulu: University of Hawai'i Press.

———. 2017a. "Girl Culture in East Asia." In *Transnational Asia: An Online Interdisciplinary Journal* 1 (2). Accessed March 20, 2022. https://transnationalasia.rice.edu/Content.aspx?id=2147483652.

———. 2017b. "Japanese Tarot Cards." *ASIA Network Exchange* 24 (1): 1–28.

———. 2018. "Searching for Charisma Queen Himiko." In *Diva Nation: Female Icons from Japanese Cultural History,* edited by Laura Miller and Rebecca Copeland, 51–79. Berkeley: University of California Press.

Miller, Laura, and Carolyn Stevens. 2021. "From Beautiful to Cute: Shifting Meanings in Japanese Language and Culture." *International Journal of Language and Culture* 8 (1): 62–83.

Miller, Richard J. 1979. *Japan's First Bureaucracy: A Study of Eighth-Century Government.* Cornell University East Asia Papers, No. 19. Ithaca, NY: China-Japan Program, Cornell University.

Miyajima, Hiroshi, 2017. "Jadeitite from Itoigawa, Niigata Prefecture, Central Japan." *Journal of Mineralogical and Petrological Sciences* 112 (5): 227–236.

Miyamoto Ryūhei. 2019. "'MANGA⇔TOKYO' ten repōto" (Manga/Tokyo exhibition report). Media geijutu karento kontentsu (Current Contents Media, Art). March 28. Web news published by the Agency for Cultural Affairs. Accessed July 13, 2021. https://mediag.bunka.go.jp/article/article-14896/.

Miyazaki nichinichi shinbun. 2021. "Aijō-ippai no hana temizu" (A flower purification basin filled with lots of love). January 12. Accessed March 6, 2022. https://www.the-miyanichi.co.jp/horou/_50428.html.

Mizuhara Atsuko. 2011. "Tarotto no kai ga watashitachi ni tsutaeru" (What the tarot community can convey to us). In *Kokoro to karada o iyasu: Serapii ōru gaido* (Healing the heart and the body: Complete therapy guide), 15–19. Tokyo: BAB Japan.

Mochizuki Takashi. 2021. "Ekiben goshuin-chō katate ni, Niigata no 'Nana ekiben meguri' o yatte mita!" (With a 'train station lunch box stamp book' in one hand, I tried the 'Seven Station Lunch Box Pilgrimage.'" Nippon Hōsō Kyōkai (NHK), December 12. Accessed October 7, 2021. https://news.1242.com/article/334859.

Moe Uranai Seisaku Iinkai, ed. 2005. *Moe uranai* (Endearing divination). Tokyo: Entāburein.

Mollier, Christine. 2009. *Buddhism and Taoism Face to Face: Scripture, Ritual, and Iconographic Exchange in Medieval China.* Honolulu: University of Hawai'i Press.

Momiji Hachimangū. 2022. Shrine website. Accessed February 19, 2022. https://momijihachimangu.or.jp/goshuinar/.

Momoki Yūko. 2015. *Magatama kassa byūtei* (Beauty with *magatama kassa* massage). Tokyo: Rinkeji wākusu.

Morgan, David. 1996. *The Sacred Gaze: Religious Visual Culture in Theory and Practice.* New Haven, CT: Yale University Press.

———. 2012. *The Embodied Eye: Religious Visual Culture and the Social Life of Feeling.* Berkeley: University of California Press.

———. 2021. *The Thing about Religion: An Introduction to the Material Study of Religions.* Durham: University of North Carolina Press.

Mori Kunihiro, dir. 2006. *Shōnen onmyōji* (The young spirit master). Anime. Tokyo: Studio Deen.

Morimoto Ryōko, Emi Suzuki, Yuko Fujimori, and Mutsumi Hidaka. 2019. "Goshuin Gāru hikken!" (Must-see for the pilgrim stamp girl). *Hanako Tokyo.* March 19. Accessed November 2, 2021. https://hanako.tokyo/news/lifestyle/81678/.

Morimura Ako. 2007. "Pawā supotto de chikara o morau" (Drawing strength from powerspots). In *Shio, pawāsutōn, ofuda: Jibun de dekiru okiyome & oharai hyakka* (Salt, powerstones, and ofuda: DIY encyclopedia of purification and exorcism), edited by Jitsugyō No Nihonsha, 36–41. Tokyo: Jitsugyō no Nihonsha.

Moron. 2015. "Jibun de tsukuru kukkii kattā de magatama kukkii" (I made *magatama* cookies with a cookie cutter I made myself). *Shiawase na tokage, omoni kēki o tsukuttemasu* (Even though I'm mainly a happy lizard, I'm making cakes) (blog). July 22. Accessed July 28, 2021. https://moro1217.exblog.jp/24274137/.

Moto Haruka. 2009. *Tonari no koakuma boy* (The devilish boy next door). Tokyo: Shōgakukan.

Mūnpurinsesu Himiko. 1989. *Mūnpurinsesu tarotto uranai* (Moon Princess tarot divination). Tokyo: Ikeda shoten.

———. 2008. *Mekuru dake de kōun o yobu: Mahō no tarotto* (Invite good fortune just by turning them over: Magical tarot). Tokyo: Makino shuppan.

———. 2010. *Mūnpurinsesu himiko no seiza uranai daijiten* (Moon Princess Himiko's big dictionary of Western astrology). Tokyo: Chūkei shuppan.

Murakami Tetsuki. 2022. *Kokon goshuin kenkyūshitsu* (Laboratory of ancient to modern pilgrim stamps). (blog). Accessed June 23, 2021. https://goshuin.net/.

Murata, Satoru. 2012. "Fortunetelling Addiction Spreads among the Insecure." *Asahi shinbun,* April 11.

Murayanimasumifutsuhime Jinja. 2022. "Goshuin gyararii" (Goshuin gallery). Accessed April 14, 2022. http://murayajinja.com/goshuin/.

Mynet Inc. 2014. *Seishinkai varukirī* (Valkyrie crusade, overseas title). RPG/simulation game set. Tokyo: Mynet Inc.

Nagakubo Takakazu. 2012. *Karura mau! Shiki pawā supotto junrei* (Dance of the celestial being Karura! Blueprint for a powerspot pilgrimage). Tokyo: Akita shoten.

Nagano Eishun. 2005. "Yogenjū Amabiko kō: Umihiko o tegakari ni" (Considering the prophetic creature Amabiko—using Umihiko as a clue). *Jakuetsu Kyōdoshi Kenkyū* 49 (2): 1–30.

Nagano Tsuyoshi. 2017. "Bachiatari?! Goshuin netto tenbai, Jinja to otera no nayami wa" (Bad karma?!! *Goshuin* net resale, shrines and temples are worried). *Asahi shinbun,* February 9.

Nagoya Broadcasting Network. 2017. "Nagoya-shi Kita-ku Wakeoe Jinja no goshuin (The *goshuin* from Wakeoe shrine in Nagoya City Kita Ward). Part of *Dō desu ka!* (What do you think?) morning TV program. Aired November 7, 2017. Accessed June 23, 2021. https://www.youtube.com/watch?v=i0lXzu2ZynM.

Nakamura Kōichi. 1999. *Ichiban daikichi: Omikuji no fōkuroa* (The best of great luck: The folklore of lottery fortunes). Tokyo: Taishūkan shoten.

Nakayama Hideaki. 2019. "Minna no kokoro de, shiawase ni narō yo" (Let's all become happy, together with everyone's heart.) (blog). Kuriru dezain kōbō (Krill Design Studio, Utsunomiya). Accessed December 18, 2022. http://minnade-happy-mind.seesaa.net/.

Namatame Hiromi. 2010. "Fū sui omamori kādo" (Feng shui amulet cards). *Koiunreki,* no. 114:19.

Nanae Hirotaka. 2007. *Tarotto no goshujin-sama* (The tarot master). Tokyo: Asukī Media Wākusu/ Kadokawa Group.

Nanao Mio. 2017. *Mugen sowaka: Tokyo shōjo onmyōji.* Vol. 5. (Mantra dreams: Tokyo maiden wizard). Cheese Flower Comics. Tokyo: Shōgakukan.

Naumann, Nelly. 1993. "Religion or Magic? Some Remarks concerning Divinatory Practices Mentioned in the Oldest Japanese Literature." Nachrichten of OAG 154:7–20.

Ngai, Sianne. 2020. *Theory of the Gimmick: Aesthetic Judgment and Capitalist Form.* Cambridge, MA: Harvard University Press.

Nihon Daiichi Kumano Jinja. 2006. Shrine website. Accessed June 5, 2021. https://kumano-jinjya.com/juyohin.html.

Nihon Juyohin Kenkyūkai. 2005. *Nihon no kawaii omamori* (The cute amulets of Japan). Tokyo: Byakuya shobō.

Nikaidō, Yoshihiro. 2015. *Asian Folk Religion and Cultural Interaction.* Göttingen: V&R Unipress. Reprinted in 2015 by Taipei: National Taiwan University Press.

Nikan Sports. 2018. "Hanyū Yuzuru fan no '*seichi junrei*'" (Holy pilgrimage by fans of Hanyū Yuzuru). *Nikan Sports*, February 17.

Ninja Studio. 2006. *Gōma reifu den Izuna* (Devil-conquering *reifu*-legend Izuna; Izuna: Legend of the unemployed ninja, overseas title). Nintendo DS video game. Tokyo: Success.

Nippon Hōsō Kyōkai. 2018. "NHK News." Television news program. Aired June 24, 2018, 8:23 a.m.

Nishide, Takeshi. 2014. "Women's Entry into Shinto Priesthood Is on the Rise." *Japan Times*, March 6. Accessed October 2015. https://www.japantimes.co.jp/life/2014/03/06/lifestyle/womens-entry-into-shinto-priesthood-is-on-the-rise/.

Nishimura, Yoko. 2018. "The Evolution of Curved Beads (*Magatama*) in *Jōmon* Period Japan and the Development of Individual Ownership." *Asian Perspectives: Journal of Archeology for Asia and the Pacific* 57 (1): 105–158.

Nishimura Yumiko. 2016. "Nihon no saiko ikemen butsu-sama, Nara Asukadera" (Japan's oldest handsome Buddha, Nara Asukadera). *Yumimi's Hatena blog Hare tokidoki goshuin*. November 10. Accessed May 5, 2023. https://yumimi-kyoto.hatenablog.com/entry/2016/11/10/000000.

———. 2018. *Kawaii Nara goshuin bukku* (The cute Nara pilgrim stamp book). Tokyo: Shufu no tomosha.

Nishiyama Yuki. 2014. "Goshuin gāru būmu, netto de wa hihan sattō mo, jisha wa kangei 'Josei ga kyōmi o motte kurereba'" (Pilgrim Stamp Girl boom, even with intense criticism on the internet, are welcomed by shrines and temples 'as long as woman have an interest'"). *Business Journal* post 5939, September 5. Cyzo. Accessed July 20, 2020. https://biz-journal.jp/2014/09/post_5939.html.

Noguchi Satoko. 2009. "Kami no shizuku: Magatama no omajinai" (Droplets of the kami: *Magatama* magic). *Koiunreki* 96, May, 148–151.

Nornes, Markus. 2021. *Brushed in Light: Calligraphy in East Asian Cinema*. Ann Arbor: University of Michigan Press.

Obata Karindo. 2010. *Kyōun ni naru onmyōji no kotodama* (Become lucky: The spirit-words of the wizard). Mook with CD and DVD included. Tokyo: Makino shuppan.

Odaira Mika. 2009. *Josei shinshoku no kindai* (Female priests in the modern era). Tokyo: Perikansha.

———. 2015. "Modern Women's Education and Religion in Yamaguchi Prefecture." *Journal of Religion in Japan* 4 (2–3): 212–239.

Ohishi Manabu and Akira Himekawa. 2012. *Gakken manga NEW Nihon no rekishi 1: Kuni no naritachi* (Gakken comic new Japanese history vol. 1: How the country came about), 81. Tokyo: Gakushū kenkyūsha kyōiku shuppan.

Ōishi Chuni. 2012. *Kaiun! Omamori garu!* (Good fortune! Good luck amulet girl!). Tokyo: Takeshobō.

Oka Manami. 2007. *Kyōto no"goriyaku" tettei gaido* (Complete guide to Kyoto blessings and benefits). Tokyo: PHP kenkyūjo.

Okada Takumi. 2020. "Pikachū no dezainā, Amabie no ema, Kasuga Taisha ni" (Pikachu's designer, an Amabie votive plaque at Kasuga Taisha). *Asahi shinbun digital*, October 5. Accessed March 7, 2022. https://www.asahi.com/articles/ASNB573JMNB5POMB001.html.

Okamoto, Ryōsuke. 2019. *Pilgrimages in the Secular Age from El Camino to Anime*. Translated by Deborah Stuhr Iwabuchi and Kazuko Enda. Tokyo: Japan Publishing Industry Foundation for Culture.

Okayama University e-Bulletin. 2013. "Japan's Oldest Votive Tablets Showing Monkey Leading a Horse, and a Cow Are Unearthed." *Okayama University e-Bulletin* 4, September 23. Accessed July 28, 2021. http://www.okayama-u.ac.jp/user/kouhou/ebulletin/pdf/vol4/news_002.pdf.

Omamori.com World Co. n.d. Home page. Accessed March 18, 2022. https://www.omamori.com/en/.

Ōmichi, Haruka. 2016. "The 'Itako' as Mass Culture." *Journal of Religion in Japan* 5 (1): 22–46.

Omikuji Gaido. 2019. Omikuji guide. Accessed July 21, 2021. https://omikuji-guide.com/nationwide/.

Ōmiya Shirō. 2007a. *Kiseki o yobu reifushū* (Collection of *reifu* that call on the miraculous). Tokyo: Gakushū kenkyūsha.

———. 2007b. *Shosha reifu hiden: Nazotte kaite goriyaku zōdai* (Secret guides for Taoist paper charms penmanship: Enhancing benefits). Tokyo: Biingunetto puresu.

———. 2011. *Reifu zensho* (Compendium of Taoist paper charms). Tokyo: Gakushū kenkyūsha māketingu.

———. 2013. *Gensen shōzai reifu shū: Kitte sugu ni tsukaeru reifu gojūkyū mai o shūroku* (A curated collection of requested Taoist paper charms: An album of fifty-nine *reifu* that can be used immediately). Tokyo: Gakushū kenkyūsha.

Omura, Hiroshi. 2002. "Trees, Forests and Religion in Japan." *Mountain Research and Development* 24 (2): 179–182.

Ono Toden. 2007. *Pengin uranai* (Penguin divination). Tokyo: Orange Page Mooks.

Ōno Yuriko. 2008. *Nihon no Kamisama kādo: Gods and Goddesses of Japan* (bilingual title). Oracle card deck. Tokyo: Visionary.

Ōsumi Yū. 2015. "Shōgeki no nakami! 'Omamori' no nakami o katappo shikara tashikamete mita" (Shocking contents! I tried to systematically ascertain what is inside an *omamori*) *Goo ima topi: Sugoi kōkishin no saito* (Goo current topics: Site for super inquisitiveness) (blog). November 3. Accessed July 28, 2021. https://ima.goo.ne.jp/column/article/3764.html.

Ōtawa Fumie. 2006. *Choi yaba onna ni tsukeru kusuri* (Medicine for super hideous women). Tokyo: PHP.

Ōtsuka Eiji. 1997. *Shōjo minzokugaku* (Ethnology of the girl). Tokyo: Kōbunsha.

Ōura Shundo. 2019. *Goshuin to goshuin-cho de tabisuru jinja otera* (Traveling to shrines and temples with pilgrim stamps and pilgrim stamp books). First published in 2016. Tokyo: Mainabi shuppan.

Owada, Aneyuki. 2013. "Interview with Aya Inoue, Kichijitsu Brand Designer." *Najimu Japan*. November 27. Accessed July 28, 2021. http://najimu-japan.com/aya-inoue-kichijitsu-brand/.

Paine, Crispin. 2013. *Religious Objects in Museums: Private Lives and Public Duties.* London: Bloomsbury.

Pony Canyon Media Lab. 2011. *Virtual trip pawā supotto e ikō* (Let's take a virtual trip to powerspots). DVD. Tokyo: Pony Canyon.

Primavera, Marie. 2008. *Dōbutsuen uranai* (Zoo divination). In *Seda* (mook), 30–37. Tokyo: Hinode.

Prough, Jennifer. 2011. *Straight from the Heart: Gender, Intimacy, and the Cultural Production of Shōjo Manga.* Honolulu: University of Hawai'i Press.

Reader, Ian. 1991. "Letters to the Gods: The Form and Meaning of *Ema*." *Japanese Journal of Religious Studies* 18 (1): 24–50.

———. 2006. *Making Pilgrimages: Meaning and Practice in Shikoku.* Honolulu: University of Hawai'i Press.

Reader, Ian, and George Tanabe. 1998. *Practically Religious: Worldly Benefits and the Common Religion of Japan.* Honolulu: University of Hawai'i Press.

Rigia Mōrisu. 2003. *Onmyōji komikku ansorojī* (Anthology of wizard comics). Tokyo: Gakushū kenkyūsha.

Rika Riko Twins. 2017. "Terebī de wa kesshite hanasanai, Shūhei Shimada totte oki no pawā supotto. Shūhei Shimada Ōtsuma Joshi Daigaku kōgi 29" (Shūhei Shimada's valued powerspot that was never discussed at all on television. Shuhei Shimada's Ōtsuma Women's University Lecture 29). YouTube video, 5:27. June 25. Accessed August 3, 2018. https://www.youtube.com/watch?v=wSNf6Rfpck0.

Rinoie Yūchiku. 2012. *Rinoie Yūchiku pawā supotto karendā* (Rinoie Yūchiku's powerspot calendar). Tokyo: Yamakeisha.

Ritō Akisato. 1801. *Kawachi meisho zue* 6 (Illustrated guide to famous sites in Kawachi). Illustrated by Tōkei Niwa. Naniwa (Osaka): Morimoto Tasuke.

Robertson, Jennifer. 2008. "*Ema*-gined Community. Votive Tablets (*Ema*) and Strategic Ambivalence in Wartime Japan." *Asian Ethnology* 67 (1): 43–77.

Robson, James. 2008. "Signs of Power: Talismanic Writing in Chinese Buddhism." *History of Religions* 48 (2): 130–169.

Rose, Alexander. 2019. "Long-Term Building in Japan." *Infrastructure Blog for the Long Now Foundation.* September 10. Accessed March 20, 2022. https://blog.longnow.org/02019/09/11/long-term-building-in-japan/.

Rosenberger, Nancy. 2013. *Dilemmas of Adulthood: Japanese Women and the Nuances of Long-Term Resistance.* Honolulu: University of Hawai'i Press.

Roth, Carina. 2019. "Essays in Vagueness: Aspects of Diffused Religiosity in Japan." In *Spirits and Animism in Contemporary Japan: The Invisible Empire,* edited by Fabio Rambelli, 95–108. London: Bloomsbury Academic.

Rots, Aike P. 2019. "This Is Not a Powerspot: Heritage Tourism, Sacred Space, and Conflicts of Authority at Sēfa Utaki." *Asian Ethnology* 78 (1): 155–180.

Ruppert, Brian D. 2000. *Jewel in the Ashes: Buddha Relics and Power in Early Medieval Japan.* Cambridge, MA: Harvard University Asia Center.

Rurubi. 2021. *Zenkoku no kawaii goshuin atsumemashita! Goshuin joshi tokushū 2021* (A collection of cute red seals from all over Japan! Special feature on Goshuin Girls 2021). *Rurubi* magazine.

Saitō Chōshū and Shōsei Suzuki, eds. 2000. *Edo meisho zue* (Guide to famous spots in Edo). Compiled by Saitō (ca. 1737–1799). Painted by Hasegawa Settan (1834–1836). Tokyo: Yumani shobō.

Sakai Tōru. 2016. *Anime ga chihō o sukuu! Seichi junrei no keizai kōka o kangaeru* (Anime is saving Japan's regions! A consideration of the economic effect of "holy pilgrimages"). Tokyo: Wani Purasu.

Sakamoto M. 2020. "Jinja bukkaku aikō kai" (Shrine and temple lover's circle). Facebook, April 11. Accessed February 3, 2022. https://www.facebook.com/groups/213967488627299/permalink/3197211263636225/.

Sakimi Jōato. 2006. "Iku dake de pawā chāji! Iyashi no seikai isan e" (Just going there gives you a power charge! Going to healing world's heritage sites). *AnAn* 1641 (December): 85–91.

Saler, Michael. 2006. "Modernity and Enchantment: A Historiographic Review." *American Historical Review* 111 (3): 692–716.

Sankar, Andra. 1985. "Sisters and Brothers, Lovers and Enemies: Marriage Resistance in Southern Kwangtung." *Journal of Homosexuality* 11 (3–4): 69–81.

Sanraizu Paburikēshon (Sunrise Production). n.d. "Omamori masukotto" (Omamori mascot). Accessed March 18, 2022. https://www.sunrisep.co.jp/03_goods/omamori.html.

Satō Mikio, dir. 2001. *Shōtoku Taishi* (Prince Shotoku). TV miniseries (2 episodes). Osaka: NHK Osaka.

Satō Mitsuyuki. 2020. "Nihon Daiichi Kumano Jinja de karada no bui ya zōki nado o natsuketa 'karada no omamori' ga wadai" (The topic is "body amulet" for named parts of the body, organs and so on at the Nihon Daiichi Kumano shrine). Kei Esu Bii Nyūzu (KSB news). May 19. Accessed July 23, 2021. https://news.ksb.co.jp/article/13852291.

Screech, Timon. 2006. "Going to the Courtesans: Transit to the Pleasure District of Edo Japan." In *The Courtesan's Arts: Cross-Cultural Perspectives,* edited by Martha Feldman and Bonnie Gordon, 255–279. Oxford: Oxford University Press.

Semba Kiyoko. 2003. "Yūshima 'Kigandō'" (The Kigandō in Yūshima). *Memo: Otoko no heya,* no. 30, 54–57.

Serenyty. 2013. "Tokyo Idol Festival 2013: The Acts Part 16." *Happy Disco* (blog). October 5. Accessed August 24, 2018. http://www.intlwota.com/happydisco/?p=605.

Sheepme. 2015. "Personalized Charm." YouTube video. Produced by Ikegami Jissō-ji. Accessed June 2021. https://omamo.me/.

Shibusawa Tatsuhiko. 1961. *Kuro majutsu no techō* (A manual of black sorcery). Tokyo: Tōgensha.

Shields, James. 2010. "Beyond Belief: Japanese Approaches to the Meaning of Religion." *Studies in Religion, Sciences religieuses* 39 (2): 133–149.

Shimada Shūhei. 2010a. *Shimada shūhei osusume! Kaiun pawā supotto meguri* (Shūhei Shimada's recommendations! A good luck powerspot pilgrimage). DVD. Tokyo: E-Net Frontier.

———. 2010b. *Shimada shūhei to iku! Zenkoku kaiun pawā supotto gaido. Ketteiban* (Let's go with Shimada Shūhei! Guide to nationwide lucky powerspots. The definitive edition!) Tokyo: Kōdansha.

Shinbutsu Goriyaku Kenkyūkai, ed. 1989. *Jinja, otera goriyaku chō* (Guidebook to supplications at temples and shrines). Tokyo: KK Rongu serāzu.

Shinkai Makoto, dir. 2016. *Kimi no na wa* (Your name). Anime. Tokyo: Comix Wave Films.

Shirabē. 2016. "Kawaii! Nayami ni awasete tsukuru ōdā meido omamori 'omamo'" (Cute!!!! A made to order amulet that matches your worry! 'Omamo'). *Shirabē.* March 31. Accessed July 28, 2021. https://sirabee.com/2016/03/31/100103.

Shōgakukan. 2018. "Josei 1000 nin ga eranda enmusubi pawā suppotto BEST 3" (The top 3 powerspots for marriage and romance selected by 1000 women). *@DIME* (*Atto Daimu*) magazine. March 2. Tokyo: Shōgakukan. Accessed August 10, 2019. https://dime.jp/genre/512873/.

Shōmoji Fudōdō (@syoumonzi). 2023. "Nanchyatte onmyōji reifu de hidoi yatsu" (These bogus wizard spirit writing amulets are awful). Twitter, January 13, 7:07 p.m. Accessed May 10, 2023. https://twitter.com/syoumonzi/status/1614066586830393344.

Silicon Studios, developers. 2012. *Gyakushō no fantashika* (Counterattack fantastic). Released as *Fantasica* in English. Tokyo: Mobage.

Silvio, Terri. 2019. *Puppets, Gods, and Brands: Theorizing the Age of Animation from Taiwan.* Honolulu: University of Hawai'i Press.

Smith, Jordan. 2021. "Rebuilding Ise." *Heart and Soul.* BBC. September 24. Podcast. Accessed September 27, 2021. https://www.bbc.co.uk/sounds/play/w3ct2lcq.

Smyers, Karen. 1999. *The Fox and the Jewel: Shared and Private Meanings in Contemporary Japanese Inari Worship.* Honolulu: University of Hawai'i Press.

Snow, Hilary Katherine. 2010. "*Ema:* Display Practices of Edo Period Votive Paintings." PhD dissertation, Stanford University.

Soga Jinja. 2023. Facebook, April 20. Accessed May 7, 2023. https://www.facebook.com/sogajinja.

Southern DS Create. 2016. "Omamori netsuke" (Omamori and netsuke). Accessed June 5, 2021. http://southern-dsc.co.jp/oem/omamori.html.

Spaeth, Ryu. 2020. "How *The New Yorker* Fell into the 'Weird Japan' Trap." *New Republic,* December 17. Accessed March 5, 2022. https://newrepublic.com/article/160595/new-yorker-japan-rent-family-fabricated.

Spiro, Melford. 1990. "On the Strange and the Familiar in Recent Anthropological Thought." In *Cultural Psychology: Essays on Comparative Human Development,* edited by James W. Stigler, Richard Shweder, and Gilbert Herdt, 47–61. Cambridge: Cambridge University Press.

Stark, Rodney, and William Sims Bainbridge. 1987. *A Theory of Religion.* New York: Peter Lang.

Stevens, John. 1995. *Sacred Calligraphy of the East.* 3rd ed. Boston: Shambhala.

Suetsugu Yuki. 2012. *Chihayafuru* 1. Tokyo: Kōdansha.

Sukeno Yoshiaki. 2013. *Sōsei no onmyōji* (Twin star exorcists). Tokyo: Shūeisha.

———. 2018. *Twin Start Exorcists.* Vol. 11. Translated by Tetsuichiro Miyaki. San Francisco: VIZ Media.

Sutā Supirichuaru (Star Spiritual). n.d. Accessed March 18, 2022. https://spiritual config.com/gokinendou-gohu/.

Suzuki, Kentarō. 1995. "Divination in Contemporary Japan." *Japanese Journal of Religious Studies* 22 (3–4): 249–266.

Swanger, Eugene R., and K. Peter Takayama. 1981. "A Preliminary Examination of the '*Omamori*' Phenomenon." *Asian Folklore Studies* 40 (2): 237–252.

Tada Takuya, dir. 2016. "LadyBaby taibō no mejā debyū shinguru 'Sampai! Goshuin girl' no music clip" (LadyBaby's long-awaited major debut single "Worship! Pilgrim Stamp Girl" music clip). YouTube video, 3:23. Accessed February 3, 2022. https://www.youtube.com/watch?v=IuNXiUyQRZ0.

Taguchi Shindō. 2002. *Abe no Seimei chokuban uranai* (Divination with the Abe no Seimei cosmograph). Tokyo: Futami shobō.

Takahashi, Rumiko 2010. *Inuyasha.* Vol. 51 Translated by Mari Morimoto. San Francisco: VIZ Media.

Takako and Mirey. 2008. *Gārii fû sui majikku meiku* (Girly feng shui magic make-up). Tokyo: Takeda Random House.

Takeda Sōun. 2005. *Shoyudō* (The art of calligraphy). Tokyo: Ikeda shoten.

Takeda Tsuneyasu. 2011. *Gendaigo* Kojiki (Modern-language *Kojiki*). Tokyo: Hatsubaimoto gakken.

Tamagawa Masato. 2021. *Guji ga kataru jinja saikō hiwa, Part two* (The hidden tale of the shrine reconstruction related by the priest, part two). *Kokoro ne,* July 4. Accessed July 7, 2021. http://so-shin.jp/kokorone-web/hoshidamyokengu02/.

Tamamoto Yōko. 2012. *Tamafuri to kaiun no hōsoku: Japanese Spiritual Magic. Un o hikiyose ganbō o kanaeru nihon korai no pawā sutōn magatama no tadashii tsukaikata* (Spirit beckoning and the laws of good fortune: Japanese spiritual magic. The correct way to use *magatama* powerstones from ancient times to attract fortune and grant your desires). Tokyo: Aiikusha.

Tambiah, Stanley J. 1968. "The Magical Power of Words." *Man* 3 (2): 175–208.

Tanabe, George J. 2007. "Playing with Religion." *Nova Religio* 10 (3): 96–101.

Tanaka, Kathryn M. 2022. "The Amabie Boom: From Mizuki Shigeru Fandoms to COVID-19." Historifans. July 21. https://historifans.org/2022/07/21/the-amabie-boom-from-mizuki-shigeru-fandoms-to-covid-19/.

Tanaka Kazuki. 2021. "Shōtoku Taishi no 'aiken' mochiifu" (Prince Shotoku's "pet dog" motif). *Sankei shinbun,* February 18. Accessed March 30, 2021. https://www.sankei.com/article/20210218-QNKF7LBMHVOGHLBUBUM5U2RTYM/.

Tanaka Toshitsugu. 1918. *Ema no bi* (The beauty of votive plaques). Kyoto: Ema kenkyūkai.

Taneda, Hiroyuki. 2000. "Fortune-Telling and Women: Contemporary Characteristics of Fortune Telling in Japanese Society." *Journal of UOEH* 22 (4): 351–362.

Tanoden. 2018. "Kodai no hōseki magatama o tsukutte miyō" (Let's make an ancient jewel, *magatama*). Kurafuteria/Crafteriaux. September 15, 2001. https://tanoden.fun/magatama_making/.

Teeuwen, Mark, and John Breen. 2017. *A Social History of the Ise Shrines: Divine Capital.* London: Bloomsbury Academic.

Terai Hiroki. 2021. *Okaruto kaii jiten* (Dictionary of occult mysteries). Tokyo: Kasama shoin.

Terashima, Emika. 2021. "Shrine's Amulet Sells Out after Osaka Likely Had One in Australia." *Asahi shinbun,* February 26.

Thomas, Jolyon Baraka. 2007. "*Shūkyō asobi* and Miyazaki Hayao's Anime." *Nova Religion* 10 (3): 73–95.

———. 2013. *Drawing on Tradition: Manga, Anime, and Religion in Contemporary Japan.* Honolulu: University of Hawai'i Press.

———. 2017. "Review Essay: Big Questions in the Study of Shinto." H-Japan International Digital Network. November 13. Accessed May 5, 2023. https://networks.h-net.org/node/20904/discussions/837862/review-jolyon-thomas-studies-shinto.

Thomas, William Isaac, and Dorothy Swaine Thomas. 1928. *The Child in America: Behavior Problems and Programs.* New York: Alfred A. Knopf.

Tobe Tamio and Takamuro Miki. 2006. *Kamigami no monogatari: Gekiga Kojiki* (Tales of the deities: Kojiki dramatic comic). Tokyo: Bajiriko.

Tokai Television Broadcasting. 2021. "'Zenkoku Ichi' no ninki jinja. Sanpai kyaku yobikomu josei shinshoku no aidea ryoku to sono gensen tōsho hantai no ujiko mo 'motto yatte'" (A popular shrine 'ranked No. 1 in the country.' The power of the female priest's ideas to attract worshippers and even the parishioners originally opposed say 'do more'). *Nyūzu one,* Tōkai Terebī. Aired February 27.

Tøllefsen, Inga Bårdsen, and Giudice, Christian, eds. 2017. *Female Leaders in New Religious Movements.* London: Palgrave Macmillan.

Tomono Kōji. 2007. *Neko kyara uranai* (Cat characters divination). Tokyo: Kōdansha.

Tsukada, Hotaka, and Toshihiro Ōmi. 2011. "A Deluge of "Religious" Information on New Religions, Power Spots, Funeral Services, and Buddhist Statues." *Religious Issues in Japan 2010. Bulletin of the Nanzan Institute for Religion and Culture* 35:24–47.

Umehara Sueji. 1965. "*Jōko no kinjū gyokei magatama*" (On the bird or animal shaped *magatama*). *Shigaku* 38 (1): 1–48. Accessed July 28, 2021. https://ci.nii.ac.jp/naid/110007409979/.

Ury, Marian B., trans. 1985. *Tales of Times Now Past: Sixty-Two Stories from a Medieval Japanese Collection.* Berkeley: University of California Press.

von Siebold, Heinrich. 1879. *Notes on Japanese Archaeology with Especial Reference to the Stone Age.* Yokohama: Typography of C. Lévy.

Wagenaar, Wester. 2016. "Wacky Japan: A New Face of Orientalism." *Asia in Focus* 3:46–54.

Wakeoe Jinja. 2019. "Wakeoe Jinja Bekki no shintaku" (The oracle from Bekki at Wakeoe Jinja). YouTube video, 3:55. February 25. Accessed February 10, 2022. https://www.youtube.com/watch?v=YwVdlBRVXtE.

Watanabe Masaharu. 2020. "Densha to basu to aruite goshuin tabi Masaharu" (Masaharu who does pilgrim stamp travel by train, bus, and walking). Twitter, December 18. Accessed February 10, 2022. https://note.com/wtrnet/n/ndb91609a4eb3.

Weber, Max. 1946. "Science as a Vocation." In *From Max Weber: Essays in Sociology,* edited and translated by Hans. H. Gerth and C. Wright Mills, 129–156, New York: Oxford University Press.

Wijers-Hasegawa, Yumi. 2007. "Flaky or Fact? Are 'Power Spots' Wacky . . . or What?" *Japan Times,* March 18. Accessed November 10, 2018. https://www.japantimes.co.jp/life/2007/03/18/to-be-sorted/flaky-or-fact-are-power-spots-wacky-or-what/#.XVA6bEdOmAY.

Yagi Tōru. 2015. *Zenkoku goshuin zukan* (Catalog of pilgrim stamp books for all Japan). Tokyo: Esubī kurieitibu.

Yagi Tōru and Masaoka Nobushirō. 2004. *Zukai zatsugaku konnani omoshiroi minzokugaku* (Such amusing folklore, miscellaneous illustrated). Tokyo: Natsumesha.

Yamada Momoko. 2016. "Betsumei tama no koshi jinja?? Kyōto pawā supotto 'Imamiya Jinja' no pointo & shōhen jōhō" (Another name is "Tama no koshi jinja"?? Aspects of and information about the environs around the Kyoto powerspot Imamiya Jinja). *Mī taimuzu* (Me Times) (blog). February 8. Accessed June 20, 2021. https://metimes.jp/articles-938.

Yamada Yōji, dir. 1969. *Otoko wa tsurai yo* (It's tough being a man). Feature film. Tokyo: Shōchiku.

Yamamichi Kiitsu. 2010. *Fūsui pawā supotto kikō* (Feng shui powerspot traveler's journal). Tōkyō: Media Sōgōkenkyūjo.

Yamamoto Naoki. 2014. *Nihon shinwa tarotto* (Japanese mythology tarot). Self-published by the artist. Accessed March 13, 2022. https://yamamoto-naoki.stores.jp/.

Yamashita, Katsuaki. 2012. "The Characteristics of On'yōdō and Related Texts." Translated by Joseph Elacqua. *Cahiers d'Extrême-Asie* 21:79–105.

Yanada Yoshiaki, ed. 2010. "Watashitachi, konna 'supi' o motometemasu!" (We are looking for this is the kind of "spiritual"!). In *Fortune Guide Book: Nayameru otona joshi no kaiun ōru gaido* (Fortune guide book: All fortune guide for worried adult women), 122–123. Tokyo: Gyappu Japan.

Yanagi Watei. 2005. *Onna o ageru! Hanryū "kao uranai"* (Just for women! Korean Wave-style face divination). Tokyo: Goma Books.

Yasokawa Keiichi. 2014. *Nihon mukashi banshi tarotto* (Tarot of Japanese fairytales). Osaka: Hatkei Artwork.

Ynao Otaku Blog. 2014. "How to Make an Omamori." March 25. Accessed July 28, 2021. http://ynaotaku.blogspot.com/2014/03/how-to-make-omamori.html.

Yoda, Hiroko (@Ninetail_fox). 2022. "A While Back I Visited the Tomb of Jesus Christ . . . in Aomori." Twitter, June 7. https://twitter.com/Ninetail_foxQ/status/1534388165007790080?fbclid=IwAR3Yw11mQzpYi3ZyvptvV_uCynm8nXr9fR2hLK7cvnnL5XlP19TzskZBOlM.

Yomiuri shinbun. 2009. "Koigokuro utsusu 'kagami no ike' ninki" (Popular "mirror pond" for casting away love). *Yomiuri shinbun*, April 16, 7.

Yoshida, Kazuhiko. 2006. "Religion in the Classical Period." In *Nanzan Guide to Japanese Religions*, edited by Paul L. Swanson and Clark Chilson, 144–159. Honolulu: University of Hawai'i Press.

Index

Page numbers in boldface type refer to illustrative matter.

About the Author

Laura Miller is the Ei'ichi Shibusawa-Seigo Arai Endowed Professor of Japanese Studies and a professor of history at the University of Missouri-Saint Louis. She has published widely on Japanese language and culture and in the field of linguistic anthropology. Miller is the author of *Beauty Up: Exploring Contemporary Japanese Body Aesthetics* (2006) and coeditor of four other books, including *Diva Nation: Female Icons from Japanese Cultural History* (with Rebecca Copeland, 2018).